An Apple for the Teacher
Fundamentals of Instructional Computing

Brooks/Cole Series in Computer Education

An Apple for the Teacher: Fundamentals of Instructional Computing, 2nd Ed.
George H. Culp and Herbert Nickles

Instructional Computing with the TRS-80
Herbert Nickles and George H. Culp

Instructional Computing Fundamentals for IBM Microcomputers
George H. Culp and Herbert Nickles

Instructional Computing Fundamentals for the Commodore 64
Herbert Nickles and George H. Culp

RUN: Computer Education
Dennis O. Harper and James H. Stewart

AN APPLE FOR THE TEACHER

Fundamentals of Instructional Computing

SECOND EDITION

GEORGE H. CULP
University of Texas at Austin

HERBERT L. NICKLES
California State University, San Bernardino

BROOKS/COLE PUBLISHING COMPANY
Monterey, California

Brooks/Cole Publishing Company

A Division of Wadsworth, Inc.

Printed in the United States of America

10 9 8 7 6 5 4 3 2 1

Library of Congress Cataloging-in-Publication Data

Culp, George H.
  An Apple for the teacher.

  (Brooks/Cole series in computer education)
  Includes index.
    1. Computer-assisted instruction—Teacher training.
2. Computer managed instruction—Teacher training.
3. Microcomputers—Teacher training. I. Nickles,
Herbert. II. Title. III. Series.
LB1028.5.C78 1985   371.3'9445   85-30001

ISBN 0-534-05832-9

This product is neither endorsed nor coproduced by Apple Computer, Inc.
Apple II is a registered trademark of Apple Computer, Inc.

Sponsoring Editor: Neil Oatley
Editorial Assistant: Gabriele Bert
Production Service: Greg Hubit Bookworks
Manuscript Editor: Patricia Talbot Harris
Permissions Editor: Carline Haga
Interior Design: Rodelinde Albrecht
Cover Illustration: Andrew Myer
Typesetting: Vera Allen Composition
Printing and Binding: Malloy Lithographing, Inc.

This is the philosophy we must preach
When using the computer to teach.
Expel the tinker's dam.
Do learn to program!
Much more will be within your reach.

PREFACE

This is a practical book for preservice and in-service teachers that presents the fundamentals of the BASIC programming language for the Apple II series of microcomputers and explains how to apply them to the design and development of instructional computing programs. In 15 years of teaching instructional computing courses to more than 2,000 students, it has been our experience that, given these fundamentals, teachers are able to expand on them and develop efficient programs to meet their specific needs.

The book focuses on the following elements:

■ *Direct instructional computing application*   The majority of programs designed and discussed may be easily adapted for actual classroom use.

■ *Top-down design of programs*   We believe that teachers can be introduced to structured design of programs, regardless of the programming language used. We incorporate this using techniques familiar to teachers who have been exposed to general instructional design strategies in their professional education.

■ *Step-by-step solution for coding programs*   Example programming "problems" incorporating the BASIC statements discussed in each chapter are solved in a step-by-step manner.

■ *Frame-by-frame program format*   Programs are designed in a frame (or screen) format, further emphasizing a top-down, structured method for development.

■ A *systems approach to instructional design*   Ten steps necessary for the design and development of instructional computing materials, along with suggested guidelines, are discussed in detail.

Although the book is directed to teachers who have little or no experience with computers, we want to emphasize that we are not attempting to teach general computer literacy. There is little mention of the history, architecture, or function in society of computers. Nor is this book for educating computer scientists or programmers. Several language statements common to programming texts are omitted because their application is not typical of the *instructional* use of computers. Rather, in keeping with our goal of providing fundamentals, we present what a teacher needs to know in order to begin designing and developing instructional computing materials.

The book consists of ten chapters and five appendices, divided into two parts. In Part One, the first four chapters discuss the BASIC programming language statements and commands common to five areas of instructional computing use: problem solving, drill, tutorial dialog, simulation, and testing. Chapter 5 presents an introduction to string functions that are relevant to instructional computing applications. Chapters 6 and 7 give example programs in each of the five areas. In addition, Chapter 7 includes a series of teacher "utility programs" related to information storage and retrieval. With the exception of the simulation examples, each of the programs in these chapters may be easily modified or used directly in actual classroom applications. Chapter 8 discusses and demonstrates some simple uses of color and graphics as instructional techniques.

In Part Two, Chapters 9 and 10 discuss the specific steps needed to first design and then develop instructional computing materials. Ten criteria for evaluation of instructional computing programs are also included. The appendices include instructions for the general operation of the microcomputer and its disk operating system, a summary of the commands and statements and their uses, answers to selected questions and problems given in the chapters, instructions for making music with the Apple, and listings of programs given as solutions to certain problems.

As a matter of personal preference, some readers may wish to study Part Two on design and development before the chapters on BASIC. However, we believe that practical design and development can occur only after a working knowledge of the language is established. Thus, BASIC fundamentals are presented before instructional design. We want to emphasize again, however, that *program design* considerations are introduced early and followed throughout in Part One. We have found that presentation, demonstration, and discussion of the entire book requires 30 to 40 class contact hours. An equal or greater amount of student contact with the microcomputer is needed. Our general course format is to assign the design and development of one or more instructional computing units in the student's area of interest as a term project.

We discuss more than 30 programs related to instructional computing use. These programs are contained on a "text diskette" that is provided without cost by the publisher to adopters who order ten or more copies of the book. We believe that access to this disk is an *integral* and *important* consideration for those using the book. Therefore, we urge its use. Permission is given to copy the disk for class-related applications.

We extend our appreciation and acknowledgment to Carey Van Loon of California State University, San Bernardino, to Dee Dee Watkins and her husband, Morgan, of the University of Texas, Austin, and to Carla Cramer for her lasting or valuable enthusiasm. Special thanks go to Dennis Harper and Jeffrey Marcus, University of California, Santa Barbara; Sister Mary K. Keller, Clark College; Sylvia Pattison, University of Cincinnati; Frederick Schneider, Virginia Commonwealth University; Carl R. Stutzman, California State University, Fresno; Edward B. Wright, Western Oregon State College; and to the publication staff at Brooks/Cole Publishing Company. An extra measure of gratitude, and apologies for the burned steak, are given to our editor, Neil Oatley of Brooks/Cole.

CONTENTS

PROGRAMS

Application Programs: Testing

Teacher Utility Programs Using Text Files

Graphics

Music

Listings of Answers to Posers and Problems Questions

An Apple for the Teacher
Fundamentals of Instructional Computing

Introduction

This book describes an approach to using a common programming language, BASIC, for the design and development of instructional computing programs for Apple II series microcomputers. Its ten chapters discuss certain fundamentals of BASIC and the design and developmental processes that provide a foundation for the production of instructional computing programs.

More than a hundred books are available that teach BASIC (the **Beginner's** All-purpose Symbolic Instruction Code, developed by John G. Kemeny and Thomas E. Kurtz at Dartmouth College). Although most of these books are very thorough in describing the language, they usually emphasize problem-solving applications. Our emphasis, on the other hand, is on instruction in the use of BASIC to design and develop materials for instructional computing.

Simply put, any use of computing techniques within the classroom may be broadly defined as instructional computing (sometimes known as *computer-assisted instruction* or *CAI*). Specifically, it includes:

1. *Problem solving,* in which computer programs are written to solve discipline-oriented problems.

2. *Drill and practice* on fundamental concepts using computer programs in a given discipline.

3. *Tutorial dialog,* in which computer programs provide "tutorlike" assistance in pointing out certain types of mistakes, providing review if needed, skipping areas in which proficiency is shown, and so on.

4. *Simulation,* in which computer programs allow manipulation and interpretation of certain elements related to given physical or social phenomena without the constraints of time, space, equipment, and environmental or logistic limits.

5. *Testing,* in which computer programs ask the questions, check the answers, and record the performance.

For our purposes, the term *instructional computing* includes all of these applications.

The Use of BASIC. An introduction to some of the fundamentals of BASIC is provided in this book. This introduction is not intended to produce highly accomplished and skilled programmers. Rather, it gives only the fundamentals needed to write simple programs for instructional computing applications.

Model programs are described that illustrate this use. Most of these programs may be easily modified for, or used directly with, actual classroom activities.

Although many different programming languages may be used in instructional computing, there are several reasons for using BASIC:

1. It is easy to learn and easy to use.

2. It is a common interactive language (see Section 1.3), available on large computer systems costing millions, medium-sized systems costing hundreds of thousands, minisystems costing tens of thousands, and small systems (commonly called *micros* or *personal* computers) costing a few hundred to a few thousand dollars.

3. It may be used in all applications of instructional computing.

4. It is one of the introductory computer languages used in most secondary and many elementary schools.

5. It is the most common language of microcomputers—an area of computer technology making the major impact on education in this decade.

Top-Down Design.   Following the introduction to BASIC, a method for designing instructional materials called the *systems approach* is outlined. This approach, in essence, is a logical, step-by-step process for identifying the tasks and activities needed in the production of validated instructional materials. However, this general concept of a logical approach to program design is introduced in the early chapters of the book. Beginning with PROGRAM 3 in Chapter 2, each of the programs is designed in a "top-down," step-by-step, frame-by-frame approach. This is a familiar approach to instructional design for educators and facilitates program development, even for the novice computer user.

Development.   The development of instructional computing programs by you is the ultimate goal of this book. Initially, the development phase overlaps the design phase, in which paper, pencil, and brain power are the principal ingredients. This process involves outlining the rationale, objectives, and instructional sequence of one or more instructional computing programs. After this program design is outlined step by step, frame by frame on paper, it is translated into the BASIC programming code. The last steps are to spend considerable time at a computer entering, testing, refining, and evaluating what has been designed and developed on paper.

As a final introductory note, we emphasize that this book assumes no previous experience whatsoever with computers. On the other hand, the book does not provide detailed information on computers in general or how they operate. Rather, it introduces the ways and means by which the Apple II® series of microcomputers* may be used within the instructional process.

Now, let us begin by getting down to the BASICs . . .

---

*Apple II is a registered trademark of Apple Computer, Inc.

PART ONE

AN INTRODUCTION TO THE BASIC PROGRAMMING LANGUAGE

THINK ABOUT THIS . . .

. . . FOR FUN

Rearrange the letters of NEW DOOR to form one word. (Note: Answers to Think About This for Fun *questions may be found in Appendix C.)*

. . . SERIOUSLY

Does a computer possess intelligence?

Chapter 1

A
BASIC Program
of My Very Own

1.1 OBJECTIVES

For the successful completion of this chapter, you should be able to:

1. List five general applications of instructional computing (Introduction).

2. Define two ways in which computers may be accessed (Section 1.3).

3. List the steps necessary to "boot up" (power up) a computer system (Appendix A).

4. State how a BASIC program may be entered on that system after the booting up (Section 1.6 and Appendix A).

5. Define what (not who) composes a BASIC program (Section 1.4.1).

6. Distinguish between BASIC statements and commands (Sections 1.4.1–1.4.2).

7. Define the actions of the following BASIC commands: NEW, RUN, LIST, and SAVE (Section 1.4.2).

8. Define and give at least one example of both a *numeric* variable and a *string* variable (Section 1.4.3).

9. Describe the use of commas and semicolons in BASIC for purposes other than punctuation (Section 1.4.4).

10. Define the purpose and give at least one example of the following BASIC statements: PRINT, INPUT, LET, and END (Sections 1.5.1–1.5.4).

11. Describe three simple techniques for editing BASIC programs (Section 1.6 and Appendix B, Section B.9).

1.2 COMPUTER USE: A BRIEF HISTORY AND RATIONALE

Electronic computers have been in use since the late 1940s. In the period from 1948 to 1965, they were used primarily for what their name implies: computing, or "number crunching," as it is sometimes called. Starting about the mid-sixties, however, educators began experimenting with applications of computers in the instructional process that involved more than just computing.

In the decade following, this use expanded, and, just as computers have become ingrained in our society, instructional computing is becoming commonplace in our schools. (These points may be emphasized by the fact that since 1975 over 12,000,000 microcomputers have been purchased, many for home or school use.)

It is very important to recognize that computers are not replacing teachers! The fundamental principle underlying the use of computers—regardless of the profession using them—is that they are incredibly fast and accurate tools, and they allow people to do certain activities in a manner that has never before been possible. Thus, the use of computers in instruction is basically (no pun intended) that of *supplemental* applications. Computers allow teachers and students to do certain educational processes faster, with greater accuracy, and in a manner not possible before.

Computer programs can be very helpful in providing patient, routine drill on fundamental concepts, in generating and grading tests in a given discipline, and in many other applications. In any of these cases, the most effective programs, we believe, are those designed by teachers: the professionals in the field who are aware of what is to be taught and how to teach it. As yet, there is no computer program that can lead an intelligent and sensitive discussion on any given abstract concept. There are no teachers out of work because they have been replaced by a computer! That is something worth remembering.

1.3 ACCESS TO COMPUTERS

A computer is an extremely fast and accurate processor of data. In the simplest sense, most common computer systems may be viewed as four units connected electronically:

1. An *input* unit (such as a computer terminal keyboard), through which data is entered.

2. A *processor* unit, which stores the data input and processes it electronically.

3. An *output* unit (such as a computer terminal screen or printer), which shows the results of processing the data input.

4. A *data storage/retrieval* unit (such as a disk drive), which stores data on, and retrieves data from, some magnetic medium (such as a floppy disk).

Figure 1.1 shows these units.

Until the late 1960s, the primary means of access involved punching program statements, data, and commands onto computer cards. This "batch" of cards was read (input) by a card reader and eventually a printout (output) of the program "run" was retrieved. This type of access is commonly referred to as *batch access* or *batch processing.*

Since the early 1970s, there has been a very strong trend toward accessing computers via computer terminals. In the simplest sense, a terminal consists of a keyboard, similar to that of a typewriter, for input of statements, data, commands, and so forth, with output displayed either on a cathode ray tube (CRT) screen or paper (hardcopy) at the terminal. This type of access is known as *interactive* (a user is interacting directly with the computer or a program) or *timesharing* (there may be literally scores of terminals in remote locations "sharing the time" of one computer). In most instances, the terminal is connected to the computer via standard telephone lines.

Microcomputers may be considered an exception to this, although they may be connected to larger computers. Here the computer, terminal, display, and other components are usually provided as a unit small enough to fit on a desk top (Figure 1.2). There are no telephone connections or sharing of computer time. These features make the unit more portable, less prone to equipment failure, less expensive, and, consequently, well suited to the classroom.

For our use here, only microcomputers are discussed. The examples and assignments in the book assume that the reader has access to an Apple II series microcomputer with BASIC, one floppy disk drive, a video monitor or television, and at least 48K of random access memory (RAM).

It is very important that the reader, particularly the reader new to microcomputers, become familiar with the processes needed to access (use) the system. This first involves gaining confidence in booting up the system. Refer to Appendix A for a step-by-step procedure to accomplish this.

1.4   A BIT ABOUT BASIC BEFORE BEGINNING

There are a few general points about BASIC that should be made early. Consider these as some of the "rules of the game" to follow for BASIC.

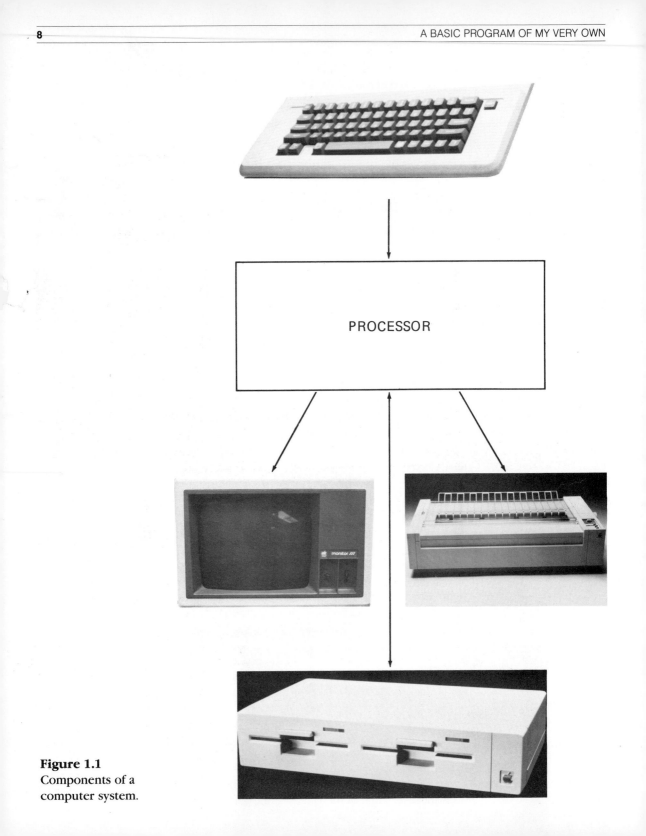

PROCESSOR

Figure 1.1
Components of a
computer system.

1.4.1 Statements

A BASIC program may be defined as at least one "instruction" performed (executed) by the computer. Instructions are written in the form of statements. These statements are words (often verbs), such as PRINT, INPUT, and so on, that make some degree of sense to both the user and the computer. (Of course, the computer has been programmed by people to "understand" these words.) The length of a BASIC statement must not exceed 255 total characters, including spaces.

BASIC statements for the Apple II series microcomputers are always numbered, generally by tens (10, 20, 30, etc.). They could be numbered 1, 2, 3, and

Figure 1.2
Apple IIe series microcomputer system: keyboard, monitor, two disk drives, and printer.

so on, but no additional statements could be inserted into the program, say, between statements numbered 1 and 2. Statements can be inserted between lines numbered 10 and 20 (11, 12, etc.). Thus, the numbering convention is usually in increments of ten.

1.4.2 Commands

BASIC commands issue specific information to the computer system *about* the program. For example, the command NEW instructs the system to prepare for a new BASIC program to be entered at the terminal by "erasing" any program statements that are currently in the system's memory. The command LIST will produce a listing of the BASIC statements comprising the program in memory.

The command RUN executes (RUNs) the BASIC statements in their increasing numeric sequence unless one of those statements transfers the execution to another part of the program. (This process is called *branching* and will be discussed later.) The command SAVE <filename> instructs the system to save on the disk the program in memory under the name <filename>. The program is stored on a floppy disk placed in the disk drive. (The <filename> may be just about any name, but short, descriptive names should be considered.)

1.4.3 Variables

All BASIC programs described in this text will include values that may *vary* as the program is executed (RUN). These values, called *variables,* could be students' names, test scores, responses for correct or incorrect answers, and so forth.

In BASIC, a variable may be *represented* (named) simply by any letter of the alphabet. However, the name could be as long as 255 characters *if* the *first* character in the name is a letter, and the rest of the name contains only letters or numbers. However, only the first *two* characters are considered by the Apple. Realistically, variable names should be short and descriptive. Initially (for simplicity), we will use only one or two characters for variable names in our example programs. Later, where appropriate, longer variable names that better describe their values will be used. However, care should be taken. Variable names such as AVERAGE and AVENUE appear to be different, but are really the same, since both have the same first two characters (AV). Names such as LETTER and FIEND cannot be used, since they contain LET and END. These are two of the "reserved words" for BASIC. Most of the reserved words are those shown in Appendix B.

For our purposes, there are two types of variables:

1. *Numeric.* The value of the variable is always numeric: 1.0, 2, 110.5, −3.1365, and so on.

2.   *String* (or *alphanumeric*). The value of the variable may be alphabetic characters or numbers or a mixture of both. Such values are always enclosed in quotation marks: "ABCDEF", "CS395T", "JOHN JONES", "NOW IS THE TIME", and so on.

A dollar sign ($) is added to the name of a string variable to distinguish it from a numeric variable. N$, A1$, Z9$, and FL$ all represent string variable names, while N, A1, Z9, and FL all represent numeric variable names.

Examples   `A  =  123`

(The *numeric* variable named A has a value of 123 assigned to it.)

`A$  =  "ABC"`

(The *string* variable named A$ (pronounced "A-string") has a value of ABC assigned to it.)

1.4.4   Commas (,) and Semicolons (;)

Commas and semicolons have specific uses in BASIC. They can be used in the normal fashion as punctuation marks, or they can be used to instruct the system to display information in special ways. For example, every so often in a BASIC program there may be a need to have information printed in columns. Suppose a list of student names, test score averages, and final numeric grades were to be displayed (PRINTed). Assume the values are stored in the variables N$, T1, and F, respectively. The BASIC statement

`PRINT N$,T1,F`

would display this information in columns fifteen spaces apart from the start of the first value to the start of the second value, and so on. Here, the comma acts as an automatic tabulator of fifteen spaces. Thus, any line can have "fields" of display starting at column 1, column 16, and so on. This can be useful when certain types of information (e.g., name and grade for a series of students) are to be displayed. (See Sections 1.5.1 and 1.5.3.)

If one wished the above information to be *close-packed* (printed without any separating spaces), the semicolon would be used in place of the comma. In essence, then, the comma, when *not* used as a punctuation mark, instructs the system to tab fifteen spaces before printing; similarly, the semicolon instructs the system not to skip *any* spaces before printing.

These and other examples of their use will be shown shortly, but for now be aware that the comma and semicolon can have special meanings when not used as punctuation.

1.5 BASIC STATEMENTS FOR THIS CHAPTER

1.5.1 Statement PRINT

Purpose
Displays (PRINTs) information at the computer terminal. This information may be text, numeric variable values, or string (alphanumeric) variable values (see Section 1.5.3). When text is to be displayed, it must be enclosed in quotation marks (") in the PRINT statement.

Example
```
PRINT "Hello, What's your first name"
```

Result of Execution
```
Hello, What's your first name
```

In addition, certain shorthand conventions are available for the Apple II series microcomputer. For example, the shorthand for the statement PRINT is the question mark (?). Thus. PRINT statements may be literally typed as:

```
10 ? "Hello, What is your first name"
```

The system will automatically interpret the ? as the word PRINT. Note that the question mark is *outside* the quotation marks!

Example
```
10 A = 123
20 A$ = "ABC"
30 ? A,A$
```

Result of Execution
```
123                 ABC
```
$\leftarrow$15 spaces$\rightarrow$

1.5.2 Statement INPUT

Purpose
Allows numeric or alphanumeric information to be entered (INPUT) into a BASIC program during its execution. The information is entered through the terminal keyboard and is assigned to a variable specified by the program author. The variable will have the assigned value until changed by another INPUT or LET (see Section 1.5.3) statement for that variable.

Examples
```
INPUT N  (for numeric information)
INPUT N$  (for alphanumeric information)
INPUT "Enter your name ";N$  (text with statement)
INPUT "Enter your age ";N  (text with statement)
```

Note: Most BASIC systems automatically display a question mark when the INPUT statement is executed. In computer terms, the question mark is called the *input indicator* or *prompt*. Program execution is stopped until the RETURN key is pressed. Also, note that the use of quotes discussed earlier for string variables (Section 1.4.3) is *not* required when string information is *input*. The dollar sign instructs the system that *any* input will be assigned as a string variable. Also notice that text may be enclosed within quotation marks with the INPUT statement. In this form, the question mark will *not* be displayed and a semicolon *must* come before the variable name.

Program Example
```
10 PRINT "Hello, What's your first name"
20 INPUT N$
30 PRINT N$ " is a nice name,"
40 END
```

Result of Execution
```
Hello, What's your first name
```
?SAMMY (The question mark appears as a prompt, SAMMY is typed, and the
    RETURN key is pressed.)
```
SAMMY is a nice name,
```

1.5.3 Statement LET

Purpose Assigns values to variables. This action may be "direct," as in LET X = 20 (X would have a value of 20), or it may be "indirect," as in LET X = (2 * Y)/3 (X would have a value equal to the result of dividing 3 into the product of 2 times the value of Y). The "*" is the symbol (character) used for multiplication; the "/" is the symbol used for division. LET may also be used to assign alphanumeric values, as in:

```
LET A$ = "Here's the answer!"
```

Note: The term LET is optional; the statement X = 20 would be equivalent to LET X = 20. Also, note here that assignment to a string variable requires the use of quotes. The string content *must* be enclosed in quotes.

Example
```
10 LET N$ = "JOHN JONES"
20 LET T1 = 100
30 FL = 89  (Note: LET is omitted.)
40 PRINT "STUDENT","TEST 1","FINAL"
50 PRINT "-------","------","-----"
60 PRINT N$,T1,FL
70 END
```

Result of Execution
```
STUDENT         TEST 1          FINAL
JOHN JONES      100             89
```

What would happen if the commas in statements 40–60 were replaced by semicolons? *Note:* Answers to this and other questions found within the book are supplied under their respective chapter and section numbers in Appendix C.

1.5.4   Statement END

Purpose   Ends program execution. However, the END statement is not required for program execution. (See also the statement STOP in Appendix B.)

1.5.5   PROGRAM 1: Years-to-Days Conversion

Note: In this book we will be discussing more than thirty sample programs. The programs are named in the sequence of their discussion: PROGRAM 1 comes before PROGRAM 2, and so on.

The statements discussed thus far can be combined to make a program. But what is the program to do? Some stage of program design must be defined that illustrates the use of these statements. Arbitrarily, suppose we wanted to design a program that will ask for a person's name, greet that person by the name entered, ask for their age in years, convert that age to age in days, display the results of the conversion, then give a farewell message. The program, designed in a step-by-step fashion, could be:

Step 1.   Ask for a person's (the program user's) name (PRINT).

Step 2.   Assign the name entered to a string variable (INPUT).

Step 3.   Greet that person with the name entered (PRINT).

Step 4.   Skip a line so that the screen is not too crowded (PRINT).

Step 5.   Ask for the person's age in years (PRINT).

Step 6.   Assign the age entered to a numeric variable (INPUT).

Step 7.   Convert the age in years to the age in days (LET).

Step 8.   Skip a line to avoid crowding on the screen (PRINT).

Step 9.   Display this age in days (PRINT).

Step 10.   End the program (END).

In creating any new program, the following sequence should be followed:

1.   Enter NEW.

2.   Enter the program statements.

3.   Enter SAVE <filename>.

4.   RUN the program to test it.

5.   Make any needed modifications.

6.   If modified, enter SAVE <same filename>.

Step 6 *replaces* the old version of the program <filename> with the new (modified) version. If a copy of *both* versions is desired, then simply enter SAVE <different filename>. Also, the statements comprising a program in memory may be seen by entering LIST. If a specific line (statement) number or a range of line numbers is desired, enter LIST <line number> or LIST <beginning line,ending line>, respectively.

RUN from disk and refer to the listing and run of PROGRAM 1.

PROGRAM 1
Creation

```
] NEW
] 10 PRINT "Hello, What's your first name"
] 20 INPUT N$
] 30 PRINT "Howdy, "N$
] 40 PRINT
] 50 PRINT "Tell me...what is your age in years";
] 60 INPUT A
] 70 D = A * 365
] 80 PRINT
] 90 PRINT "Well, "N$", you have been breathing"
] 100 PRINT "for at least "D" days!"
] 110 PRINT, "Bye-bye, "N$
] 120 END
] SAVE PROGRAM 1
```

PROGRAM 1
Sample Run

```
] RUN
Hello, What's your first name
?GEORGE
Howdy, GEORGE

Tell me...what is your age in years? 46

Well, GEORGE, you have been breathing
for at least 16790 days!
                    Bye-bye, GEORGE


]
```

Statement-by-statement discussion of PROGRAM 1:

Step 1. Statement 10 displays a greeting and asks for the user's first name.

Step 2. Statement 20 automatically displays a "?" and waits for input from the terminal keyboard. Whatever is typed is assigned as a value to the variable N$ when the RETURN key is pressed.

Step 3. This value is displayed with the text, "Howdy, " in statement 30. Carefully note that the variable N$ is *not* enclosed within the quotation marks. (Why is the blank space included within the quotation marks?)

Steps 4 and 5. Statement 40 prints a blank line, and statement 50 requests the user's age in years.

Step 6. Statement 60 automatically displays a "?" and waits until some number is typed and the RETURN key is pressed. This value is assigned to variable A.

Step 7. Statement 70 assigns a value to variable D equal to the value of A times 365 (converting years to days).

Step 8. Statement 80 prints a blank line.

Step 9. The value of variable D, with appropriate text, is then displayed in statements 90 and 100. Again, carefully note that *only* the text to be displayed, *not* the variable names (N$ and D), is enclosed within the quotation marks.

Step 10. Statement 110 skips over fifteen spaces and displays a farewell. Statement 120 ends program execution.

1.6 EDITING BASIC PROGRAMS

Most BASIC systems have some means by which programs may be edited. For example, a PRINT statement with a misspelled word or typographic error may be corrected by editing. Three simple editing techniques are:

1. *Left arrow key (←).* A typographic error may be corrected by using this key to backspace the cursor (the "flashing" box) over the error, entering the correction, and then completing the line being typed. This type of editing can be used only before the RETURN key is pressed for the line currently being entered.

2. *Retyping the statement.* A statement may be replaced by simply retyping the line number followed by the correct statement.

3. *Deleting lines.* A statement may be deleted entirely by typing the line number *only* and then pressing the RETURN key. Inclusive line num-

bers may be deleted by typing DEL, followed by the beginning and ending line numbers to be deleted, separated by a comma. For example,
the command

```
DEL 20,50
```

would delete lines 20–50, inclusive.

   Although these are only three simple techniques for editing, they will get
you started and can be extremely useful. Also, knowledge of the use of the ESC
and arrow keys described in Appendix B, Section B.9, will be particularly helpful. Practice using these editing keys as you become more familiar with the
system.

1.7 POSERS AND PROBLEMS

Note: Many of the "Posers and Problems" given in this book may be entered
and run as programs. Where possible, this should be done, since it will be of
help in arriving at the solutions. As a last resort, or to check your work, refer
to Appendix C. Problems headed by an asterisk (*) may be considered as more
difficult problems.

1. Correct any errors found in the following BASIC statements:

```
10 PRIMT "Hello
20 PRIMT What's your height in inches"
30 INPUT
40 M = 2.54 *
50 PRINT You are M centimeters tall!
60 FINISH
```

2. Mentally determine the value of X in each of the following if Y = 6.

```
X = 25
X = (2 * Y)/3
X = Y
X = (2 * Y)/(3 * Y)
X = (Y * Y)/(Y * 2)
```

3. Why is a space included within the quotation marks before or after the
    variable names in statements 90, 100, and 110 in PROGRAM 1? Are the
    variables N$ and D actually enclosed in quotation marks as they might
    appear in statements 90 and 100?

4. Note the different positions of the two question marks in the sample
    RUN of PROGRAM 1. What caused the difference? *Hint:* Carefully exam-
    ine statements 10 and 50.

5. Modify PROGRAM 1 to output the user's age in "heartbeats" (use H as the variable), assuming a pulse rate of 72 beats per minute (and 60 minutes per hour, 24 hours per day).

6. What would result if the following statements were executed?

```
10 A$ = "NAME"
20 B$ = "SCORE"
30 C$ = "AVERAGE"
40 PRINT A$,B$,C$
50 END
```

7. What would result if the following statements were executed? (Assume you input your own name and weight.)

```
10 PRINT "Your first name is";
20 INPUT N$
30 PRINT "Your weight in pounds is";
40 INPUT P
50 K = P/2.2
60 Z = P * 16
70 PRINT,"Wow, " N$ "!"
80 PRINT "That's only " K " kilograms, but, see,"
90 PRINT,"it's " Z " ounces!"
100 END
```

*8. Write a program that converts a temperature in Celsius to a temperature in Fahrenheit. The user should enter the temperature for conversion from the keyboard. *Hint:* The formula for conversion is

$$F = (C * \tfrac{9}{5}) + 32.$$

*9. Write a program that converts two variables, cups and ounces, into ounces. For example, 2 cups and 3 ounces equal 19 ounces.

*10. Write a program that inputs two string variables, first name and last name, and prints out a salutation of your choice using the person's full name.

THINK ABOUT THIS . . .

. . . FOR FUN

What do you sit on, sleep on, and brush your teeth with?

. . . SERIOUSLY

Can computer programs teach?

Chapter 2
Now Tell It Where to Go and What to Do with It

2.1 OBJECTIVES

For the successful completion of this chapter, you should be able to:

1. Define the purpose and give at least one example of each of the BASIC statements HOME, REM, GOTO, IF-THEN, and ON-GOTO (Sections 2.2.1–2.2.5).

2. Define the purpose and give at least one example of each of the BASIC functions RND(1) and INT (Section 2.3).

3. Define the purpose of the BASIC command LOAD (Section 2.4.1).

4. Define the purpose and give at least one example of the PRINT TAB statement (Section 2.5.1).

5. Define the purpose and give at least one example of "multiple statements per line" (Section 2.5.1).

6. Alone and unafraid, boot up a microcomputer system (Appendix A).

7. Design, enter, and RUN a BASIC program that includes the statements discussed in Chapters 1 and 2.

2.2 BASIC STATEMENTS FOR THIS CHAPTER

2.2.1 Statement HOME

Purpose   HOME erases all display and places the cursor in the upper left corner of the monitor screen. This use is particularly appropriate in instructional computing, since it allows information, examples, questions, and so on to be displayed in a screen-by-screen or frame-by-frame fashion.

Example   `HOME`

2.2.2 Statement REM

Purpose   Used as a REMinder or REMark to document the listing of BASIC programs. That is, REM gives a means by which internal notes may be made in the program listing. These notes will provide information about the program and will identify special program routines or strategies, separating the program into segments so that the program listing is easy to read. The REM statement is not executed during a program RUN; thus, the only time these are displayed is after a LIST command. We will primarily use the REM statement to show the frame-by-frame and step-by-step design in the listing of each program.

Example
```
REM  ------------------------------------------------------
REM                    Step 1 - Display a Title
REM
```

2.2.3 Statement GOTO

Purpose   *Unconditionally* transfers (branches) program execution to the specified statement number.

Example   `GOTO 100`

Note: Use of the GOTO statement in programs should be minimized. If this statement is used excessively, following the design flow of a program in a frame-by-frame fashion can become very difficult.

2.2.4 Statement IF-THEN

Purpose   *Conditionally* transfers (branches) program execution to the specified statement number if, and only if, the defined variable relationship is *true*. (Note the uses and combinations of the symbols $=$, $<$, and $>$ and their meanings.)

Examples   `IF X = 1 THEN 100`

(Transfer to statement 100 will occur only if X is *equal* to 1.)

`IF Y <> Z THEN 100`

(Transfer to statement 100 will occur only if the value of Y is *not equal* to the value of Z.)

`IF A <= 2 THEN 100`

(Transfer to statement 100 will occur only if the value of A is *less than* or *equal* to 2.)

`IF A >= 2 THEN 100`

(Transfer to statement 100 will occur only if the value of A is *greater than* or *equal* to 2.)

`IF A$ = "YES" THEN 100`

(Transfer to statement 100 will occur only if the value of A$ is *equal* to [the same value as] the character string YES.)

Also, note that IF-OR-THEN and IF-AND-THEN statements are possible:

`IF A < 1 OR A > 10 THEN 100`

(Transfer to statement 100 will occur only if the value of A is *less than* 1 *or greater than* 10.)

`IF A = 2 AND B = 3 THEN 100`

(Transfer to statement 100 will occur only if the value of A is *equal* to 2 *and* the value of B is *equal* to 3.)

Combinations of string and numeric variables also may be used:

`IF Z$ = "YES" AND C > 8 THEN 100`

(Transfer to statement 100 will occur only if the value of Z$ is *equal* to the string YES *and* the value of C is *greater than* 8.)

Make special note that many statements, such as PRINT, (LET), and others to be seen in later chapters, can be included in the IF-THEN statement. If the condition defined by the IF-THEN statement is *true,* the statement included will be executed; otherwise, execution continues with the next statement in the program.

`IF S > 69 THEN PRINT "You passed!"`

(If the value of S is greater than 69, then "You passed!" will be PRINTed.)

```
IF Z$ = "N" THEN A = 0
```

(If the value of Z$ is equal to the string N, then the numeric variable A is set to zero.)

2.2.5   Statement ON-GOTO

Purpose   Transfers (branches) program execution to a specified statement number based on the rounded value of a variable or numeric relationship.

Example   `ON X GOTO 100,300,600`

(Transfer to statement 100 will occur if the value of X is 1; transfer to statement 300 will occur if this value is 2; transfer to statement 600 will occur if this value is 3. If X is 0 or greater than 3 in the foregoing example, execution continues with the first statement following the ON-GOTO.)

This example of the ON-GOTO is equivalent to the following three IF-THEN statements:

```
IF X = 1 THEN 100
IF X = 2 THEN 300
IF X = 3 THEN 600
```

By using the ON-GOTO statement, the same instructions can be given to the system by just one statement:

```
ON X GOTO 100,300,600
```

2.3 SOME VERY BASIC FUNCTIONS

Functions in BASIC are essentially mathematical routines that either come with the computer system (as a library of routines or functions) or are defined by the user. Once a function has been defined, it may be used over and over again without the bother of writing out the entire routine.

Two of the most common library functions used in instructional computing applications are RND(1) and INT. When executed, the RND(1) function automatically gives some random numeric value between 0.0 and 0.99999999. The INT function reduces any number with a decimal fraction (called a *real* number) to a whole number (called an *integer*).

By using a combination of these functions in BASIC statements, it is possible to generate random numbers within any range desired. This may be used in generating different values for questions containing numbers, randomly selecting questions by number from a "bank" of questions, randomly branching to specified line numbers using ON-GOTO statements, and so on. The following illustration shows how this combination may be used to generate numbers in the range of 1–10, inclusive.

Suppose a BASIC statement looked like this:

```
X = INT(10 * RND(1) + 1)
```

and suppose RND(1) comes up with a random value of 0.58. BASIC is set up so that numeric operations enclosed in parentheses are performed first. Thus, the steps the system follows in computing the value of X would be:

1. $10 * 0.58 = 5.8$

2. $5.8 + 1 = 6.8$

3. INT of $6.8 = 6$

Thus, X will have a value of 6 in this example. What would be the value of X if RND(1) = 0.99999999? What would be the value of X if RND(1) = 0.01? What is the *range* of random numbers that could result from the statement:

```
X = INT((100 * RND(1) + 1) * 10) / 10
```

What would be the statement that would generate random numbers in the range of 1.00–100.00, inclusive? *Hint:* Note the two decimal places. How is an integer value changed to a real value containing two decimal places? *Answer:* By dividing the integer value by 100.

A general formula may be derived that will give any desired range of positive random numbers:

```
N = INT((H - L + 1) * RND(1) + L)
```

where N is the random number generated and H and L are the highest and lowest numbers, respectively, in the desired range. For example, a range of random numbers is desired between 100 and 25.

```
Highest number = 100
Lowest number = 25
100 - 25 + 1 = 76
```

The statement to generate this range of random numbers is:

```
N = INT(76 * RND(1) + 25)
```

What statement would produce random numbers in the range of 5–95, inclusive?

2.4 MODIFICATION OF EXISTING PROGRAMS

In Chapter 1, Problem 5 asked you to modify PROGRAM 1 to output (PRINT) the number of heartbeats equivalent to a user's age in years, assuming there were 72 beats per minute. To do this, it is necessary to:

1. Retrieve PROGRAM 1 from the disk (LOAD PROGRAM 1).

2. Examine the LISTing for needed changes (LIST).

3. Make the modifications.

4. Save the modified version of PROGRAM 1 as PROGRAM 2 (SAVE PRO-GRAM 2).

By saving the *modified* program as PROGRAM 2, both the old version (PRO-GRAM 1) and the new version (PROGRAM 2) are on the disk. If only the new version is wanted, the same name (PROGRAM 1, in this case) should be used (SAVE PROGRAM 1).

In summary, we have the following commands:

Command	Example	Action
NEW	NEW	Clears memory of statements.
RUN	RUN	Executes statements in memory.
LOAD <name>	LOAD PROGRAM 1	LOADs the program <name> from the disk to memory.
LIST	LIST	LISTs the entire program.
LIST nn	LIST 10	LISTs line nn.
LIST nn–mm	LIST 10–100	LISTs lines nn–mm, inclusive.
SAVE <name>	SAVE PROGRAM 1	SAVEs a NEW program in memory on the disk as <name>.

2.4.1 PROGRAM 2: Adding Heartbeats

Recall that PROGRAM 1 was created by first typing NEW to erase any program in memory and then entering each line, statement by statement. The program was SAVEd, then RUN was entered to test it. Once a program has been SAVEd, it may be retrieved by the command

```
LOAD <name>
```

where <name> is the name of the program. If any changes are made that are to be permanent in the program, the command SAVE <name> must be entered.

Step by step then, we must:

1.   LOAD PROGRAM 1.

2.   LIST it to see where insertions or changes must be made.

3.   Insert a statement that will convert the age in days to the age in heartbeats.

4.   Insert a statement(s) that will display the result of this conversion.

5.   SAVE as PROGRAM 2.

6.   Test the program.

7.   Make any changes indicated from the results of testing the program, then repeat Steps 5 and 6 until satisfied.

PROGRAM 2
Creation from
Program 1

```
] LOAD PROGRAM 1
] 101 REM ---------------------------------------------
] 102 REM          THESE ARE CHANGES TO PROGRAM 1
] 103 REM
] 104 PRINT
] 105 H = D * 24 * 60 * 72
] 107 PRINT "and that's a lifetime of"
] 108 PRINT H "total heartbeats!"
] 109 PRINT
] 70 D = A * 365.25
] SAVE PROGRAM 2
```

PROGRAM 2
Sample Run

```
] RUN
Hello, What's your first name
?GEORGE
Howdy, GEORGE

Tell me...what is your age in years? 46

Well, GEORGE, you have been breathing
for at least 16801.5 days!

And that's a lifetime of
1.74197952E+09 total heartbeats!

                    Bye-bye, GEORGE
```

Step-by-step discussion of PROGRAM 1 modification:

PROGRAM 1 is first LOADed and then LISTed. Statements 101–109 are entered. (Statement 105 converts the age in days, D, to heartbeats, H, since there are 24 hours per day, 60 minutes per hour, and 72 heartbeats per minute.)

Statements 107 and 108 display the value of the variable H, along with appropriate text.

Computers can be programmed to appear friendly, as if talking back to students.

Note that statement 70 is reentered to reflect a more accurate value for the number of days per year (365.25 versus 365).

The program is SAVEd as PROGRAM 2.

The program is RUN. *Note:* In the RUN of the program, the value of H is expressed as 1.74197952E + 09. This is the method by which the system displays a value of 1,741,979,520. It is also the system's way of expressing scientific notation, that is, 1.741979520×10^9. This amounts to one billion, seven hundred forty one million, nine hundred seventy nine thousand, five hundred and twenty heartbeats! Though easily broken, 'tis still a powerful muscle!

RUN from disk and refer to the modification and run of PROGRAM 2.

2.5 INCORPORATING THE NEW STATEMENTS

The content design of any BASIC program is at the discretion of its author (programmer). The program can be as simple or as complex as the author desires. For example, BASIC may be used in trivial Fahrenheit-to-Celsius temperature conversions or in sophisticated modeling of population dynamics. The point is that a program does only what an author has designed it to do—nothing more or less. However, for any program, regardless of its simplicity or complexity, the author must first outline the design and "flow" of the program. On that note, the following program (PROGRAM 3) is designed to illustrate a use of the statements discussed in this unit, and to introduce the frame-by-frame, step-by-step format we will use throughout the book.

2.5.1 PROGRAM 3: Appropriate Responses

Suppose we wish to design a program that will ask a question and give only one chance for a correct answer. "Appropriate" responses will be made for either a correct or incorrect answer. The program will then ask a final question related to age. The user will be informed if the answer is too low or too high. For answers that are too high, an additional comment will be randomly selected from three choices. The question will be repeated until the correct answer is given.

The preceding paragraph outlines what we want the program to do. But how is this to be translated into BASIC code? A logical, step-by-step approach is the answer. Design the overall programming "problem" as a series of small, independent steps, each accomplishing a specific task related to the complete "problem" solution. Thus, for this program we could have:

Step 1   Clear the screen and show a title (HOME, PRINT).

Step 2   Ask a question and get an answer (PRINT, INPUT [with text]), and check the answer for accuracy. If correct, respond positively, then ask the next question (IF-THEN-PRINT). If incorrect, give the correct answer, then ask the next question (IF-THEN-PRINT).

Step 3   Ask the next question and get an answer (PRINT, INPUT [with text]). Here, we will check the answer for a range of possible numbers.

Step 4   If correct, respond positively and END the program (IF-THEN-PRINT, GOTO Step 7).

Step 5   If the answer is too low, respond accordingly, then repeat the question (IF-THEN-PRINT, GOTO Step 3).

Step 6   If the answer is too high, respond accordingly (IF-THEN-PRINT). Then use a method to randomly select an additional comment (LET, IF-THEN-LET, PRINT), and repeat the question (GOTO Step 3).

Step 7   Give a closing comment and conclude the program (PRINT, END).

Carefully examine the listing of PROGRAM 3 on the opposite page to see how these steps are accomplished.

Note: This program also uses another "shorthand" method in BASIC: the use of multiple statements per line (statements 270, 310, 400, and 440). We have combined different BASIC statements on one line, rather than using a separate line number for each statement. The colon is used as a "delimiter," or separator, for each statement. Use of multiple statements per line makes more efficient use of the system's memory, but it can have the disadvantage of making the LISTing of the program more difficult to "read" in terms of its design. Therefore, the program examples will make minimal use of multiple statements on one line. However, remember that as you become more experienced, this is a handy shorthand method. Also, remember that the total length of a multiple-statement line must not exceed 255 characters.

Carefully note statements 150, 160, and 270 in the program listing. Each of these incorporates the PRINT TAB statement. This statement allows an automatic tabulation to a defined space before display or PRINTing occurs.

RUN from disk and refer to the listing and run of PROGRAM 3.

PROGRAM 3 Sample Run— Steps 1 and 2

```
STRING AND NUMERIC ANSWER CHECKING

What state follows Alaska
in total land area? TEXAS

   YEEE-HAA          THAT'S IT!
-------------------------------------------
STRING AND NUMERIC ANSWER CHECKING

What state follows Alaska
in total land area? CALIFORNIA

        NO...IT'S TEXAS
```

PROGRAM 3 Sample Run— Steps 3, 5, and 6

```
What was the perpetual age
of the late Jack Benny? 29

Too low...

What was the perpetual age
of the late Jack Benny? 50

Too high...have you no sympathy?

What was the perpetual age
of the late Jack Benny? 40

Too high...are you trying to be cruel?
```

```
] LIST

10 REM        PROGRAM 3
20 REM
30 REM -----------------------------------------------------------------
40 REM        STEP 1 - CLEAR THE SCREEN AND SHOW A TITLE
50 REM
60 HOME
70 PRIN] "STRING AND NUMERIC ANSWER CHECKING"
80 REM -----------------------------------------------------------------
90 REM        STEP 2 - ASK FIRST QUESTION; CHECK STRING INPUT FOR ACCURACY
100 REM
110 PRINT
120 PRINT "WHAT STATE FOLLOWS ALASKA"
130 INPUT "IN TOTAL LAND AREA? ";REPLY$
140 PRINT
150 IF REPLY$ = "TEXAS" THEN PRINT TAB( 3)"YEEE-HAA" TAB( 25)"THAT'S IT!"
160 IF REPLY$ < > "TEXAS" THEN PRINT TAB( 10)"NO...IT'S TEXAS"
170 REM -----------------------------------------------------------------
180 REM        STEP 3 - ASK SECOND QUESTION; CHECK NUMERIC INPUT FOR RANGE
190 REM
200 PRINT
210 PRINT "WHAT WAS THE PERPETUAL AGE"
220 INPUT "OF THE LATE JACK BENNY? ";REPLY
230 PRINT
240 REM -----------------------------------------------------------------
250 REM        STEP 4 - CORRECT ANSWER? IF SO, FEEDBACK GIVEN & END PROGRAM
260 REM
270 IF REPLY = 39 THEN PRINT "DIDN'T LOOK IT..." TAB( 25)"DID HE?": GOTO
    440
280 REM -----------------------------------------------------------------
290 REM        STEP 5 - WAS ANSWER TOO LOW? IF SO, SAY SO & REPEAT QUESTION
300 REM
310 IF REPLY < 39 THEN PRINT "TOO LOW...": GOTO 200
320 REM -----------------------------------------------------------------
330 REM        STEP 6 - TOO HIGH? IF SO, SAY SO WITH RANDOM FEEDBACK &
    REPEAT
340 REM
350 IF REPLY > 39 THEN PRINT "TOO HIGH...";
360 RANUM = INT (3 * RND (1) + 1)
370 IF RANUM = 1 THEN FEEDBK$ = "NOW THAT IS OLD!"
380 IF RANUM = 2 THEN FEEDBK$ = "ARE YOU TRYING TO BE CRUEL?"
390 IF RANUM = 3 THEN FEEDBK$ = "HAVE YOU NO SYMPATHY?"
400 PRINT FEEDBK$: GOTO 200
410 REM -----------------------------------------------------------------
420 REM        STEP 7 - GIVE A FINAL COMMENT AND END THE PROGRAM
430 REM
440 PRINT : PRINT
450 PRINT ,"BYE-BYE, FRIENDS..."
460 END
```

Chapter 3

Take a Ride
on the Loop-D-Loop

3.1 OBJECTIVES

For the successful completion of this chapter, you should be able to:

1. Define and give at least one example of each of these BASIC statements: VTAB, HTAB, DATA-READ, RESTORE, and FOR-NEXT (Sections 3.2.1–3.2.5).

2. Enter and RUN each of the BASIC programs used as statement examples in this chapter.

3. Design, enter, and RUN a BASIC program of your choosing that contains the statements discussed in Chapters 1–3.

3.2 BASIC STATEMENTS FOR THIS CHAPTER

3.2.1 Statement VTAB n

Purpose VTAB vertically positions the cursor n lines on the screen, where n may be 1–24, inclusive.

Example   VTAB 12 (The cursor would be positioned on the twelfth line in its current
          column.)

3.2.2   Statement HTAB n

Purpose   HTAB horizonally positions the cursor to column n on the screen, where n
          may be 1–40, inclusive.

Example   HTAB 10 (The cursor would be positioned in the tenth column on its current
          line.)

Example   ```
          10 HOME : VTAB 12 : HTAB 18
          20 PRINT "TEST 1"
          ```

          (TEST 1 would appear in the approximate center of the screen.)

## 3.2.3   Statement Pair DATA-READ

Purpose   DATA allows information (numeric or string) to be stored in a program for use
          at various stages throughout its execution. The pieces of information are gen-
          erally referred to as *data elements,* with each element separated (*delimited*) by
          a comma. READ assigns the defined value of a data element to a specified
          variable and "moves" a data "marker" or "pointer" to the next data element.
          The data type (numeric or string) *must* match the variable type (numeric or
          string). For example, "ABC" cannot be assigned to a numeric variable!
              One additional important note should be made in regard to the elements
          in the DATA statements: *Never* place a comma at the end of the DATA statement.
          The system may take the space character following the comma as the next data
          element!

Example   ```
          10 HOME
          20 READ P1$ : PRINT P1$
          30 READ A : PRINT A
          40 READ P2$ : PRINT P2$
          50 VTAB 22 : HTAB 30 : INPUT "RETURN =>";Z$
          60 PRINT P1$; A; P2$
          999 DATA "Help! I'm ",47," and sinking fast!"
          ```

          What caused the display to change from vertical to horizontal? Did the values
          of the variables change from one display to the next?
              This example also demonstrates one method to "hold" the screen display
          for an indefinite period *until* the RETURN key is pressed. Note how the posi-
          tioning is set in line 50. Also note that spaces are included within the quotation
          marks of the string DATA elements to prevent close-packing when the variable
          values are PRINTed in statement 60.

Example
```
10 HOME : C = 0
20 READ N
30 C = C + N
40 PRINT "N = " N TAB(20) "C = " C
50 READ N
60 C = C + N
70 PRINT "N = " N TAB(20) "C = " C
80 DATA 10,15
```

Why did the values of variables N and C change? Note that variable C is, in effect, a cumulative total of the values assigned to variable N. (After mentally tracing the program execution, enter and RUN the preceding examples to check your mental interpretations.)

3.2.4   Statement RESTORE

Purpose   Moves the data pointer to the first data element in the first DATA statement.

Example
```
10 HOME : C = 0
20 READ A$,B$,C$ : PRINT A$;B$;C$   (Note the commas and the
30 C = C + 1                           semicolons.)
40 PRINT "The value of C is " C
60 IF C <> 2 THEN 20
70 VTAB 22 : HTAB 30 : PRINT "Sigh..."
80 DATA "I'm a ","prisoner of ","LOVE!"
```

Enter and RUN the preceding program and note what happens. Add the statement 50 RESTORE and RUN again. Note the results.

What is the position of the data pointer after statement 20 has been executed but before the RESTORE statement is added? What caused the error message in the first RUN? What caused the program to stop execution after the statement 50 RESTORE was added? What would the program do if statement 30 were deleted (after 50 RESTORE was included in the program)? Think this through before RUNning; otherwise, remember that pressing the CTRL and RESET keys simultaneously will halt the execution of a "runaway" program!

Note: On many BASIC systems, statements such as 10 ... C = 0 (as in the previous programs, for example) are not needed, because all numeric variables are automatically "initialized" (set) to zero, and string variables are set to a null value (""). However, it is good programming practice to initialize any numeric variable used to zero.

3.2.5   Statement Pair FOR-NEXT

Purpose   Defines the number of times (loops) a series of consecutive BASIC statements is to be repeated. FOR defines the variable used as a counter for the repeats and the lower and upper limits of the count. NEXT increases the variable count

The Apple IIc is a portable computer in the Apple II family. It is functionally compatible with the Apple IIe.

by 1 (or the defined STEP size) and checks to see if the upper limit of the FOR is exceeded. If not, execution is transferred to the statement immediately following the FOR statement. If the upper limit is exceeded, execution is transferred to the statement immediately following the NEXT statement.

The variable names in the loop defined by a FOR-NEXT must be identical. Note that the start and/or limit of the loop may be defined by variable names, as in FOR X = Y TO Z.

Note also that loops may be defined in *decreasing* order:

```
FOR I = 10 TO 1 STEP -1
 ◆
 ◆
 ◆
NEXT I
```

In this example, the counter begins at 10 and decreases to 1 in increments (steps) of −1.

Examples

```
10 HOME
20 FOR C = 1 TO 10
30    PRINT C,C * C
40 NEXT C
50 PRINT "That's doing a loop ten times . . ."
```

```
10 HOME
20 FOR C = 1 TO 30 STEP 3
30    PRINT C
40 NEXT C
50 PRINT "That's a loop in steps of threes . . ."
```

```
10 HOME : VTAB 12
20 INPUT "Enter your first name ";NAME$
30 FOR C = 1 TO 30
40    HOME : VTAB 12 : HTAB C
50    PRINT NAME$
60 NEXT C
70 VTAB 20 : HTAB 10 : PRINT "Wow! You move fast!"
```

```
10 HOME
20 A = 10 : B = -10
30 FOR C = A TO B STEP -2
40    PRINT C " ";
50 NEXT C
60 PRINT "And we counted backward by twos . . ."
```

Note: The indentations are for clarity. Mentally trace the execution, and then enter and RUN each program.

The FOR-NEXT loop also may be used to produce a "pausing" effect while the loop "counts" to the specified value. Approximately 1 second is required for the loop to "count" to 1000.

Example

```
10 HOME : VTAB 12 : HTAB 10
20 PRINT "THE VANISHING TITLE"
30 FOR P = 1 TO 3000 : NEXT P
40 HOME
```

In the preceding example, the title will be displayed in the center of the screen for approximately 3 seconds.

3.3 INCORPORATING THE NEW STATEMENTS

With the addition of the statements in this chapter, a BASIC program may be designed that provides more utility than the earlier programs. In these programs we will also introduce "framing" into our design. Consider frames as separate screens displaying a title, information, questions, etc. For our purposes, each frame will begin with a HOME statement.

One of the many uses of computer programs involves searching a list of information (commonly called a *data base*) for key elements that may be specified by a user. For example, data bases may be searched for financial accounts that are overdue by 30, 60, or 90 days; address lists may be searched for ZIP codes; employee rolls may be searched for persons who have special deductions; and so on. The following program illustrates one search technique.

3.3.1 PROGRAM 4: Searching for a Range of Values

This program contains a list of DATA elements representing pairs of hypothetical names and scores. This list is to be searched for scores that fall within a specified maximum and minimum range. A list of names and scores that are within this range is printed. Following this, the user is given an option to do another search.

What will this require as the program is mentally designed? In outline form, there could be:

Frame 1   Center and display a title a moment or two for the program (HOME, VTAB, HTAB, PRINT, FOR-NEXT).

Frame 2   Present an introduction until the RETURN key is pressed [HOME, VTAB, PRINT(s), VTAB, HTAB, INPUT].

Frame 3   Initialize a counter for the number of matches found in a given search; get the maximum and minimum scores sought [HOME, (LET), VTAB, HTAB, INPUT(s)].

Frame 4, Step 1   Display a heading for the names and scores of any matches found (HOME, PRINT).

Frame 4, Step 2   Use a loop (FOR) to:

1. READ the DATA.
2. Check (IF-THENs) to see if the current score read is the last data element in the list and, if not, to see if it is in the maximum-minimum range.
3. Display (PRINT) the name and score if in the range.
4. Continue the search (NEXT).

Frame 4, Step 3   Prompt the user for another search option (INPUT). Move the data pointer back to the first data element if another search is to be done (RESTORE), followed by repetition of the total process (GOTO Frame 3).

```
] LIST


10 REM         PROGRAM 4
20 REM
30 REM -----------------------------------------------------------------------
40 REM         FRAME 1 - TITLE DISPLAY WITH PAUSE
50 REM
60 HOME : VTAB 12: HTAB 8
70 PRINT "SCORE DATA SEARCHING"
80 FOR P = 1 TO 4000: NEXT P
90 REM -----------------------------------------------------------------------
100 REM        FRAME 2 - INTRODUCTION
110 REM
120 HOME : VTAB 4
130 PRINT "THIS PROGRAM WILL SEARCH A DATA LIST": PRINT
140 PRINT "CONSISTING OF STUDENT NAMES AND SCORES": PRINT
150 PRINT "FOR A MATCH WITHIN A MAXIMUM AND": PRINT
160 PRINT "MINIMUM RANGE THAT YOU SPECIFY."
170 VTAB 20: HTAB 30: INPUT "RETURN =>";Z$
180 REM -----------------------------------------------------------------------
190 REM        FRAME 3 - INITIALIZE A COUNTER; GET MAXIMUM & MINIMUM VALUES
200 REM
210 HOME : VTAB 10: HTAB 6:COUNT = 0
220 INPUT "MAXIMUM SCORE SOUGHT IS? ";MAX
230 VTAB 12: HTAB 6
240 INPUT "MINIMUM SCORE SOUGHT IS? ";MIN
250 REM -----------------------------------------------------------------------
260 REM        FRAME 4, STEP 1 - DISPLAY A HEADING
270 REM
280 HOME
290 PRINT "SCORES IN THE RANGE OF "MIN" TO "MAX: PRINT
300 PRINT "NAME","SCORE"
310 PRINT "----","-----"
320 REM -----------------------------------------------------------------------
330 REM        FRAME 4, STEP 2 - DO A LOOP, SEARCHING THE DATA FOR A MATCH
340 REM
350 FOR I = 1 TO 50
360 READ NAME$,SCRE
370 IF NAME$ = "END OF NAMES" THEN 400
380 IF SCRE > = MIN AND SCRE < = MAX THEN PRINT NAME$,SCRE:COUNT = COUNT
    + 1
390 NEXT I
400 PRINT : PRINT "THIS SEARCH FOUND "COUNT" MATCH(ES).": PRINT
410 REM -----------------------------------------------------------------------
420 REM        FRAME 4, STEP 3 - GIVE AN OPTION FOR ANOTHER SEARCH
430 REM
440 INPUT "DO YOU WISH ANOTHER SEARCH (Y OR N)? ";Z$
450 IF Z$ = "Y" THEN RESTORE : GOTO 210
```

Frame 5 An end to the program (HOME, PRINT and END).

- -

DATA List Include a list of names and scores as DATA at the end of the program.

Carefully examine the listing of PROGRAM 4 on pages 41 and 43 to see how these steps are incorporated into BASIC code.

Note: Two LISTings of PROGRAM 4 are shown. The first is representative of how we will design programs in a frame-by-frame and step-by-step manner. The second reflects the version stored on the disk. In this version, we have incorporated the HOME, INVERSE, PRINT, and NORMAL statements in place of certain REM statements. This allows each frame and step to be displayed on the screen "black on white" so that you may "see" each sequence as it is executed. Compare both listings for the changes that were made. PROGRAM 4 is the only program in which the disk version is different from the listing shown in the book.

RUN from disk and refer to the listing and run of PROGRAM 4.

```
460 REM  -------------------------------------------------------------------
470 REM         FRAME 5 - CONCLUSION OF THE PROGRAM
480 REM
490 HOME : VTAB 12: HTAB 8
500 PRINT "* SEARCH COMPLETED *"
510 END
520 REM  -------------------------------------------------------------------
530 REM         DATA LIST - HYPOTHETICAL NAMES AND SCORES
540 REM
550 DATA "SUE",67,"BOB",55,"JACK",98,"MARY",99,"STAN",50,"ROB",72
560 DATA "LETA",77,"ALEX",66,"SUSAN",85,"MARIA",99,"FRAN",70
570 DATA "BOBBIE",100,"CHARLES",64,"BILLY",66,"MAGGIE",86
580 DATA "DONNA",91,"YANCY",77,"TRACY",89,"KARYN",100,"BUCK",90
590 REM  -------------------------------------------------------------------
600 REM         SPACE FOR ADDITIONAL DATA PAIRS TO BE INSERTED
970 REM  -------------------------------------------------------------------
980 REM         THE FINAL DATA PAIR TO IDENTIFY THE END OF THE DATA LIST
990 REM
1000 DATA     "END OF NAMES",0


] LIST


10 REM        PROGRAM 4
20 REM
30 REM  -------------------------------------------------------------------
40 HOME : INVERSE : PRINT "FRAME 1 - TITLE DISPLAY WITH PAUSE": NORMAL
50 REM
60 VTAB 12: HTAB 8
70 PRINT "SCORE DATA SEARCHING"
80 FOR P = 1 TO 4000: NEXT P
90 REM  -------------------------------------------------------------------
100 HOME : INVERSE : PRINT "FRAME 2 - INTRODUCTION": NORMAL
110 REM
120 VTAB 4
130 PRINT "THIS PROGRAM WILL SEARCH A DATA LIST": PRINT
140 PRINT "CONSISTING OF STUDENT NAMES AND SCORES": PRINT
150 PRINT "FOR A MATCH WITHIN A MAXIMUM AND": PRINT
160 PRINT "MINIMUM RANGE THAT YOU SPECIFY."
170 VTAB 20: HTAB 30: INPUT "RETURN =>";Z$
180 REM  -------------------------------------------------------------------
190 HOME : INVERSE : PRINT "FRAME 3 - INITIALIZE COUNTER; GET VALUES":
    NORMAL
200 REM
210 VTAB 10: HTAB 6:COUNT = 0
220 INPUT "MAXIMUM SCORE SOUGHT IS? ";MAX
230 VTAB 12: HTAB 6
240 INPUT "MINIMUM SCORE SOUGHT IS? ";MIN
250 REM  -------------------------------------------------------------------
```

```
260 HOME : INVERSE : PRINT "FRAME 4, STEP 1 - DISPLAY A HEADING": NORMAL
270 REM
280 VTAB 4
290 PRINT "SCORES IN THE RANGE OF "MIN" TO "MAX: PRINT
300 PRINT "NAME","SCORE"
310 PRINT "----","-----"
320 REM ----------------------------------------------------------------
330 INVERSE : PRINT "FRAME 4, STEP 2 - DATA SEARCH LOOP": NORMAL
340 REM
350 FOR I = 1 TO 50
360 READ NAME$,SCRE
370 IF NAME$ = "END OF NAMES" THEN 400
380 IF SCRE > = MIN AND SCRE < = MAX THEN PRINT NAME$,SCRE:COUNT = COUNT
    + 1
390 NEXT I
400 PRINT : PRINT "THIS SEARCH FOUND "COUNT" MATCH(ES).": PRINT
410 REM ----------------------------------------------------------------
420 INVERSE : PRINT "FRAME 4, STEP 3 - OPTION FOR ANOTHER": NORMAL
430 REM
440 INPUT "DO YOU WISH ANOTHER SEARCH (Y OR N)? ";Z$
450 IF Z$ = "Y" THEN RESTORE : GOTO 190
460 REM ----------------------------------------------------------------
470 HOME : INVERSE : PRINT "FRAME 5 - CONCLUSION OF THE PROGRAM": NORMAL
480 REM
490 VTAB 12: HTAB 8
500 PRINT "* SEARCH COMPLETED *"
510 END
520 REM ----------------------------------------------------------------
530 REM         DATA LIST - HYPOTHETICAL NAMES AND SCORES
540 REM
550 DATA "SUE",67,"BOB",55,"JACK",98,"MARY",99,"STAN",50,"ROB",72
560 DATA "LETA",77,"ALEX",66,"SUSAN",85,"MARIA",99,"FRAN",70
570 DATA "BOBBIE",100,"CHARLES",64,"BILLY",66,"MAGGIE",86
580 DATA "DONNA",91,"YANCY",77,"TRACY",89,"KARYN",100,"BUCK",90
590 REM ----------------------------------------------------------------
600 REM         SPACE FOR ADDITIONAL DATA PAIRS TO BE INSERTED
970 REM ----------------------------------------------------------------
980 REM         THE FINAL DATA PAIR TO IDENTIFY THE END OF THE DATA LIST
990 REM
1000 DATA    "END OF NAMES",0
```

```
                    SCORE DATA SEARCHING
```

```
This program will search a data list

consisting of student names and scores

for a match within a maximum and

minimum range that you specify.

                                RETURN  =>
```

```
            Maximum score sought is? 60

            Minimum score sought is? 50
```

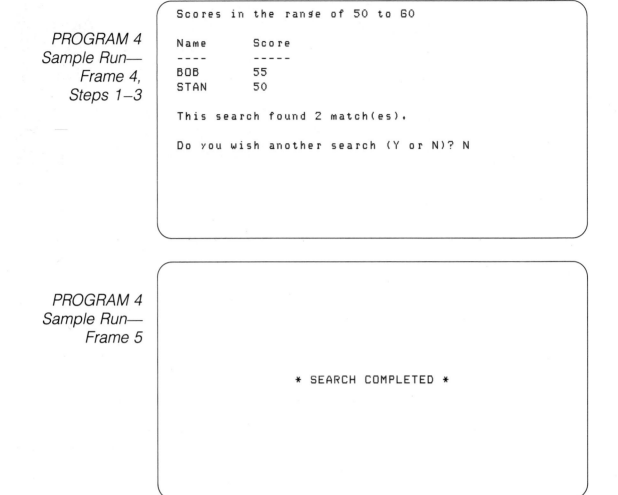

PROGRAM 4
Sample Run—
Frame 4,
Steps 1–3

```
Scores in the range of 50 to 60

Name        Score
----        -----
BOB         55
STAN        50

This search found 2 match(es).

Do you wish another search (Y or N)? N
```

PROGRAM 4
Sample Run—
Frame 5

```
            * SEARCH COMPLETED *
```

3.3.2   Additional Comments
on PROGRAM 4

DATA statements may be included anywhere in a BASIC program. They are not executed as, for example, a PRINT or INPUT statement would be. Their only use is to contain data (information) that is to be READ and assigned to variables. The DATA statements in PROGRAM 4 are placed at the end of the program so that additional DATA statements may be added if desired. The last data element pair, "END OF NAMES" and 0, is given the highest number possible for a DATA statement (1000 in this case). Thus, additional DATA statements could be inserted between statements 580–1000 if there were a need to add more data.

Students using the
Apple IIe in school
can transfer their
skills to small
businesses that use
computers to do
accounting and
record keeping.

In RUNning the program, how could the DATA in PROGRAM 4 be searched for only *one* user-specified score, listing all the names with that score?

3.4   A TIMESAVING TECHNIQUE

There may be times when a user wishes to SAVE both the "old" and "new" versions of a program. The "new" (modified) version of a program may be SAVEd by simply giving it a new (unique) name when the SAVE command is issued. We did this earlier in Chapter 2 when PROGRAM 1 was modified (with the heartbeats) and SAVEd as PROGRAM 2.

To further illustrate this, PROGRAM 5 will be created and SAVEd. Then it will be modified and SAVEd as PROGRAM 5A. This means that both the old (PROGRAM 5) and the new (PROGRAM 5A) programs will be available for future use.

3.4.1   PROGRAM 5: Subtraction Drill

Arbitrarily, this new program will be a drill on subtraction practice. Then it will be modified to be a drill on addition practice.

We will have the program display a title for a few seconds, then let the user select the number of problems (within limits) and the range of values (again, within limits). The program will present that number of problems, randomly selecting the values from within the requested range. If the problem is answered correctly, a "correct counter" will be incremented by 1, and the next problem will be presented. Otherwise, the correct answer will be displayed until the RETURN key is pressed. At the conclusion of the program the number of problems answered correctly will be displayed.

Here is the program design by frames and steps.

Frame 1   Erase the screen and center and display a title for a few seconds (HOME, VTAB, HTAB, PRINT, FOR-NEXT).

Frame 2, Step 1   Erase the screen and ask for the number of problems the user wishes (HOME, VTAB, INPUT).

Frame 2, Step 2   Check that the value INPUT is within our defined limits (IF-THEN-PRINT, GOTO Frame 2, Step 1).

Frame 2, Step 3   Ask for the maximum and minimum values for the problems (INPUTs).

Frame 2, Step 4   Check that these values are within our defined limits (IF-THEN-PRINT, GOTO Frame 2, Step 3).

Now we begin a loop asking the requested number of problems.

Loop Frames, Step 1   Erase the screen and position the cursor for each problem (FOR, HOME, VTAB, HTAB).

Loop Frames, Step 2   Randomly select two numbers within the range requested by the user [(LET), INT, RND], and check (IF-THEN) to ensure that the first random number is larger than the second. This is done arbitrarily, since the program is a *subtraction* drill.

Loop Frames, Step 3   Assign the difference of the second number from the first number to a variable (LET). This is the correct answer to the problem. Display the problem (PRINT).

Loop Frames, Step 4   Get the user's answer and check it for accuracy. If it is correct, increase a counter by 1 and ask the next question [INPUT, IF-THEN (LET), GOTO, NEXT].

] LIST


```
10 REM         PROGRAM 5
20 REM
30 REM  -----------------------------------------------------------------
40 REM         FRAME 1 - DISPLAY A TITLE FOR ABOUT 3 SECONDS
50 REM
60 HOME : VTAB 12: HTAB 10
70 PRINT "SUBTRACTION DRILL"
80 FOR P = 1 TO 3000: NEXT P
90 REM  -----------------------------------------------------------------
100 REM        FRAME 2, STEP 1 - ASK FOR THE NUMBER OF PROBLEMS
110 REM
120 HOME : VTAB 12
130 INPUT "HOW MANY PROBLEMS DO YOU WANT? ";NUMBER
140 REM  ----------------------------------------------------------------
150 REM        FRAME 2, STEP 2 - CHECK FOR A REASONABLE NUMBER
160 REM
170 IF NUMBER < 5 OR NUMBER > 20 THEN PRINT ,"SELECT 5 TO 20!": GOTO 130
180 REM  ----------------------------------------------------------------
190 REM        FRAME 2, STEP 3 - ASK FOR HIGH AND LOW RANGE OF NUMBERS
200 REM
210 PRINT : INPUT "WHAT'S THE LOWEST NUMBER YOU WANT? ";LOW
220 PRINT : INPUT "WHAT'S THE HIGHEST NUMBER YOU WANT? ";HIGH
230 REM  ----------------------------------------------------------------
240 REM        FRAME 2, STEP 4 - CHECK FOR REASONABLE LIMITS
250 REM
260 IF LOW < 10 OR HIGH > 100 THEN PRINT ,"SELECT 10 TO 100": GOTO 210
270 IF HIGH < = LOW THEN PRINT "HIGH IS LESS OR = LOW NUMBER!": GOTO 210
280 REM  ----------------------------------------------------------------
290 REM        LOOP FRAMES, STEP 1 - START THE LOOP; POSITION CURSOR
300 REM
310 FOR I = 1 TO NUMBER
320 HOME : VTAB 12: HTAB 10
330 REM  ----------------------------------------------------------------
340 REM        LOOP FRAMES, STEP 2 - RANDOMLY SELECT TWO NUMBERS
350 REM
360 N1 = INT (((HIGH - LOW) + 1) * RND (1) + LOW)
370 N2 = INT (((HIGH - LOW) + 1) * RND (1) + LOW)
380 REM  ----------------------------------------------------------------
390 REM        LOOP FRAMES, STEP 3 - CHECK N1 > N2; ASSIGN ANSWER; DISPLAY
400 REM
410 IF N1 < = N2 THEN 360
420 ANSWER = N1 - N2
430 PRINT N1" - "N2" = ";
440 REM  ----------------------------------------------------------------
450 REM  LOOP FRAMES, STEP 4 - CHECK REPLY; IF CORRECT, COUNT IT; ASK NEXT
460 REM
470 INPUT REPLY
480 IF REPLY = ANSWER THEN CRCT = CRCT + 1: GOTO 540
```

Loop Frames,   If the answer is incorrect, display the correct answer until the RETURN key is
Step 5   pressed, then ask the next question (PRINT, VTAB, HTAB, INPUT, NEXT).

Final Frame   Erase the screen and center and display the number of problems answered
correctly (HOME, VTAB, PRINT, END).

Carefully examine the listing of PROGRAM 5 on pages 49 and 51 and note
how each frame and step is translated into BASIC code.

RUN from disk and refer to the listing and run of PROGRAM 5.

```
490 REM -----------------------------------------------------------------
500 REM        LOOP FRAMES, STEP 5 - IF INCORRECT, SHOW ANSWER UNTIL RETURN
510 REM
520 PRINT : PRINT "THE CORRECT ANSWER IS "ANSWER
530 VTAB 20: HTAB 30: INPUT "RETURN =>";Z$
540 NEXT I
550 REM -----------------------------------------------------------------
560 REM        FINAL FRAME - PERFORMANCE REPORT
570 REM
580 HOME : VTAB 12
590 PRINT "YOU WERE CORRECT ON "CRCT" OF "NUMBER" PROBLEMS"
600 END
```

PROGRAM 5
Sample Run—
Frame 2, Steps
1–4

```
How many problems do you want? 100
               SELECT 5 TO 20!
How many problems do you want? 7

What's the lowest number you want? 12

What's the highest number you want? 12
HIGH IS LESS THAN OR = LOW NUMBER!

What's the lowest number you want? 12

What's the highest number you want? 50
```

PROGRAM 5
Sample Run—
Loop Frame,
Steps 1–4

```
               32 - 14 =? 18
```

PROGRAM 5
Sample Run—
Loop Frame,
Steps 1–5

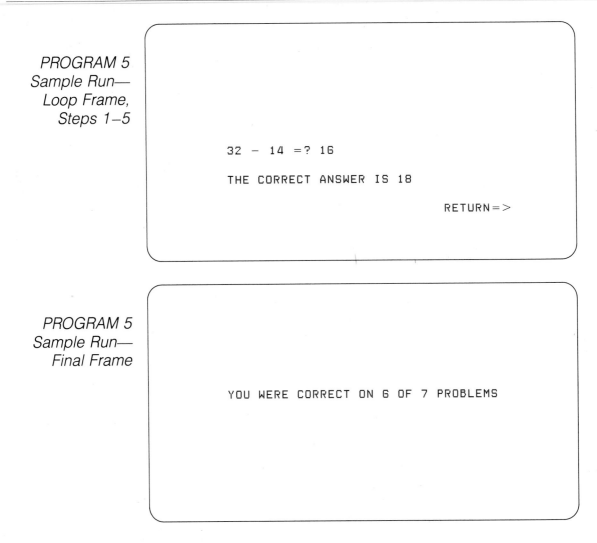

```
32  -  14  =?  16

THE CORRECT ANSWER IS 18

                                        RETURN = >
```

PROGRAM 5
Sample Run—
Final Frame

```
YOU WERE CORRECT ON 6 OF 7 PROBLEMS
```

3.4.2   PROGRAM 5A: Addition Drill
(A Modification of PROGRAM 5)

For the two previous programs, we took a concept for the general design, broke it down into a series of steps from "top to bottom," outlined the BASIC statements needed to accomplish each step, and translated each step into program code. Now, let us see what would be necessary to take an existing program and make a minimum of modifications so that the program would present material in a similar design, but of different content.

PROGRAM 5 presented drill on subtraction. We will modify this program to present drill on addition, then SAVE it as PROGRAM 5A. Careful examination of the listing of PROGRAM 5 shows that the *minimum* changes needed are statements 70, 420, and 430. After PROGRAM 5 has been LOADed from the disk, the following is entered:

```
70 PRINT "A D D I T I O N   D R I L L"
420 ANSWER = N1 + N2
430 PRINT N1 " + " N2 " = ";
SAVE PROGRAM 5A
```

However, statement 10 was retyped to reflect the new program name and statement 410 was deleted, since, arbitrarily, it no longer matters if the first random number is smaller than the second.

Thus, a new program, PROGRAM 5A, based on PROGRAM 5, has been created and SAVEd without the time and trouble required to completely retype the new version.

RUN from disk and refer to the listing and run of PROGRAM 5A.

PROGRAM 5A
Creation from
PROGRAM 5

```
] LOAD PROGRAM 5

] 10 REM        PROGRAM 5A

] 70 PRINT "ADDITION DRILL"

] 410

] 420 ANSWER = N1 + N2

] 430 PRINT N1 " + " N2 " = ";

] SAVE PROGRAM 5A
```

```
] LIST


10 REM        PROGRAM 5A
20 REM
30 REM --------------------------------------------------------------
40 REM        FRAME 1 - DISPLAY A TITLE FOR ABOUT 3 SECONDS
50 REM
60 HOME : VTAB 12: HTAB 10
70 PRINT "ADDITION DRILL"
80 FOR P = 1 TO 3000: NEXT P
```

```
90 REM  -------------------------------------------------------------------
100 REM        FRAME 2, STEP 1 - ASK FOR THE NUMBER OF PROBLEMS
110 REM
120 HOME : VTAB 12
130 INPUT "HOW MANY PROBLEMS DO YOU WANT? ";NUMBER
140 REM  -------------------------------------------------------------------
150 REM        FRAME 2, STEP 2 - CHECK FOR A REASONABLE NUMBER
160 REM
170 IF NUMBER < 5 OR NUMBER > 20 THEN PRINT ,"SELECT 5 TO 20!": GOTO 130
180 REM  -------------------------------------------------------------------
190 REM        FRAME 2, STEP 3 - ASK FOR HIGH AND LOW RANGE OF NUMBERS
200 REM
210 PRINT : INPUT "WHAT'S THE LOWEST NUMBER YOU WANT? ";LOW
220 PRINT : INPUT "WHAT'S THE HIGHEST NUMBER YOU WANT? ";HIGH
230 REM  -------------------------------------------------------------------
240 REM        FRAME 2, STEP 4 - CHECK FOR REASONABLE LIMITS
250 REM
260 IF LOW < 10 OR HIGH > 100 THEN PRINT ,"SELECT 10 TO 100": GOTO 210
270 IF LOW = HIGH THEN PRINT "HIGH IS LESS OR = LOW NUMBER!": GOTO 210
280 REM  -------------------------------------------------------------------
290 REM        LOOP FRAMES, STEP 1 - START THE LOOP; POSITION CURSOR
300 REM
310 FOR I = 1 TO NUMBER
320 HOME : VTAB 12: HTAB 10
330 REM  -------------------------------------------------------------------
340 REM        LOOP FRAMES, STEP 2 - RANDOMLY SELECT TWO NUMBERS
350 REM
360 N1 = INT (((HIGH - LOW) + 1) * RND (1) + LOW)
370 N2 = INT (((HIGH - LOW) + 1) * RND (1) + LOW)
380 REM  -------------------------------------------------------------------
390 REM        LOOP FRAMES, STEP 3 - CHECK N1 > N2; ASSIGN ANSWER; DISPLAY
400 REM
420 ANSWER = N1 + N2
430 PRINT N1" + "N2" = ";
440 REM  -------------------------------------------------------------------
450 REM        LOOP FRAMES, STEP 4 - CHECK REPLY; IF CORRECT, COUNT IT; ASK
    NEXT
460 REM
470 INPUT REPLY
480 IF REPLY = ANSWER THEN CRCT = CRCT + 1: GOTO 540
490 REM  -------------------------------------------------------------------
500 REM        LOOP FRAMES, STEP 5 - IF INCORRECT, SHOW ANSWER UNTIL RETURN
510 REM
520 PRINT : PRINT "THE CORRECT ANSWER IS "ANSWER
530 VTAB 20: HTAB 30: INPUT "RETURN =>";Z$
540 NEXT I
550 REM  -------------------------------------------------------------------
560 REM        FINAL FRAME - PERFORMANCE REPORT
570 REM
```

```
580 HOME : VTAB 12
590 PRINT "YOU WERE CORRECT ON "CRCT" OF "NUMBER" PROBLEMS"
600 END
```

3.5 POSERS AND PROBLEMS

1. Correct any errors (if, in fact, there are any) in the following three programs:

    ```
    10 FOR X = 1 TO 10
    20    PRINT Y,Y * Y
    30 NEXT Y
    40 END
    ```

    ```
    10 DATA "How old is George",47," (in 1985)"
    20 READ Q$,A,C
    30 PRINT Q$;C;
    40 INPUT R
    50 IF A$ = R THEN 70
    60 PRINT "No...!"
    70 PRINT A " is correct!"
    80 END
    ```

    ```
    10 DATA 4,5,6
    20 FOR X = 1 TO 3
    30    READ A
    40    PRINT, A
    50 NEXT X
    60 READ A
    70 PRINT A
    80 END
    ```

2. Following are some student data for a name and test score. Complete the program so that the name and score are printed in columnar form.

    ```
    10 DATA "CHUCK",95,"MARY",80,"PHIL",95,"JEANNIE",35
    20 FOR I = 1 TO 4
    30    READ S$,S
    ??
    ```

3. Modify your program from Problem 2 to print the average of the scores after printing the list of names and scores. *Hint:* Review "cumulative total" techniques shown in Section 3.2.3.

4. Write a search program in which a list of data elements consists of hy-

pothetical names, hair colors, and eye colors. A list is to be printed that shows the foregoing information based on a search of a user-specified eye color. For example, if BLUE is input in response to EYE COLOR?, the names, hair colors, and eye colors of all the blue-eyed people would be printed. The program should also give the option to conduct another search.

Note: This program may be easily completed by modifying PROGRAM 4. For example, PRINT statements describing the program and prompting for eye color will have to be modified and/or added. The INPUT will have to be a string variable. The READ statement will need to READ three DATA elements. The IF-THEN check will have to compare the INPUT variable and the eye color variable just read. The PRINT statement showing a match will have to be written so that three variable values are displayed on one line. Finally, the DATA statements will have to contain three string elements (name, hair color, and eye color).

5. Enter and RUN the following program. Be prepared to discuss its flow.

```
10 FOR R = 10 TO 1 STEP -1
20     HOME : VTAB 12
30     PRINT R " little rabbit(s)...see the tail(s)!"
40     PRINT ,
50       FOR T = 1 TO R
60         PRINT "* ";
70       NEXT T
80     PRINT
90     VTAB 20 : HTAB 12 : PRINT "FRAME " 11 - R
100    VTAB 22 : HTAB 30 : INPUT "RETURN =>";Z$
110 NEXT R
120 HOME : VTAB 12 : HTAB 10
130 PRINT "And then there were NONE..."
```

In particular, what is the purpose of STEP −1 in statement 10, the comma in statement 40, the semicolon in statement 60, and PRINT in statement 80? After RUNning the program, delete statements 90–100 and 120. RUN the program again and note the results.

6. Write a program that converts Celsius to Fahrenheit and PRINTs an equivalence table for every five Celsius degrees from 0–100, inclusive. *Hint:* F = 32 + (C * ⅘).

7. Write a program that will PRINT the cube of the numbers 1–10, inclusive.

8. Modify PROGRAM 5 to present a drill on multiplication.

9. Modify PROGRAM 5 to present a drill on division. Use random numbers that will *not* have a remainder after division. *Note:* This task may be accomplished by incorporating the statement:

```
410 IF N1/N2 <> INT(N1/N2) THEN 360
```

This will ensure that any quotient derived from dividing N1 by N2 will be a whole number, that is, an integer value with no remainder.

THINK ABOUT THIS . . .

. . . FOR FUN

I have two U.S. coins that total $0.55. One of them is not a nickel. What are the coins?

. . . SERIOUSLY

Could the proliferation of microcomputers in the school and home alter the traditional classroom setting as we now know it? If so, how?

Chapter

DIM It!
There Must Be
an Easier Way!
Array! Array!
There Is!

4.1 OBJECTIVES

For the successful completion of this chapter, you should be able to:

1. Define and give at least one example of a subscripted variable (Section 4.2.1).

2. Define and give at least one example of both a one- and a two-dimensional array (Sections 4.2.1 and 4.2.2).

3. Define and give at least one example of each of the BASIC statements DIM and GOSUB-RETURN (Section 4.4).

4. Give examples that indicate how *commands* may be incorporated as *statements* in a BASIC program (Section 4.4.4).

5. Design, enter, and RUN a BASIC program of your own choosing that includes a one-dimensional array and the BASIC statements for this chapter.

4.2 ARRAYS

4.2.1 One-Dimensional Arrays

For our purposes, a one-dimensional array is just an organized LIST of information stored in a new type of variable. That information could be any string and/or numeric values: student names, states, chemical names, school districts, test scores, ages, weights, years, and so on. This list of information may be assigned to variables using any of the methods previously discussed, such as (LET), INPUT, and DATA-READ statements. As you will see, once we have assigned this information to lists, we may apply a variety of uses without having to RESTORE and READ as we did in earlier programs.

Recall the four names and test scores given in Problem 2 of Chapter 3. Using one-dimensional arrays in BASIC, we can easily make lists of those names and scores.

Consider the BASIC statements needed. First, there is information (names and scores) that will be used; thus, there will be a need for DATA statements. Of course, if there is DATA, it will need to be READ. Also, a FOR-NEXT loop could be used to do the READing. Thus:

```
10 DATA "Chuck","Mary","Phil","Jeannie"
20 FOR I = 1 TO 4
30    READ N$(I)
40 NEXT I
```

This should appear somewhat familiar, with the exception of statement 30, READ N$(I). N$(I) is an example of another type of variable. This type, however, uses an "internal" variable, (I), to distinguish one value of N$(I) from the others. Remember, the variable I is going to have a value that may be 1, 2, 3, or 4 (FOR I = 1 TO 4). Thus, the variable values in this example are:

```
N$(1) = Chuck
N$(2) = Mary
N$(3) = Phil
N$(4) = Jeannie
```

Or, said another way, there is a four-item list (one-dimensional array) of N$(I) values:

I	N$(I)
1.	Chuck
2.	Mary
3.	Phil
4.	Jeannie

The name given to these types of variables is *subscripted variables*. The value of N$(1), pronounced "N-string sub 1," is equal to the string Chuck; the value of N$(2) is equal to the string Mary, and so on.

It is quite simple to build a series of lists using subscripted variables. Consider:

```
10 DATA "Chuck",95,"Mary",80,"Phil",95,"Jeannie",35
20 FOR I = 1 TO 4
30    READ N$(I),S(I)
40 NEXT I
```

If these statements were to be executed, what would be the value of N$(3)? Of S(4)? If the following statements were added to the preceding statements, what would be the result of execution?

```
50 FOR I = 4 TO 1 STEP -1
60    PRINT N$(I),S$(I)
70 NEXT I
80 END
```

(Mentally trace the execution; then enter and RUN to check your mental interpretation.)

Enter and RUN the following program:

```
10 HOME : VTAB 2 : HTAB 8
20 PRINT "Here's a list of 5 names:" : PRINT
30 FOR I = 1 TO 5 : READ N$(I) : PRINT,N$(I) : NEXT I
40 PRINT : PRINT "Let's randomly choose 4 sets of 2
   names"
44 VTAB 22 : HTAB 30 : INPUT "RETURN =>";Z$ : HOME
50 FOR I = 1 TO 4
60    FOR J = 1 TO 2 : VTAB I + 1 : HTAB J * 10
70       X = INT(5 * RND(1) + 1)
80          PRINT N$(X)
90    NEXT J
100 NEXT I
110 PRINT : PRINT "And here's the list in reverse" :
    PRINT
120 FOR I = 5 TO 1 STEP -1 : PRINT, N$(I) : NEXT I
130 DATA "Kay","Buck","Karyn","Tracy","George"
```

As you can see (and will see again), one advantage of using one-dimensional arrays is that, once the values have been assigned to positions in the list, we may pick and choose items from the list at will. Note that the FOR I = 1 TO 4 loop has another loop (FOR J = 1 TO 2) "nested" within it. In this example, the "inner" J loop, which randomly selects and displays two names, will be executed four times by the "outer" I loop. Thus, a total of eight names will be randomly selected and displayed. Some will be repeated, of course, since there are only five names in the list. Also note how the VTAB and HTAB in statement 60 use the values of I and J, respectively, in positioning the display of the names.

4.2.2   Two-Dimensional Arrays

A one-dimensional array is nothing more than a *list* of data; a two-dimensional array is a *table* of data in rows and columns.

Assume there are two test scores for each of the students in the preceding example. A table, consisting of four rows and two columns, might look like this:

Name	Test 1	Test 2
Chuck	95	80
Mary	80	82
Phil	95	93
Jeannie	35	98

Note: The table in this example is composed of the test scores. The names of the students cannot be included in the table, because they are *string* variables, and the two-dimensional array is defined as a *numeric* array. In other words, variable types (string and numeric) cannot be mixed in an array. However, just as it is possible to define a two-dimensional numeric array, a two-dimensional string array may also be defined. Just don't mix them!

How could a two-dimensional array of this information be formed? Again, there is information (names and scores) that will be used, so DATA statements are appropriate. This information in statement form would be:

```
10 DATA "Chuck",95,80
20 DATA "Mary",80,82
30 DATA "Phil",95,93
40 DATA "Jeannie",35,98
```

(The DATA statements could be combined into one or two statements. However, they are listed as four separate statements and at the beginning of the "program" for the sake of clarity.)

The difficulty is in determining how the DATA should be READ. Examine the sequence of information: one name, followed by two scores, then the next name, followed by two scores; and so on. Since there are four rows (names) and each must be READ, the first loop to be defined will be FOR ROW = 1 TO 4. However, before the next name is READ, there are two scores to be assigned (READ). So, another loop, FOR COL = 1 TO 2, needs to be defined. Thus:

```
50 FOR ROW = 1 TO 4
60     READ N$(ROW)
70         FOR COL = 1 TO 2
80             READ S(ROW,COL)
90         NEXT COL
100 NEXT ROW
```

Note: The indentation is for clarity only.

The variable ROW is READing the rows of the table and the variable COL is READing columns. Again, one loop (COL) is *nested* within another loop (ROW). Examine the table. What is the value of S(ROW,COL) when ROW = 1 and COL = 1? When ROW = 3 and COL = 2? The most important point to remember is that ROW and COL are nothing more than *numbers* that define a row and a column, respectively.

We will not make extensive use of two-dimensional arrays in this book. However, some of the later program examples will include this type of array. Thus, it is important that you have some awareness of two-dimensional arrays.

4.3 EXAMPLES OF THE USE OF ONE-DIMENSIONAL ARRAYS

There are many more applications of one- and two-dimensional arrays in instructional computing than just building lists or tables of names and scores. The following two programs give examples of some of these uses.

4.3.1 PROGRAM 6: Random Sentences, Questions, and Responses

One use of one-dimensional arrays may be seen in PROGRAM 6. This program demonstrates the use of one-dimensional arrays in forming random sentences. One array will contain the subjects, another the verbs, and another the direct objects. Using random numbers, a subject, verb, and direct object will be selected from each list and printed as a sentence. Since each list will contain five items, a total of 125 (5 × 5 × 5) different sentences is possible. A one-dimensional array is also used to randomly select the "question" to be asked; that is, "Identify the ([SUBJECT]/[VERB]/[DIRECT OBJECT])." Another one-dimensional array will contain the "positive feedback" comments given for a correct answer. This feedback will also be randomly selected from the list. Thus, the use of one-dimensional arrays provides a method of increasing the variety of questions, answers, and feedback in instructional computing programs without extensive programming.

Frame by frame and step by step, the design of this program is:

Frame 1   Present a title for a moment or two, then dimension the size of the arrays and assign the lists of subjects, verbs, direct objects, and sentence parts to identify and feed back to their appropriate arrays.

Frame 2   Present an introduction until the RETURN key is pressed.

Frame 3   Let the user select the number of sentences to practice (within defined limits).

Frame 4, Step 1   Begin the question loop by randomly selecting each part of the sentence (subject, verb, and direct object).

Frame 4, Step 2   Assign the randomly selected part to identify as the correct answer.

Frame 4, Step 3   Display the sentence and get a reply from the user.

```
] LIST


10 REM        PROGRAM 6
20 REM
30 REM -------------------------------------------------------------------
40 REM        FRAME 1 - TITLE AND ASSIGNMENTS
50 REM
60 HOME : VTAB 12: HTAB 8
70 PRINT "RANDOM SENTENCES"
80 FOR P = 1 TO 3000: NEXT P
90 DIM SUBJ$(5), VERB$(5),DIROBJ$(5)
100 FOR I = 1 TO 5: READ SUBJ$(I),VERB$(I),DIROBJ$(I): NEXT I
110 PART$(1) = "SUBJECT":PART$(2) = "VERB":PART$(3) = "DIRECT OBJECT"
120 FDBK$(1) = "PERFECT":FDBK$(2) = "GREAT":FDBK$(3) = "A-OK"
130 REM -------------------------------------------------------------------
140 REM        FRAME 2 - INTRODUCTION
150 REM
160 HOME : VTAB 4
170 PRINT "I'LL GIVE YOU SOME SENTENCES AND YOU": PRINT
180 PRINT "WILL BE ASKED TO IDENTIFY EITHER THE": PRINT
190 PRINT "SUBJECT, VERB, OR DIRECT OBJECT. YOU": PRINT
200 PRINT "MAY SELECT 3-25 SENTENCES TO PRACTICE.": PRINT
210 VTAB 20: HTAB 30: INPUT "RETURN =>";Z$
220 REM -------------------------------------------------------------------
230 REM        FRAME 3 - NUMBER OF SENTENCES FOR PRACTICE
240 REM
250 HOME : VTAB 12
260 INPUT "HOW MANY SENTENCES DO YOU WANT (3-25)?";NUMBER
270 IF NUMBER < 3 OR NUMBER > 25 THEN 250
280 REM -------------------------------------------------------------------
290 REM FRAME 4, STEP 1 - RANDOM SELECTIONS: SENTENCE PARTS & QUESTION
300 REM
310 FOR I = 1 TO NUMBER: HOME : VTAB 8
320 PRINT "GIVEN THE SENTENCE:": PRINT
330 SBJ = INT (5 * RND (1) + 1)
340 VRB = INT (5 * RND (1) + 1)
350 DOB = INT (5 * RND (1) + 1)
360 PRT = INT (3 * RND (1) + 1)
370 REM -------------------------------------------------------------------
380 REM        FRAME 4, STEP 2 - ASSIGN RANDOM PART SELECTED TO ANSWER$
390 REM
400 IF PRT = 1 THEN ANSWER$ = SUBJ$(SBJ)
410 IF PRT = 2 THEN ANSWER$ = VERB$(VRB)
420 IF PRT = 3 THEN ANSWER$ = DIROBJ$(DOB)
430 REM -------------------------------------------------------------------
440 REM        FRAME 4, STEP 3 - DISPLAY RANDOM SENTENCE, CHECK REPLY
450 REM
460 PRINT SUBJ$(SBJ)" "VERB$(VRB)" THE "DIROBJ$(DOB)".": PRINT
470 PRINT "WHAT IS THE "PART$(PRT);
480 INPUT REPLY$: PRINT
```

Frame 4, Step 4   If the reply is correct, assign a random feedback to the correct answer variable.
Otherwise, display the correct answer as feedback. In either case, display the
result until the RETURN key is pressed.

Final Frame   Display a performance report to the user.
DATA List   Include a list of DATA for the subjects, verbs, and direct objects at the end of
the program.

Examine the listing of PROGRAM 6 on pages 65 and 67 carefully to see how
these concepts are translated frame by frame and step by step into BASIC code.

Run from disk and refer to the listing and run of PROGRAM 6.

*PROGRAM 6
Sample Runs—
Frame 4,
Steps 1–4*

```
Given the sentence:

SAM SOLD THE CAR.

What is the DIRECT OBJECT? SOLD

The answer to that question is CAR!

------------------------- RETURN =>
Given the sentence:

TRACY LIKES THE BIRD.

What is the VERB? LIKES

The answer to that question is A-OK!
```

```
490 REM ---------------------------------------------------------------
500 REM          FRAME 4, STEP 4 - IF CORRECT, ASSIGN FEEDBACK TO ANSWER$
510 REM
520 IF REPLY$ = ANSWER$ THEN ANSWER$ = FDBK$(PRT):COUNT = COUNT + 1
530 PRINT "THE ANSWER TO THAT QUESTION IS "ANSWER$"!"
540 VTAB 20: HTAB 30: INPUT "RETURN =>";Z$
550 NEXT I
560 REM ---------------------------------------------------------------
570 REM          FINAL FRAME - PERFORMANCE REPORT
580 REM
590 HOME : VTAB 12: HTAB 6
600 PRINT "YOU CORRECTLY ANSWERED "COUNT"."
610 END
620 REM ---------------------------------------------------------------
630 REM          DATA FOR SUBJECTS, VERBS, AND DIRECT OBJECTS
640 REM
650 DATA "SAM","LIKES","DOG","MARY","LOVES","CAT","TRACY","KISSED","FISH"
660 DATA "HERB","SOLD","BIRD","LISA","BOUGHT","CAR"
```

4.3.2   PROGRAM 7: Random Selection Without Repetition

The primary purpose of this program is to demonstrate building one-dimensional string arrays (lists) and then randomly selecting from the lists without repeating an item once it has been selected. A user is given the option of making the length of the list from 3 to 15 elements. The lists, containing names and sexes, are then assigned using INPUT statements. The user then has the option of deciding on the number of names to be randomly selected from the list. Each randomly selected name will appear only once. A message will be displayed if a random number previously selected is selected again. The randomly selected list (with any "previously selected" message) is printed. The complete list is displayed with an asterisk shown by each name that was randomly selected. Finally, the user has the opportunity to produce another randomly selected list or to stop.

The frame-by-frame design of this program is shown on pages 68–71.

Frame 1   Present a title and dimension the variables to be used.

Frame 2   Present a brief introduction until the RETURN key is pressed.

Frame 3   Prompt the user for the number of names to enter. Check this value to be within the defined limits.

Frame 4   The user INPUTS that number of names and the sex for each.

Frame 5   Prompt the user for the number of names to be randomly selected. Check this value to be within limits.

] LIST

```
10 REM        PROGRAM 7
20 REM
30 REM -----------------------------------------------------------------
40 REM        FRAME 1 - PRESENT A TITLE AND DIMENSION VARIABLES
50 REM
60 HOME : VTAB 12: HTAB 4
70 PRINT "RANDOM SELECTION WITHOUT REPETITION"
80 FOR P = 1 TO 2000: NEXT P
90 DIM NAME$(15),SEX$(15),FLAG(15)
100 REM ----------------------------------------------------------------
110 REM        FRAME 2 - INTRODUCTION
120 REM
130 HOME
140 PRINT "THIS PROGRAM DEMONSTRATES ASSIGNING": PRINT
150 PRINT "INFORMATION TO ONE-DIMENSIONAL ARRAYS": PRINT
160 PRINT "AND THEN RANDOMLY SELECTING FROM THE": PRINT
170 PRINT "LISTS. YOU WILL BE ASKED TO ENTER": PRINT
180 PRINT "THE NAMES AND SEXES OF AT LEAST 3 BUT": PRINT
190 PRINT "NO MORE THAN 15 HYPOTHETICAL PEOPLE.": PRINT
200 PRINT "AFTER THESE HAVE BEEN ENTERED, YOU": PRINT
210 PRINT "WILL BE ASKED TO ENTER THE NUMBER OF": PRINT
220 PRINT "NAMES TO BE RANDOMLY SELECTED. ONCE": PRINT
230 PRINT "A NAME HAS BEEN SELECTED, IT WILL NOT": PRINT
240 PRINT "BE REPEATED IN THE RANDOM SELECTION."
250 VTAB 24: HTAB 30: INPUT "RETURN =>";Z$
260 REM ----------------------------------------------------------------
270 REM        FRAME 3 - INPUT WITH CHECKING OF THE NUMBER TO BE ENTERED
280 REM
290 HOME : VTAB 12
300 INPUT "HOW MANY NAMES DO YOU WISH TO ENTER? ";ENTRDNUM
310 IF ENTRDNUM < 3 OR ENTRDNUM > 15 THEN PRINT ,"*ENTER 3-15*": GOTO 300
320 REM ----------------------------------------------------------------
330 REM        FRAME 4 - INPUT OF NAMES AND SEXES TO ARRAYS
340 REM
350 HOME : VTAB 4
360 FOR I = 1 TO ENTRDNUM
370 PRINT "NAME "I" IS";: INPUT NAME$(I)
380 PRINT NAME$(I)"'S SEX IS (M/F)";: INPUT SEX$(I)
390 IF SEX$(I) < > "M" AND SEX$(I) < > "F" THEN PRINT "THAT'S A STRANGE
    SEX!": GOTO 380
400 NEXT I
410 REM ----------------------------------------------------------------
420 REM        FRAME 5 - INPUT WITH CHECKING OF NUMBER TO BE SELECTED
430 REM
440 HOME : VTAB 12
450 PRINT "YOU HAVE ENTERED "ENTRDNUM" NAMES. HOW MANY"
460 INPUT "DO YOU WISH TO SELECT? ";SELCT
470 IF SELCT < 1 OR SELCT > ENTRDNUM THEN PRINT "*NOT POSSIBLE*": GOTO
    450
```

Frame 6   Display a heading

Frame 6, Step 1   Begin the loop to randomly select names from the user's list. Generate a random number within the limits of the list of names.

Frame 6, Step 2   Check to see if this number has been previously selected. If it has, display a message and randomly select another number.

Frame 6, Step 3   "Flag" the number selected and display the corresponding name and sex from the list. Continue the loop.

Frame 7   Display the complete list, placing an asterisk by each name selected.

Frame 8   The user is then given the option to randomly select names from this list again. If so, reinitialize FLAG() to zero.

Examine the listing of PROGRAM 7 on pages 68–71 to see how these concepts are translated frame by frame and step by step into BASIC code.

RUN from disk and refer to the listing and run of PROGRAM 7.

```
480 REM ---------------------------------------------------------------
490 REM          FRAME 6 - DISPLAY A HEADING
500 REM
510 HOME
520 PRINT "HERE ARE "SELCT" RANDOMLY SELECTED NAMES:": PRINT
530 PRINT "NAME","SEX"
540 PRINT "----","---"
550 REM ---------------------------------------------------------------
560 REM          FRAME 6, STEP 1 - BEGIN LOOP; SELECT RANDOM NUMBER
570 REM
580 FOR I = 1 TO SELCT
590 X = INT (ENTRDNUM * RND (1) + 1)
600 REM ---------------------------------------------------------------
610 REM          FRAME 6, STEP 2 - HAS THIS RANDOM NUMBER APPEARED BEFORE?
620 IF FLAG(X) = 1 THEN PRINT "OOPS...GOT "NAME$(X)" AGAIN": GOTO 590
630 REM ---------------------------------------------------------------
640 REM    FRAME 6, STEP 3 - FLAG THE NUMBER; DISPLAY NAME AND SEX SELECTED
650 REM
660 FLAG(X) = 1
670 PRINT NAME$(X),SEX$(X)
680 NEXT I
690 VTAB 24: HTAB 30: INPUT "RETURN =>";Z$
700 REM ---------------------------------------------------------------
710 REM          FRAME 7 - DISPLAY OF COMPLETE LIST SHOWING SELECTED NAMES
720 REM
730 HOME
740 PRINT "HERE IS THE COMPLETE LIST OF NAMES"
750 PRINT "WITH A * BY THOSE RANDOMLY SELECTED:": PRINT
760 FOR I = 1 TO ENTRDNUM
770 PRINT NAME$(I)" ";
780 IF FLAG(I) = 1 THEN PRINT "*";
790 PRINT
800 NEXT I
810 VTAB 24: HTAB 30: INPUT "RETURN =>";Z$
820 REM ---------------------------------------------------------------
830 REM          FRAME 8 - OPTION TO SELECT AGAIN; IF SO, RE-INITIALIZE FLAG
840 REM
850 HOME : VTAB 12
860 INPUT "DO YOU WISH TO SELECT AGAIN (Y/N)? ";R$
870 IF R$ = "Y" THEN FOR I = 1 TO 15:FLAG(I) = 0: NEXT I: GOTO 440
880 END
```

PROGRAM 7
Sample Run—
Frame 3

```
How many names do you wish to enter? 20

        ENTER A NUMBER BETWEEN 3 AND 15

How many names do you wish to enter? 5
```

PROGRAM 7
Sample Run—
Frame 4

```
Name 1 is? FRANK
FRANK'S sex is (M/F)? M
Name 2 is? FRAN
FRAN'S sex is (M/F)? N
THAT'S A STRANGE SEX!
FRAN'S sex is (M/F)? F
Name 3 is? BILL
BILL'S sex is (M/F)? M
Name 4 is? BARB
BARB'S sex is (M/F)? F
Name 5 is? BUCK
BUCK'S sex is (M/F)? M
```

PROGRAM 7
Sample Run—
Frame 5

```
You have entered 5 names. How many
do you wish to randomly select? 7

IMPOSSIBLE! YOU ENTERED 5 NAMES.

You have entered 5 names. How many
do you wish to randomly select? 4
```

PROGRAM 7
Sample Run—
Frame 6,
Steps 1–3

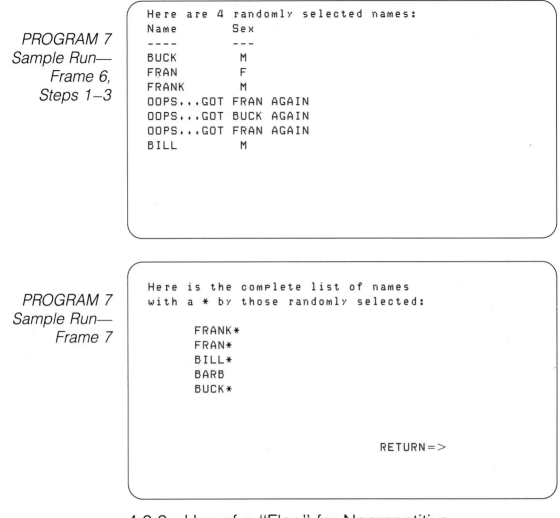

```
Here are 4 randomly selected names:
Name          Sex
----          ---
BUCK           M
FRAN           F
FRANK          M
OOPS...GOT FRAN AGAIN
OOPS...GOT BUCK AGAIN
OOPS...GOT FRAN AGAIN
BILL           M
```

PROGRAM 7
Sample Run—
Frame 7

```
Here is the complete list of names
with a * by those randomly selected:

        FRANK*
        FRAN*
        BILL*
        BARB
        BUCK*




                        RETURN=>
```

4.3.3 Use of a "Flag" for Nonrepetitive Random Selection

In PROGRAM 7, all values for FLAG(X) are initialized to zero by the DIMension statement (90). Thus, a partial list of the information INPUT in Frame 4 of the sample RUN of PROGRAM 7 would be:

X	N$(X)	S$(X)	FLAG(X)
1	Frank	M	0
2	Fran	F	0
3	Bill	M	0
4	Barb	F	0
.	.	.	.
.	.	.	.
.	.	.	.

If, for example, a random value for X is 2 (statement 590 in Frame 6, Step 1), FLAG(2) is set to 1, that is, "flagged" (statement 660 in Frame 6, Step 3), and the list is now:

X	N$(X)	S$(X)	FLAG(X)
1	Frank	M	0
2	Fran	F	1
3	Bill	M	0
4	Barb	F	0
.	.	.	.
.	.	.	.
.	.	.	.

Since FLAG(2) is now equal to 1, any subsequent random value in which X is equal to 2 would cause statement 620 in Frame 6, Step 2 to transfer execution *back* to statement 590, where another random value for X would be generated. Therefore, any randomly selected name in this program example will be displayed only one time.

4.4 BASIC STATEMENTS FOR THIS CHAPTER

4.4.1 Statement DIM

Purpose   DIMensions (defines the size needed) for one- and two-dimensional arrays. On most BASIC systems, it is unnecessary to use the DIM statement, since space is automatically allocated for ten or fewer elements. However, it is good programming practice to DIMension all arrays, even those containing ten or fewer elements.

Examples   `DIM NAM$(12),FLAG(5)`

(Dimensions space for a list of twelve string variables and a list of five numeric variables.)

`DIM SCRE(20,3)`

(Dimensions space for a 20-row, 3-column table containing numeric data.)

4.4.2 Statement Pair GOSUB-RETURN

Purpose   This statement pair is very useful for programs in which a sequence of statements is repeated several times throughout program execution. Whenever GO-

SUB is encountered, program execution is transferred to the statement number specified in the GOSUB. Execution continues from that statement until the RETURN *statement* (not the RETURN key) is encountered. Execution is then transferred (RETURNed) to the statement number *immediately following* the GOSUB statement that caused the transfer in the first place.

A typical example in instructional computing would be an answer-checking sequence for student input in a program containing several questions. Rather than writing an identical answer-checking sequence for each question, it is written only once as a subroutine. GOSUB may then be used after each question to check the answer.

Example

```
10 REM        FRAME 1 - TITLE
20 REM ------------------------------------------------
30 HOME : VTAB 12 : HTAB 8
40 PRINT "Examples of GOSUB-RETURN Use"
50 FOR P = 1 TO 2000 : NEXT P
60 REM ------------------------------------------------
70 REM        FRAME 2 - 1ST QUESTION/ANSWER ASSIGNMENT
80 QUES$ = "Identify the capital of Texas"
90 ANS$ = "AUSTIN"
100 GOSUB 5000
110 REM ------------------------------------------------
120 REM        FRAME 3 - NEXT QUESTION/ANSWER ASSIGNMENT
130 QUES$ = "X marks the --?--"
140 ANS$ = "SPOT"
150 GOSUB 5000
160 REM ------------------------------------------------
170 REM        ADDITIONAL FRAMES MAY BE ADDED
4930 REM ------------------------------------------------
4940 REM        FINAL FRAME
4950 HOME : VTAB 12 : HTAB 8
4960 PRINT "You answered " C " question(s) correctly."
4970 END
4980 REM ------------------------------------------------
4990 REM        THE SUBROUTINE
5000 HOME : VTAB 12 : PRINT QUES$
5010 VTAB 14 : HTAB 10 : INPUT REPLY$
5020 IF REPLY$ <> ANS$ THEN 5050
5030 HOME : VTAB 12 : HTAB 18 : PRINT "GREAT!"
5040 C = C + 1 : FOR P = 1 TO 1000 : NEXT P : RETURN
5050 PRINT : PRINT "The correct answer is " ANS$
5060 VTAB 22 : HTAB 30 : INPUT "Return =>";Z$ : RETURN
```

Mentally execute this program before entering and RUNning it. Note that the program has room to incorporate other questions between statements 150 and 4930, that RETURN may be with different statements in the subroutine, and that END may come before the subroutine.

4.4.3 PROGRAM 8: Question Sets and Hints, Using GOSUB-RETURN Statements

The following program illustrates the use of GOSUB-RETURN in a "muscle quiz." Note that alternate correct answers are used; note how the questions, hints, and answers are assigned and presented; and note that credit is given only for those answers that are correct on the first try.

Carefully review the listing of PROGRAM 8 for a frame-by-frame, step-by-step analysis of the program design. These design steps will be shown only in the program LISTings for the remaining examples in this book.

RUN from disk and refer to the listing and run of PROGRAM 8

```
] LIST


10 REM        PROGRAM 8
20 REM
30 REM --------------------------------------------------------------
40 REM        FRAME 1 - TITLE AND CORRECT COUNT INITIALIZATION
50 REM
60 HOME : VTAB 12: HTAB 10
70 PRINT "A SHORT MUSCLE QUIZ"
80 FOR P = 1 TO 3000: NEXT P:CNT = 0
90 REM --------------------------------------------------------------
100 REM        FRAME 2 - FIRST QUESTION PRINT AND ASSIGNMENT SEQUENCE
110 REM
120 HOME : VTAB 8
130 PRINT "WHAT IS THE LARGEST MUSCLE IN THE"
140 PRINT "HUMAN BODY";
150 A1$ = "GLUTEUS MAXIMUS":A2$ = "BUTTOCKS":A3$ = "DERRIERE"
160 HNT$ = "YOU MAY BE SITTING ON IT!": GOSUB 10000
170 REM --------------------------------------------------------------
180 REM        FRAME 3 - SIMILAR SEQUENCE FOR THE SECOND QUESTION
190 REM
200 HOME : VTAB 8
210 PRINT "WHAT MUSCLE HAS MADE SOME PEOPLE RICH,"
220 PRINT "WEIGHT LIFTERS STRUT, AND DIRTY,"
230 PRINT "OLD MEN LEER";
240 A1$ = "PECTORALIS MAJORA":A2$ = "PECTORALS":A3$ = "PECTORAL"
250 HNT$ = "PALM-TO-PALM PRESSURE DEVELOPS THIS.": GOSUB 10000
260 REM --------------------------------------------------------------
270 REM        FRAME 4 - SIMILAR SEQUENCE FOR A FINAL QUESTION
280 REM
290 HOME : VTAB 8
300 PRINT "WHAT MUSCLE IS CONSIDERED BY SOME TO"
310 PRINT "HAVE AN ORIGIN BUT NO INSERTION";
```

```
320 A1$ = "TONGUE":A2$ = A1$:A3$ = A1$
330 HNT$ = "ON SOME, IT WAGS A LOT.": GOSUB 10000
340 REM ---------------------------------------------------------------
350 REM        FRAMES FOR ADDITIONAL QUESTION SEQUENCES
360 REM
9910 REM --------------------------------------------------------------
9920 REM        FINAL FRAME - PERFORMANCE REPORT
9930 REM
9940 HOME : VTAB 12
9950 PRINT "YOU GOT "CNT" CORRECT ON THE FIRST ATTEMPT."
9960 END
9970 REM --------------------------------------------------------------
9980 REM        THE INPUT AND ANSWER CHECKING SUBROUTINE
9990 END
10000 INPUT R$: PRINT
10010 IF R$ = A1$ OR R$ = A2$ OR R$ = A3$ THEN PRINT ,"CORRECT!": GOTO
      10060
10020 IF MISS = 1 THEN 10070
10030 PRINT "LET ME GIVE YOU A HINT...": PRINT
10040 PRINT HNT$: PRINT : PRINT "PLEASE ANSWER AGAIN";
10050 MISS = 1: GOTO 10000
10060 IF MISS = 0 THEN CNT = CNT + 1
10070 VTAB 20: PRINT "ACCEPTABLE ANSWERS ARE:": PRINT
10080 PRINT A1$" "A2$" "A3$: PRINT
10090 HTAB 30: INPUT "RETURN =>";Z$
10100 MISS = 0: RETURN
```

Classroom computers can be used to initiate group discussions in addition to one-on-one instruction.

PROGRAM 8
Sample Run—
Question 1
Correct

```
What's the largest muscle
in the human body?GLUTEUS MAXIMUS

        CORRECT!


Acceptable answers are:

GLUTEUS MAXIMUS  BUTTOCKS  DERRIERE


                           RETURN =>
```

PROGRAM 8
Sample Run—
Second Attempt
Correct

```
What is the largest muscle
in the human body?THIGH MUSCLE

Let me give you a hint...

YOU MAY BE SITTING ON IT!
Please answer again?BUTTOCKS

        CORRECT!

Acceptable answers are:

GLUTEUS MAXIMUS  BUTTOCKS  DERRIERE
                           RETURN =>
```

4.4.4 Incorporating Commands into a Program

By now, you are well aware of several of the BASIC commands (LOAD, RUN, LIST, etc.) of the Apple microcomputer. Many of these commands may be incorporated within the body of a BASIC program. When these are executed they could, for example, execute (RUN) another program from the disk. This example is particularly useful in that one program can "command" another program to RUN, which could command another program to RUN, and so on. Thus, programs can be "linked" together in "chain" fashion, rather than writing, entering, and testing *one long* program.

  The Apple microcomputers require use of the following statement to incorporate these commands into programs:

```
PRINT CHR$(4) "<command>"
```

Here <command> is the command to be executed, such as RUN MENU. [The PRINT CHR$(4) statement, in simplest terms, is needed to "inform" the system that information contained on the disk will be accessed.]

A common use in instructional computing is to design one program as a "menu" of available programs on the disk. When this menu program is executed, a selection of programs is displayed, and the user may enter the choice desired.

This use of commands as BASIC statements is illustrated in the program named MENU on the disk. Carefully examine the listings of MENU, SEQUEL 1, and SEQUEL 2; then, RUN MENU and note the options and actions it provides. In particular, note the method in MENU by which program names and descriptions are assigned to one-dimensional arrays. Then note how the selected program is RUN. Compare this use of RUN as a statement with those in SEQUEL 1 and SEQUEL 2.

Also note the use of the GET R$ and PRINT statements in SEQUEL 2 (statement 150). The GET statement is similar to the INPUT statement in assigning a value to the named variable. However, GET "gets" the *first* keystroke and assigns that value to the named variable *without* the need for pressing the RETURN key. Execution continues automatically at that point. We will use this technique when we want "pressing any key" to continue to the next frame of display. Note that we use a string variable with GET; otherwise, a numeric key would need to be pressed.

The MENU program shown here may also be used as a model program for ANY "menu of programs" simply by changing the DATA statements containing the number of selections and the program names and descriptions.

Note: If this program is used when the disk *is* INITialized (or is SAVEd using the SAME name of the program used when the disk *was* INITialized), the menu of programs will appear automatically when the disk is booted.

```
] LIST


10 REM        MENU PROGRAM
20 REM
30 REM -------------------------------------------------------------------
40 REM        DATA ASSIGNMENTS
50 REM
60 READ ITEMS
70 DIM PROGM$(ITEMS),DESCRIP$(ITEMS)
80 FOR I = 1 TO ITEMS: READ PROGM$(I),DESCRIP$(I): NEXT I
90 REM -------------------------------------------------------------------
100 REM      FRAME 1, STEP 1 - DISPLAY MENU SELECTIONS
110 REM
120 HOME : VTAB 4: HTAB 8
130 PRINT "P R O G R A M   M E N U": PRINT : PRINT
```

```
140 FOR I = 1 TO ITEMS
150 PRINT I" - "DESCRIP$(I): PRINT
160 NEXT I
170 PRINT I" - STOP"
180 PRINT : PRINT TAB( 8)"ENTER YOUR CHOICE (1 TO "I")";
190 INPUT C
200 IF C < 1 OR C > I THEN 180
210 REM ------------------------------------------------------------
220 REM        FRAME 1, STEP 2 - EXECUTE CHOICE
230 REM
240 IF C = I THEN HOME : VTAB 12: HTAB 12: PRINT "*** DONE ***": END
250 PRINT CHR$ (4)"RUN "PROGM$(C)
260 REM ------------------------------------------------------------
270 REM        DATA FOR NUMBER OF ITEMS, PROGRAM NAME AND DESCRIPTION
280 REM
290 DATA 2
300 DATA "SEQUEL 1", "SEQUEL 1 FIRST PROGRAM OPTION"
310 DATA "SEQUEL 2", "SEQUEL 2 SECOND PROGRAM OPTION"
```

MENU
Sample Run

```
                    PROGRAM MENU

          1 - SEQUEL 1 First Program Option

          2 - SEQUEL 2 Second Program Option

          3 - STOP

             ENTER YOUR CHOICE (1-3) 1
```

] LIST

```
10 REM        SEQUEL 1 PROGRAM
20 REM
30 REM ------------------------------------------------------------
40 REM        FRAME 1, STEP 1 - INTRODUCTION, ETC.
50 REM
60 HOME : VTAB 4: HTAB 12
70 PRINT "SEQUEL 1": PRINT : PRINT
80 PRINT "SO, WE MADE IT TO SEQUEL 1...": PRINT
```

```
90 PRINT "IF YOU ENTER THE LETTER N, WE WILL"
100 PRINT "TRANSFER TO SEQUEL 2, ANY OTHER"
110 PRINT "LETTER WILL TRANSFER BACK TO MENU.": PRINT
120 INPUT "WHAT IS YOUR PLEASURE? ";R$
130 REM --------------------------------------------------------------
140 REM       FRAME 1, STEP 2 - TRANSFER TO THE APPROPRIATE PROGRAM
150 REM
160 IF R$ = "N" THEN PRINT CHR$ (4)"RUN SEQUEL 2"
170 PRINT CHR$ (4)"RUN MENU"
```

SEQUEL 1
Sample Run

```
                              SEQUEL 1


        So, we have made it to SEQUEL 1...

        If you enter the letter N, we will
        transfer to SEQUEL 2. Any other
        letter will transfer back to MENU.

        What is your pleasure? N
```

] LIST

```
10 REM        SEQUEL 2 PROGRAM
20 REM
30 REM --------------------------------------------------------------
40 REM        FRAME 1, STEP 1 - INTRODUCTION, ETC.
50 REM
60 HOME : VTAB 4: HTAB 12
70 PRINT "SEQUEL 2": PRINT : PRINT
80 PRINT "AND, HERE WE ARE EXECUTING SEQUEL 2.": PRINT
90 PRINT "WHEN YOU PRESS ANY KEY, WE WILL"
100 PRINT "TRANSFER BACK TO THE MENU.": PRINT
110 PRINT "I'LL WAIT UNTIL YOU DO SO...";
120 REM --------------------------------------------------------------
130 REM        FRAME 1, STEP 2 - USE THE GET AND PRINT FOR PRESSING ANY KEY
140 REM
150 GET R$: PRINT
160 PRINT CHR$ (4)"RUN MENU"
```

82

DIM IT! THERE MUST BE AN EASIER WAY! ARRAY! ARRAY! THERE IS!

SEQUEL 2
Sample Run

```
                    SEQUEL 2

And, here we are executing SEQUEL 2.

When you press ANY key, we will
transfer back to the MENU.

I'll wait until you do so....
```

4.5 POSERS AND PROBLEMS

1. Assume that you have a class of twenty students and the semester test average and final exam scores for each. Outline the BASIC statements that would make a series of lists of this information.

2. Outline the BASIC statements that will read three scores for each of twenty-five students into a two-dimensional array.

3. The following program fragment gives an error message. Why?

```
10 FOR I = 1 TO 15
20 READ NUMB(I)
30 NEXT I
        .
        .
        .
1000 DATA 1,2,3,4,5,6,7,8,9,10,11,12,13,14,15
```

4. Describe what would result from execution of the following BASIC statements:

```
10 DIM S$(5),FLAG(5)
20 FOR I = 1 TO 5
30    READ S$(I)
40 NEXT I
50 FOR K = 1 TO 3
60    X = INT(5 * RND(0) + 1)
70    PRINT S$(X)
```

```
80 NEXT K
90 END
100 DATA "TEXAS","OKLAHOMA","KANSAS","NEVADA","UTAH"
```

5. How would adding the following statements affect the execution of the program in Problem 4?

```
64    IF FLAG(X) = 1 THEN 60
66    FLAG(X) = 1
```

6. Describe the execution of the complete program in Problem 5 if statement 50 were changed to:

```
50 FOR K = 1 TO 6
```

Think this through carefully before entering and RUNning. Remember, pressing the CTRL and RESET keys simultaneously will halt a runaway program!

7. How would you modify the program in Section 4.4.2 to print a hint as a response for the first miss and give the correct answer on the second miss? *Hint:* One way to do this is shown in PROGRAM 8.

8. Write a program that creates five random sentences from lists of subjects, verbs, and objects.

9. Write a program to choose and print four random numbers between 1 and 10 without repeating any number that has been printed.

10. Modify the MENU program to be a "DRILL MENU" for the addition, subtraction, multiplication, and division programs written in Chapter 3. Modify each of the drill programs so that at their conclusions the DRILL MENU program will be RUN. *Note!!!* SAVE your DRILL MENU program before RUNning to test your design. (Why is this necessary?)

THINK ABOUT THIS . . .

. . . FOR FUN

Four men are on a raft in the middle of the ocean. Each has one carton of cigarettes but no means whatsoever of lighting them. The smartest of the four, however, devotes his full mental prowess to the problem and, within minutes, all are smoking a cigarette. How was this accomplished?

. . . SERIOUSLY

Should every student have an exposure to computers and their uses by graduation from high school?

Chapter 5
You're RIGHT$, I'm LEFT$, She's Gone . . . (But I'll STRING Along)

5.1 OBJECTIVES

For the successful completion of this chapter, you should be able to:

1. Define and give at least one example of "string concatenation" (Section 5.3).

2. Define the purpose of and give at least one example of use of the following BASIC functions: ASC, CHR$, LEN, LEFT$, RIGHT$, and MID$ (Sections 5.4.1–5.4.6).

3. Use the Minimum Answer subroutine in at least one program of your choosing (Section 5.5).

4. Use the KEYWORD subroutine in at least one program of your choosing (Section 5.6).

5.2 SOME COMMENTS ON STRINGS

As you know by now, many of the instructional computing applications use string input in a program to obtain a user's response. This response is then evaluated, and some form of appropriate feedback is given. To this point, most of this evaluation depended on an *exact* match between the user's response and some anticipated answer defined in the program. If, however, the user's response contained typographic errors, misspelling, or even something as subtle as a leading space, a match might not occur. This chapter will illustrate the use of certain BASIC functions and programming strategies to better accommodate evaluation of string input.

Some of these functions will be incorporated into two subroutines—one is simple; the other is slightly more complex. Through the use of these subroutines, a user's response may be evaluated in terms of defined "minimum acceptable" or "key phrase" answers. In essence, the subroutines provide a means by which both the response and anticipated answer strings may be examined and compared in much more detail.

5.3 STRING CONCATENATION

Strings may be joined together by simple use of the + symbol. This process is called *concatenation*. As you know, relationships between strings may be compared, as in:

```
IF A$ = R$ THEN PRINT "O. K."
```

Other comparisons also may be performed. For example, enter and RUN the following programs:

```
10 HOME : VTAB 10
20 INPUT "Enter any string of characters";F$
30 PRINT
40 INPUT "Enter another string of characters";S$
50 PRINT
60 PRINT "The combined strings are " F$ + S$
70 PRINT
80 IF F$ = S$ THEN PRINT F$ " IS THE SAME AS " S$
90 IF F$ < S$ THEN PRINT F$ " COMES BEFORE " S$
100 IF F$ > S$ THEN PRINT S$ " COMES BEFORE " F$
110 END
```

```
10 HOME : VTAB 10
20 PRINT "What's the password? ";
30 FOR I = 1 TO 5
40    GET C$ : PRINT "X";
50    PW$ = PW$ + C$
60 NEXT I
70 IF PW$ = "APPLE" THEN PRINT " O.K." : END
80 PRINT " THAT'S NOT IT"
```

5.4 BASIC FUNCTIONS RELATED TO STRINGS

5.4.1 Function ASC (STRING$)

Purpose The ASC function converts the *first* character in STRING$ to its ASCII code (see Appendix B).

Example
```
10 FOR I = 1 TO 5
20    READ S$
30    PRINT "The ASCII value for " S$ " is " ASC(S$)
40 NEXT I
50 DATA "A","P","P","L","E"
```

5.4.2 Function CHR$ (NUMBER)

Purpose The CHR$ function converts the ASCII code NUMBER to its character equivalent.

Examples
```
10 FOR C = 65 TO 90
20    PRINT CHR$(C) " ";
30 NEXT C
```

```
10 FOR BEEP = 1 TO 10
20    PRINT CHR$(7)
30    FOR P = 1 TO 100 : NEXT P
40 NEXT BEEP
```

5.4.3 Function LEN (STRING$)

Purpose The LEN function returns the NUMBER of characters in STRING$.

Example
```
10 HOME : VTAB 10 : INPUT "Enter any sentence"; R$
20 L = LEN(R$)
30 PRINT "You typed " L " characters in your response."
```

Enter and RUN the following program:

```
10 HOME : VTAB 10 : INPUT "Enter your full name"; N$
20 HOME : VTAB 12 : HTAB 8 : PRINT "WATCH THIS..."
30 FOR P = 1 TO 2000 : NEXT P : HOME : VTAB 12 : HTAB 10
40 PRINT N$
50 FOR I = 1 TO LEN(N$)
60    VTAB 12 : HTAB 8 + I : PRINT " "
70    FOR P = 1 TO 1000 : NEXT P
80 NEXT I
90 VTAB 12 : PRINT "Do you feel as if something is
   missing?"
```

5.4.4 Function LEFT$ (STRING$, NUMBER)

Purpose   The LEFT$ function returns the *leftmost* characters of "NUMBER" length from STRING$.

Enter and RUN the following examples:

```
10 HOME:VTAB 10:INPUT "Do you wish to continue...? "; R$
20 IF LEFT$(R$,1) = "Y" THEN PRINT,"Continuing..." :
   GOTO 20
30 PRINT,"Stopping..."
40 END
```

(How will you stop this "runaway" program?)

```
10 HOME:VTAB 12:INPUT "Enter your full name"; N$
   :HOME:VTAB 12
20 FOR I = 1 TO LEN(N$)
30    PRINT LEFT$(N$,I); : FOR P = 1 TO 500 : NEXT P
40 NEXT I
```

5.4.5 Function RIGHT$ (STRING$, NUMBER)

Purpose   The RIGHT$ function returns the *rightmost* characters of "NUMBER" length from STRING$.

Example
```
10 HOME : VTAB 10 : INPUT "Enter your name"; N$ : HOME
20 FOR I = 1 to LEN(N$)
30    PRINT LEFT$(N$,I) TAB(40 - I) RIGHT$(N$,I)
40 FOR P = 1 TO 500 : NEXT P
50 NEXT I
60 PRINT : PRINT "Ambidextrous, aren't I..."
```

When you enter "RUN," the program runs — but don't let it run away!

5.4.6 Function
MID$ (STRING$, CHARNUM1, CHARNUM2)

Purpose The MID$ function returns the characters from STRING$ beginning with (character number) CHARNUM1 through CHARNUM2.

Enter and RUN the following example:

```
10 HOME : VTAB 12
20 INPUT "Please enter your name ";NAM$
30 IF LEN(NAM$)/2 = INT(LEN(NAM$)/2) THEN NAM$ = NAM$
   + " "
40 L = LEN(NAM$) : HOME : VTAB 12
50 PRINT "Thank you...Now we'll 'pull out' the" : PRINT
60 PRINT "successive middle characters..."
70 VTAB 24 : HTAB 30 : INPUT "Return =>";Z$ : HOME
80 BEGIN = INT((L/2) + .5)
90 FOR CHAR = 1 TO L STEP 2
100    HTAB 10 + BEGIN : PRINT MID$(NAM$,BEGIN,CHAR)
110    FOR P = 1 TO 1000 : NEXT P : BEGIN = BEGIN - 1
120 NEXT CHAR
130 VTAB 22 : PRINT "And thus goes the MID$ function..."
```

5.5 THE MINIMUM ANSWER SUBROUTINE

Often in instructional computing situations arise in a question-answer sequence, in which one "key word" or continuous string of certain defined characters will be sufficient for a correct answer. We have seen (ad nauseam) the question:

```
What is the capital of Texas?
```

Of course, the answer anticipated is "AUSTIN," but, until now, answers such as:

```
AUSTIN TEXAS
```

or

```
IT IS THE CITY OF AUSTIN
```

would not match our defined answer. You can imagine the frustration of a student in the following program scenario:

```
What is the capital of Texas? AUSTIN TEXAS
No, the correct name is AUSTIN
```

(And the student thinks, "%$*@! Stupid computer!")

The following routine allows an author to define a "word" of continuous characters as the "minimum acceptable answer" that has been assigned to A$.

```
10000 INPUT R$
10010 L = LEN$(A$)
10020 FOR I = 1 TO LEN(R$ - L + 1)
10030    IF MID$(R$,I,L) = A$ THEN PRINT "OK" : RETURN
10040 NEXT I
10050 PRINT "The minimum answer is " A$ : RETURN
```

Review the LISTing and RUN of the MINANSWER program.

```
] LIST


10 REM         MINANSWER PROGRAM EXAMPLE
20 REM
30 REM -------------------------------------------------------------
40 REM         FRAME 1 - FIRST QUESTION SEQUENCE
50 REM
60 HOME
70 PRINT "THIS PROGRAM IS WRITTEN IN A"
80 PRINT "LANGUAGE CALLED -----";
90 A$ = "BASIC": GOSUB 10000
100 REM -------------------------------------------------------------
110 REM         FRAME 2 - SECOND QUESTION SEQUENCE
120 REM
130 PRINT "THE EPIC POEM 'HIAWATHA' WAS"
140 PRINT "WRITTEN BY ";
150 A$ = "LONGFELLOW": GOSUB 10000
160 REM -------------------------------------------------------------
170 REM         ADDITIONAL QUESTION SEQUENCES MAY BE ADDED
180 REM
9940 HOME : VTAB 12: HTAB 12
9950 PRINT "THAT'S ALL..."
9960 END
9970 REM -------------------------------------------------------------
9980 REM         THE MINIMUM ANSWER SUBROUTINE
9990 REM
10000 INPUT R$
10010 L = LEN (A$)
10020 FOR I = 1 TO ( LEN (R$) - L + 1)
10030 IF MID$ (R$,I,L) = A$ THEN 10080
10040 NEXT I
10050 PRINT : PRINT "YOUR ANSWER DID NOT CONTAIN"
10060 PRINT : PRINT TAB( 12)A$
10070 PRINT : PRINT "THE MINIMUM ANSWER I WANTED.": GOTO 10110
10080 PRINT : PRINT "YES, I'LL ACCEPT": PRINT
```

```
10090  PRINT R$: PRINT
10100  PRINT "BECAUSE IT CONTAINS "A$
10110  VTAB 22: HTAB 30: INPUT "RETURN =>";Z$
10120  HOME : RETURN
```

MINANSWER
Sample Run—
Frame 1

```
This program is written in a
language called -----?CONTROVERSIAL BASIC

Yes, I'll accept

CONTROVERSIAL BASIC

because it contains BASIC


                                        RETURN  =>
```

MINANSWER
Sample Run—
Frame 2

```
The epic poem 'Hiawatha' was
written by?THE POET HENRY LONGSTREET

Your answer did not contain

        LONGFELLOW

the minimum answer I wanted.


                                        RETURN  =>
```

5.6 THE KEYWORD SUBROUTINE

Up to this point, a variety of instructional computing program examples and
models have been presented. These programs illustrate some of the major
concepts, strategies, and techniques that may be used in program design. However, one additional technique that merits discussion is *keyword matching*.

This technique allows a program author to define a phrase or a keyword sequence of characters that, if found anywhere in the user's response in the same sequence, will constitute a match between the input and an anticipated answer. For example, assume that an author wanted to ask the following question:

```
WHAT DO WE COLLECTIVELY CALL OUR FIFTY STATES?
```

Further assume that the author anticipates the following responses as possible answers to the question:

```
UNITED STATES OF AMERICA
UNITED STATES
UNITED
AMERICA
U.S.A.
```

With the use of a keyword subroutine, the author can define a match of these anticipated answers as:

```
"*UNIT*STAT*AMER*"
"*UNIT*STAT*"
"*UNIT*"
"*AMER*"
"*U*S*A*"
```

Computers are entertaining and exciting to many students. Instructional computing materials can capitalize on these factors to motivate young learners.

In this subroutine we define the * as the "I don't care" character. In other words, we do not care what characters come before or after our defined keywords in the keyword phrase. However, the defined keyword sequence must be present in the user's response if a "match" is to occur. Thus, if the user responds with *any* phrase containing the fragments UNIT, STAT, and AMER (our first example above), then a match will be found for those defined keyword fragments. The author can have the program make appropriate responses, transfer execution back to the original question, or give the complete answer for each defined keyword sequence. If none of the anticipated answers are matched, a response (such as a hint) can be made and execution can be transferred accordingly.

Note that in defining our keyword phrases above, we go from the longest to the shortest phrase. This is the sequence that should always be followed. If, for example, "*UNIT*" was BEFORE "UNIT*STAT*AMER", any input containing "UNIT" would always match. Thus, the sequence is longest to shortest phrase.

The program fragment KEYWORD found on the text diskette is one example of a subroutine of this nature. It is based on the MINANSWER subroutine. Here, however, a "phrase" of keywords is separated into its component keywords. The user's input is then searched for each of those words in the sequence in which they were defined by the program's author. A "flag" variable is used to indicate whether or not a match occurred.

Now, referring to the listing of program KEYWORDS DEMO (containing the subroutine KEYWORD), note the following step-by-step sequence for using the subroutine:

1. Program fragment KEYWORD is loaded from the disk; that is, the KEYWORD subroutine (statements in the range of 9950–10200) is loaded into the system's memory.

2. Statements 10–80 are added to document the program and present a title.

3. Statements 90–160 are added to ask the question and assign the user's response to R$.

4. Statement 200 assigns the first anticipated answer (in this case, the correct response) to A$. Three keyword fragments must be in the reply for a match: UNIT, STAT, and AMER. These are delimited by asterisks. Transfer is then made to the subroutine beginning at statement 10000.

5. On return from the subroutine, statement 240 checks the value of FLAG. If the user's response contains *at least* the keyword fragment UNIT followed somewhere by the keyword fragment STAT, followed by the fragment AMER, a match occurred. If a match did *not* occur, FLAG is set to 1.

6. If FLAG is equal to 0, statement 240 PRINTs the program's response for the keyword defined in statement 200 (the correct answer). Transfer is

then made to 440, for the next question sequence (or the END of the program, as in our example).

7. Statement 280 is executed if no match occurred for the first keyword (FLAG = 1). A\$ is now redefined as the next keyword fragment to check in the user's response and transfer is made back to the subroutine. This same sequence of defining a keyword, going to the subroutine, checking the value of FLAG on return, and continuing or responding accordingly is repeated through statement 380.

8. Statements 390–430 are executed if none of the defined keyword fragments are matched; that is, a hint is given.

9. The program is SAVEd as KEYWORDS DEMO.

Following this same sequential strategy, a variety of both *anticipated* correct and incorrect answers may be used in a program. Carefully examine the listing of the program, frame by frame and step by step.

```
] LIST


9950 REM
9960 END
9970 REM  ---------------------------------------------------------------
9980 REM          KEYWORD SUBROUTINE
9990 REM
10000 FLAG = 0:LTRS = 0:WRD = 0
10010 L = LEN (A$):P = 2
10020 REM  --------------------------------------------------------------
10030 REM        STEP 1 - BREAK KEY PHRASE INTO KEYWORDS
10040 REM
10050 FOR J = 1 TO L
10060 IF MID$ (A$,J + 1,1) < > "*" THEN LTRS = LTRS + 1: GOTO 10090
10070 WRD = WRD + 1:KW$(WRD) = MID$ (A$,P,LTRS):L(WRD) = LTRS
10080 P = J + 2:LTRS = 0
10090 NEXT J
10100 S = 1
10110 REM  --------------------------------------------------------------
10120 REM        STEP 2 - SEARCH RESPONSE FOR EACH KEYWORD IN SEQUENCE
10130 REM
10140 FOR J= 1 TO WRD
10150 FOR I = S TO LEN (R$)
10160 IF MID$ (R$,I,L(J)) = KW$(J) THEN S = I + 1: GOTO 10190
10170 NEXT I
10180 FLAG = 1: RETURN
10190 NEXT J
10200 RETURN
```

*KEYWORDS
DEMO Creation
from KEYWORD
Subroutine*

```
] LOAD KEYWORD

] 10 REM      KEYWORDS DEMO

   .
   .      (Statements 10–460 are entered.)
   .

] 460 REM

] SAVE KEYWORDS DEMO
```

```
] LIST 10,460


10 REM        KEYWORDS DEMO PROGRAM
20 REM
30 REM ----------------------------------------------------------------
40 REM        FRAME 1 - TITLE
50 REM
60 HOME : VTAB 12: HTAB 8
70 PRINT TAB( 8) "KEYWORDS DEMONSTRATION"
80 FOR P = 1 TO 2500: NEXT P
90 REM ----------------------------------------------------------------
100 REM      FRAME 2, STEP 1 - PRESENT QUESTION; ASSIGN INPUT TO R$
110 REM
120 HOME : VTAB 3
130 PRINT
140 PRINT "WHAT DO WE COLLECTIVELY CALL"
150 PRINT "OUR FIFTY STATES";
160 INPUT R$: PRINT
170 REM ----------------------------------------------------------------
180 REM       FRAME 2, STEP 2 - ASSIGN 1ST ANTICIPATED MATCH TO A$
190 REM
200 A$ = "*UNIT*STAT*AMER*": GOSUB 10000
210 REM ----------------------------------------------------------------
220 REM       FRAME 2, STEP 3 - IF FLAG = 0 THEN MATCH OCCURRED
230 REM
240 IF FLAG = 0 THEN PRINT "YES! I'LL ACCEPT THAT ANSWER!": GOTO 440
250 REM ----------------------------------------------------------------
260 REM       FRAME 2, STEP 4 - NO MATCH; ASSIGN NEXT ANTICIPATED ANSWER
270 REM
280 A$ = "*UNIT*STAT*": GOSUB 10000
290 IF FLAG = 0 THEN PRINT "YES, BUT UNITED STATES OF WHAT?": GOTO 130
```

```
300 REM ----------------------------------------------------------------
310 REM         (FOLLOWING ILLUSTRATE OTHER ANTICIPATED MATCHES)
320 REM
330 A$ = "*UNIT*": GOSUB 10000
340 IF FLAG = 0 THEN PRINT "UNITED WHAT OF WHAT?": GOTO 130
350 A$ = "*AMER*": GOSUB 10000
360 IF FLAG = 0 THEN PRINT "WHAT OF AMERICA?": GOTO 130
370 A$ = "*U*S*A*": GOSUB 10000
380 IF FLAG = 0 THEN PRINT "I'M NOT CERTAIN OF THAT SPELLING!": GOTO 130
390 REM ----------------------------------------------------------------
400 REM        FINAL FRAME FOR THIS QUESTION SEQUENCE. GIVE A HINT
410 REM
420 PRINT "HERE'S A HINT:"
430 PRINT "UNITED ------ -- -------": GOTO 130
440 REM ----------------------------------------------------------------
450 REM        (FRAMES FOR ADDITIONAL QUESTION SEQUENCES)
460 REM
```

KEYWORDS
DEMO
Sample Run

```
What do we collectively call
our fifty states? UNITED STATES

Yes, but UNITED STATES of what?

What do we collectively call
our fifty states? AMERICA

What of AMERICA?

What do we collectively call
our fifty states? THE GREAT UNITED STATES OF
      AMERICA

Yes, I'll accept that answer!
```

5.7 POSERS AND PROBLEMS

1. Modify the "PASSWORD" program in Section 5.3 to accept an alternate password of your choosing.

2. Write a program of your choosing using the Minimum Answer subroutine.

3. Write a program of your choosing using the KEYWORD subroutine.

4. Design and develop a program that presents a "spelling word drill." The number of words possible and the words are READ from DATA. The user is to have the option of selecting the number of words to be

presented from those available. Words are to be randomly selected and displayed for either 1, 2, or 3 seconds, depending on the display time selected by the user. (Assume that a "count" of 1000 is equivalent to 1 second.) If a word is spelled correctly by the user, the next randomly selected word (without repetition) is displayed. If the word is misspelled, a "miss" counter is incremented by 1, and the same word is displayed again. The user's last incorrect spelling is assigned to a "misspelled" array. This sequence for incorrect spellings is to be repeated until the word is spelled correctly. A list of "problem words" showing the user's last misspelling and the correct spelling of missed words is to be displayed at the conclusion of the program. (Assume that a null value [""] assigned to a position in the misspelled word array means that the corresponding word in the array of possible words either was not selected or was not misspelled.)

The following frame-by-frame outline will assist in developing the program.

Frame 1, Step 1.   Title.

Frame 1, Step 2.   READ number of words possible.

Frame 1, Step 3.   Variable assignments; READ words.

Frame 2.   Introduction.

Frame 3, Step 1.   User selects number of words to attempt.

Frame 3, Step 2.   User selects the display time.

Loop frames, Step 1.   Randomly select word not given previously.

Loop frames, Step 2.   Display word, erase, get user's response.

Loop frames, Step 3.   If correct, display another word.

Loop frames, Step 4.   If incorrect, assign user's response to misspelled array; increment counter; repeat display of word.

Frame 4, Step 1.   Check for perfect score; if so, give appropriate feedback.

Frame 4, Step 2.   Otherwise, present lists of last incorrect spelling and correct spelling for each missed word.

Final frame.   Concluding comment.

"The opportunities of man are limited only by his imagination. But so few have imagination that there are ten thousand fiddlers to one composer."
—CHARLES F. KETTERING

"The most beaten paths are certainly the surest; but do not hope to scare up much game on them."
—ANDRÉ GIDE

"All that glitters is not gold."
—SHAKESPEARE

THINK ABOUT THIS . . .

. . . FOR FUN

Read this sentence slowly: "Finished files are the result of years of scientific study combined with the experience of years." Now, once and only once, count out loud the F's (and f's) in that sentence. How many are there?

. . . SERIOUSLY

Should at least one course in "Computer Literacy" be required for teacher certification in any area?

Chapter 6
Show and Tell: Problem-Solving and Drill Examples

6.1 OBJECTIVES

For the successful completion of this chapter, you should be able to:

1. Describe the purpose or application of instructional computing programs that are:
   a. problem solvers
   b. drill and practice
   (Sections 6.4–6.5).

2. Modify certain programs in this chapter to present information of your choosing.

6.2 A SUMMARY OF THE PURPOSES OF BASIC STATEMENTS

Although there are more statements in the BASIC language than those discussed to this point, the statements in Chapters 1–5 are fundamental to the construction of instructional computing programs. In essence, these statements form the foundation on which a program author has:

1. Some means of assigning and/or displaying values.

2. Some means of controlling the screen display and sequence of execution.

3. Some means of easing repetitious tasks.

Thus, most of the BASIC statements discussed may be further summarized into three categories:

Assignment	Control	Repetition
PRINT	HOME	FOR-NEXT
LET	IF-THEN	GOSUB-RETURN
INPUT	ON-GOTO	
DATA-READ	GOTO	
DIM	END	

This further generalization can be helpful in the initial design stages of program development. Once a category for a particular design task is identified, it becomes a matter of selecting the appropriate statements and defining their sequence of execution in a frame-by-frame and step-by-step process. This is what we have done in designing the programs in Chapters 1–4.

6.3 SOME EXAMPLE PROGRAMS AND PROGRAMMING STRATEGIES

One of the important factors determining the success or failure of a given human endeavor is the amount of imagination (originality, creativity, innovation, etc.) that goes into it. This applies not only to education in general and the instructional process in particular, but also to the use of computers in instruction (in general) and the successful design and development of instructional computing programs (in particular).

In Chapters 9 and 10, specific steps will be discussed in which imagination will have an opportunity to spring forth. Before these steps are discussed, however, examine a few sample programs that give an introduction to strategies and techniques for five methods by which instructional computing may be applied.

As these programs are examined, please keep in mind the quotations at the beginning of this chapter. These example programs *are* limited—by imagination and space. They are not meant to be the "well-beaten path" for those who choose to follow one. Also, they are certainly not meant to reflect the "gold" of instructional computing applications. However, they might plant an "imaginative seed" to allow one to reach greater heights in developing instructional computing programs.

Many of the examples are intentionally trivial, because their content is *not* the point to be made. Rather, the programs illustrate some of the strategies that may be used in designing instructional computing programs. The content is left to the individual author who might use or expand on these strategies.

However, it *is* very important to note that the program examples in this and the next chapter (with the exception of the simulation programs) are designed so that they may be easily modified for specific uses in the classroom. These modifications generally involve nothing more than changing DATA and PRINT statements to reflect the content of your choosing. Thus, within the design constraints of these "model" programs, you will be able to produce instructional computing materials for your own use with a minimum of time and effort.

In addition, a section at the end of Chapter 7 includes "stand-alone" programs that may be used as "teacher utilities." These programs require few or no changes for direct use.

6.4 PROBLEM-SOLVING APPLICATIONS

The heaviest use of instructional computing to date is that of problem solving—writing computer programs to solve specific discipline-oriented problems. This particular application, for all practical purposes, has no limits. It could be finding the roots of a quadratic equation in mathematics, calculating lunar orbits in physics, solving gas-law problems in chemistry, analyzing voting behavior in sociology, determining circulation trends in library science, and so on.

Most, if not all, problem-solving programs are based on some formula or mathematical expression. Known parameters (elements) of the expression are input or read from data, and the solution to an unknown parameter is calculated and output. Our two examples of problem-solving applications are related to a common teaching "problem": routine calculations that translate student numeric data into meaningful information.

6.4.1 PROGRAM 9: Class Statistics

PROGRAM 9 computes standard statistics for a set of student scores. The mean, variance, standard deviation, z-score, and percentile ranking (assuming normal distribution of scores) are determined.

The formula for the *mean* of a set of scores is:

$$\text{Mean} = \frac{\text{Sum of scores}}{\text{Number of scores}}$$

The *variance* may be found from:

$$\text{Variance} = \frac{\text{Sum of squared differences between mean and scores}}{\text{Number of scores}}$$

The *standard deviation* of a set of scores is:

$$\text{Standard deviation} = \text{Square root of the variance}$$

The *z-score* may be found from:

$$z = \frac{\text{Difference of score from mean}}{\text{Standard deviation}}$$

The *percentile ranking* is based on a "table" of *z*-scores and their corresponding percentiles.

A program may be written step by step as shown previously to solve for these unknowns, given a set of scores.

RUN from disk and refer to the listing and run of PROGRAM 9.

```
] LIST


10 REM        PROGRAM 9
20 REM
30 REM -----------------------------------------------------------------
40 REM         FRAME 1 - TITLE AND ASSIGNMENTS
50 REM
60 HOME : VTAB 12: HTAB 4
70 PRINT "STATISTICS FOR A SET OF SCORES"
80 FOR P= 1 TO 3000: NEXT P
90 DIM SCRE(100),DIST(100),ZTABLE(45),PRCNT(45)
100 SUM = 0:SMDIST = 0:LINE = 0
110 FOR I = 1 TO 45: READ ZTABLE(I),PRCNT(I): NEXT I
120 REM -----------------------------------------------------------------
130 REM       FRAME 2 - INTRODUCTION AND DIRECTIONS
140 REM
150 HOME : VTAB 4
160 PRINT "THE MEAN, VARIANCE, STANDARD DEVIATION,": PRINT
170 PRINT "Z-SCORE, AND PERCENTILE RANKING": PRINT
180 PRINT "FOR A SET OF SCORES (ASSUMING NORMAL": PRINT
190 PRINT "DISTRIBUTION) WILL BE CALCULATED.": PRINT
200 PRINT "AS MANY AS 100 SCORES MAY BE ENTERED.": PRINT : PRINT
210 PRINT "ENTER ANY NEGATIVE NUMBER TO STOP."
220 VTAB 24: HTAB 30: INPUT "RETURN =>";Z$
230 REM -----------------------------------------------------------------
```

```
240 REM        FRAME 3 - INPUT OF SCORES; CUMULATIVE SCORE SUM
250 REM
260 HOME : VTAB 10
270 FOR I = 1 TO 100
280 INPUT "SCORE (NEGATIVE TO STOP) ";SCRE(I)
290 IF SCRE(I) < 0 THEN 320
300 SUM = SUM + SCRE(I)
310 NEXT I
320 ENTRIES = I - 1
330 REM ------------------------------------------------------------------
340 REM        FRAME 4 - COMPUTATION OF MEAN, VAR, STND DEVIA
350 REM
360 HOME : VTAB 10
370 PRINT "MEAN" TAB( 15)"VARIANCE" TAB( 30)"SD"
380 PRINT "----" TAB( 15)"--------" TAB( 30)"--"
390 MEAN = INT ((SUM / ENTRIES) * 100) / 100
400 FOR I = 1 TO ENTRIES
410 DIST(I) = SCRE(I) - MEAN
420 SMDIST = SMDIST + DIST(I) ^ 2
430 NEXT I
440 VARIANCE = INT ((SMDIST / ENTRIES) * 100) / 100
450 SD = INT ( SQR (VARIANCE) * 100) / 100
460 PRINT MEAN TAB( 15)VARIANCE TAB( 30)SD
470 VTAB 24: HTAB 30: INPUT "RETURN =>";Z$
480 REM ------------------------------------------------------------------
490 REM        FRAME 5 - COMPUTATION OF Z-SCORE AND PERCENTILE RANK
500 REM
510 HOME : HTAB 8
520 PRINT "Z-SCORE AND PERCENTILE": PRINT
530 PRINT "SCORE" TAB( 15)"Z-SCORE" TAB( 30)"PERCENTILE": PRINT
540 FOR I = 1 TO ENTRIES
550 ZSCRE = INT ((DIST(I) / SD) * 10) / 10
560 PRINT SCRE(I) TAB( 15)ZSCRE TAB( 30);
570 IF ZSCRE < - 2.1 THEN PRINT "1": GOTO 630
580 IF ZSCRE > 2.3 THEN PRINT "99": GOTO 630
590 FOR MTCH = 1 TO 45
600 IF ZSCRE = ZTABLE(MTCH) THEN PRINT PRCNT(MTCH):MTCH = 45
610 NEXT MTCH
620 LINE = LINE + 1: IF LINE = 20 THEN HTAB 30: INPUT "RETURN =>";Z$
    :LINE = 0
630 NEXT I
640 VTAB 24: HTAB 30: INPUT "RETURN =>";Z$
650 REM ------------------------------------------------------------------
660 REM        FRAME 6 - OPTION FOR ANOTHER ANALYSIS
670 REM
680 HOME : VTAB 12
690 INPUT "DO ANOTHER SET OF SCORES? ";Z$
700 IF LEFT$ (Z$,1) = "Y" THEN SUM = 0:SMDIST = 0:LINE = 0: GOTO 260
710 HOME : END
720 REM ------------------------------------------------------------------
```

```
730 REM        DATA FOR Z-SCORE AND PERCENTILE TABLE
740 REM
750 DATA −2.1,2,−2,2,−1.9,3,−1.8,4,−1.7,5,−1.6,6,−1.5,7
760 DATA −1.4,8,−1.3,10,−1.2,12,−1.1,14,−1,16,−.9,18,−.8,21
770 DATA −.7,24,−.6,27,−.5,31,−.4,35,−.3,38,−.2,42,−.1,46
780 DATA 0,50,.1,54,.2,58,.3,62,.4,66,.5,59,.6,73,.7,76
790 DATA .8,79,.9,82,1,84,1.1,86,1.2,89,1.3,90,1.4,92,1.5,93
800 DATA 1.6,95,1.7,96,1.8,96.5,1.9,97,2,98,2.1,98.3,2.2,98.5,2.3,99
```

*PROGRAM 9
Sample Run—
Frame 3*

```
SCORE (NEGATIVE TO STOP) 88
SCORE (NEGATIVE TO STOP) 100
SCORE (NEGATIVE TO STOP) 76
SCORE (NEGATIVE TO STOP) 56
SCORE (NEGATIVE TO STOP) 89
SCORE (NEGATIVE TO STOP) 57
SCORE (NEGATIVE TO STOP) 60
SCORE (NEGATIVE TO STOP) 91
SCORE (NEGATIVE TO STOP) 92
SCORE (NEGATIVE TO STOP) 85
SCORE (NEGATIVE TO STOP) −1
```

*PROGRAM 9
Sample Run—
Frame 4*

```
MEAN       VARIANCE     SD
----       --------     --
79.4       235.24       15.33
```

THINK ABOUT THIS . . .

. . . FOR FUN

What is the exact opposite of not in?

. . . SERIOUSLY

Is the use of computers in instruction just another "educational fad"?

"Don't put off for tomorrow what you can do today, because if you enjoy it today you can do it again tomorrow."
—JAMES A. MICHENER

PROGRAM 3
Sample Run—
Steps 3, 4, 5,
and 7

```
What was the perpetual age
of the late Jack Benny? 35

Too low...

What was the perpetual age
of the late Jack Benny? 39

DIDN'T LOOK IT...     DID HE?

Bye-bye, friends...
```

2.6 POSERS AND PROBLEMS

1. What is the difference between the variables REPLY and REPLY$ in PRO-GRAM 3?

2. Modify statements 370, 380, and 390 in PROGRAM 3 to give comments of your choosing.

3. What should be done to PROGRAM 3 so that it would ask for your age instead of Jack Benny's?

4. What should be done to PROGRAM 3 in order to select a random com-ment from five choices instead of three?

5. What changes should be made to PROGRAM 3 in order to ask for the third largest state by land area instead of the second?

6. How should PROGRAM 3 be modified to ask for the user's first name at the start of the program and then refer to the user by name instead of the "BYE-BYE, FRIENDS . . ." at statement 450?

7. Write a statement that will randomly give a value for the variable X that is between 200 and 50, inclusive.

8. What is the *range* of numbers that could randomly be generated by the statement:

   X = INT(25 * RND(0) + 5)

*9. Write a program that asks for the user's height in inches and then prints "TALL" if the user is over 6 feet, "SHORT" if under 5 feet, or "AVER-AGE" if between 5 and 6 feet, inclusive.

*10. Write a program that inputs a number and prints "THREE" if it is a 3, "SIX" if it is a 6, "NINE" if it is a 9, or "NEITHER 3, 6, NOR 9" if it is neither 3, 6, nor 9.

PROGRAM 9
Sample Run—
Frame 5

```
                        z-SCORE AND PERCENTILES

        SCORE        z-SCORE        PERCENTILE

        88              .5              59
        100            1.3              90
        76             -.3              38
        56            -1.6               6
        89             .6               73
        57            -1.5               7
        60            -1.3              10
        91             .7               76
        92             .8               79
        85             .3               62

                                        RETURN  =>
```

6.4.2 PROGRAM 10: Semester Averages

Semester or term grade averages are often based on a cumulative total of such factors as quizzes, homework assignments, regularly scheduled exams, and a final examination. Each of these performance rating factors contributes a certain percentage to the overall semester grade.

PROGRAM 10 illustrates how each of these contributing factors may be entered into one-dimensional arrays, appropriate percentages computed, and the semester average determined and output. The number of possible scores for each factor, the contributing percentage for the factor, and the scores for each factor are entered via INPUT statements. The number of students and the student names are included in the program as DATA statements. The program may be used in a "real" situation by simply replacing the example DATA with actual DATA.

RUN from disk and refer to the listing and run of PROGRAM 10.

```
] LIST


10 REM        PROGRAM 10
20 REM
30 REM  ------------------------------------------------------------------
40 REM        FRAME 1 - TITLE AND ASSIGNMENTS
50 REM
60 HOME : VTAB 12: HTAB 12
70 PRINT "SEMESTER AVERAGES"
80 FOR P = 1 TO 2000: NEXT P
90 READ ROLL
```

```
100 DIM NAM$(ROLL),QUIZ(ROLL),HMWK(ROLL),EXAM(ROLL),FINL(ROLL)
110 REM ----------------------------------------------------------------
120 REM         FRAME 2 - GET INFO FOR QUIZ, HOMEWORK, EXAMS & FINAL
130 REM
140 HOME : VTAB 4
150 PRINT "HOW MANY QUIZZES WERE GIVEN"
160 INPUT "THIS SEMESTER? ";QNUM: PRINT
170 PRINT "THE QUIZZES CONSTITUTE WHAT PERCENT"
180 INPUT "(DECIMAL) OF THE SEMESTER GRADE? ";QPRC
190 PRINT
200 PRINT "HOW MANY HOMEWORK ASSIGNMENTS"
210 INPUT "WERE GIVEN THIS SEMESTER? ";HNUM: PRINT
220 PRINT "THE HOMEWORK CONSTITUTES WHAT PERCENT"
230 INPUT "(DECIMAL) OF THE SEMESTER GRADE? ";HPRC
240 PRINT
250 PRINT "HOW MANY REGULAR EXAMS WERE GIVEN"
260 INPUT "THIS SEMESTER? ";ENUM: PRINT
270 PRINT "THE EXAMS CONSTITUTE WHAT PERCENT"
280 INPUT "(DECIMAL) OF THE SEMESTER GRADE? ";EPRC
290 PRINT
300 PRINT "THE FINAL EXAM CONSTITUTES WHAT PERCENT"
310 INPUT "(DECIMAL) OF THE SEMESTER GRADE? ";FPRC
320 PRINT
330 REM ----------------------------------------------------------------
340 REM         FRAME 3 - CHECK FOR DECIMAL PERCENT = 1.00
350 REM
360 IF ABS ((QPRC + HPRC + EPRC + FPRC) - 1) < = .001 THEN 440
370 HOME : VTAB 12
380 PRINT "THE DECIMAL PERCENTS YOU HAVE ENTERED": PRINT
390 PRINT "DO NOT EQUAL 1.00. PLEASE TRY AGAIN."
400 VTAB 24: HTAB 30: INPUT "RETURN =>";Z$: GOTO 140
410 REM ----------------------------------------------------------------
420 REM         LOOP FRAMES, STEP 1 - GET PUPIL'S NAME; ZERO TOTALS
430 REM
440 FOR PUPIL = 1 TO ROLL
450 HOME :QT = 0:HT = 0:ET = 0
460 READ NAM$(PUPIL): HTAB 8: PRINT "FOR "NAM$(PUPIL)":": PRINT
470 REM ----------------------------------------------------------------
480 REM         LOOP FRAMES, STEP 2 - GET QUIZ SCORES; COMPUTE AVERAGE
490 REM
500 FOR Q = 1 TO QNUM
510 PRINT "QUIZ "Q" SCORE IS";: INPUT QS:QT = QT + QS
520 NEXT Q
530 QUIZ(PUPIL) = INT ((QT / QNUM) * 10) / 10: PRINT
540 REM ----------------------------------------------------------------
550 REM         LOOP FRAMES, STEP 3 - GET HOMEWORK SCORES; COMPUTE AVERAGE
560 REM
570 FOR H = 1 TO HNUM
580 PRINT "HOMEWORK "H" SCORE IS";: INPUT HS:HT = HT + HS
590 NEXT H
```

```
600 HMWK(PUPIL) = INT ((HT / HNUM) * 10) / 10: PRINT
610 REM ---------------------------------------------------------------
620 REM         LOOP FRAMES, STEP 4 - GET EXAM SCORES; COMPUTE AVERAGE
630 REM
640 FOR E = 1 TO ENUM
650 PRINT "EXAM "E" SCORE IS";: INPUT ES:ET = ET + ES
660 NEXT E
670 EXAM(PUPIL) = INT ((ET / ENUM) * 10) / 10: PRINT
680 REM ---------------------------------------------------------------
690 REM         LOOP FRAMES, STEP 5 - GET FINAL EXAM SCORE
700 REM
710 INPUT "THE FINAL EXAM SCORE IS?";FINL(PUPIL)
720 NEXT PUPIL
730 REM ---------------------------------------------------------------
740 REM         FINAL FRAME - OUTPUT WITH PRINTER OPTION
750 REM
760 HOME : VTAB 12:CLASSUM = 0
770 INPUT "DO YOU WANT TO USE THE PRINTER? ";P$
780 IF LEFT$ (P$,1) = "Y" THEN PRINT CHR$ (4)"PR#1"
790 FOR I = 1 TO ROLL
800 SUM = 0: PRINT "/////////////////"
810 PRINT NAM$(I)
820 PRINT "QUIZ AVE "QUIZ(I)" X "QPRC TAB( 20)" = "QUIZ(I) * QPRC
830 SUM = SUM + QUIZ(I) * QPRC
840 PRINT "HOMEWORK "HMWK(I)" X "HPRC TAB( 20)" = "HMWK(I) * HPRC
850 SUM = SUM + HMWK(I) * HPRC
860 PRINT "EXAM AVE "EXAM(I)" X "EPRC TAB( 20)" = "EXAM(I) * EPRC
870 SUM = SUM + EXAM(I) * EPRC
880 PRINT "FINAL EX "FINL(I)" X "FPRC TAB( 20)" = "FINL(I) * FPRC
890 SUM = SUM + FINL(I) * FPRC
900 PRINT TAB( 8)"SEMESTER SUM = "SUM:CLASSUM = CLASSUM + SUM
910 NEXT I
920 PRINT : PRINT "THE CLASS AVERAGE = " INT ((CLASSUM / ROLL) * 10) / 10
930 PRINT CHR$ (4)"PR#0"
940 END
950 REM ---------------------------------------------------------------
960 REM         DATA FOR NUMBER OF PUPILS AND THEIR NAMES
970 REM
980 DATA 5
990 DATA "ABLE","BAKER","CAIN A.","CAIN R.","OMEGA"
```

```
How many quizzes were given
this semester? 4
The quizzes constitute what percent
(decimal) of the semester grade? .25

How many homework assignments
were given this semester? 5
The homework constitutes what percent
(decimal) of the semester grade? .10

              .
              .
              .


The final exam constitutes what percent
(decimal) of the semester grade? .40
```

```
                        FOR ABLE:
Quiz 1 score is? 88
Quiz 2 score is? 90
    .
    .
    .
Homework score 1 is? 86
Homework score 2 is? 90
    .
    .
    .
Exam 1 score is? 70
    .
    .
    .
The final exam score is? 77
```

```
//////////////////
ABLE
QUIZ AVE 89    × .25 = 22.25
HOMEWORK 88    × .1  = 8.8
EXAM AVE 72    × .25 = 18
FINAL 77       × .4  = 30.8
     SEMESTER SUM    = 79.85
//////////////////
BAKER
QUIZ AVE 47.5 × .25 = 11.88
HOMEWORK 77    × .1  = 7.7
EXAM AVE 70    × .25 = 17.5
FINAL 75       × .4  = 30
     SEMESTER SUM    = 67.08
```

Computers are being used in industrial arts courses such as automotive shop to keep maintenance records.

6.5 DRILL-AND-PRACTICE APPLICATIONS

Drill-and-practice programs are second only in use to problem-solving applications in instructional computing. This technique also has wide application in any area in which certain fundamental concepts require practice for mastery, such as multiplication tables, chemical nomenclature, Latin-English word root translations, state capitals, and so on.

Drill-and-practice programs are generally very straightforward. An introduction, usually including examples, is given; drill questions are presented (either linearly or by random selection); answers are entered and checked for accuracy; appropriate feedback is given; the next question is asked; and, at the end of the program, some form of performance report is given.

The four example programs that follow illustrate use of GOSUB-RETURN, FOR-NEXT, and DATA-READ for both linear and random selection of drill questions. The programs may be easily modified for actual class use by simply changing PRINT and DATA statements accordingly.

6.5.1 PROGRAM 11:
Linear Drill Using GOSUB-RETURN

Linear drill programs are easy to design using GOSUB-RETURN. In the example shown, PRINT statement(s) are used to ask a question and the anticipated correct answer is assigned to ANSWER$, followed by a GOSUB 10000 to get the user's response and check it for accuracy. In this particular subroutine, the LEN string function is used to display a number of dashes (-) corresponding to the number of characters in the anticipated answer.

The program also illustrates how positive feedback may be assigned to an array and randomly selected for each correct answer.

By following the sequence of PRINT(s) for the question, ANSWER$ = <correct answer>, and GOSUB 10000, the program may be used to present an indefinite number of questions on any topic.

RUN from disk and refer to the listing and run of PROGRAM 11.

```
] LIST


10 REM        PROGRAM 11
20 REM
30 REM ------------------------------------------------------------
40 REM       FRAME 1, STEP 1 - TITLE
50 REM
60 HOME : VTAB 12: HTAB 2
70 PRINT "DRILL USING A SUBROUTINE FOR INPUT"
80 FOR P = 1 TO 2000: NEXT P: GOSUB 10060
90 REM ------------------------------------------------------------
100 REM       FRAME 1, STEP 2 - DATA ASSIGNMENT FOR FEEDBACK
110 REM
120 DIM FDBK$(6)
130 FOR I = 1 TO 6: READ FDBK$(I): NEXT I
140 REM ------------------------------------------------------------
150 REM       FRAME 2 - FIRST QUESTION SEQUENCE
160 REM
170 PRINT "THE STATE FLOWER OF TEXAS IS THE"
180 ANSWER$ = "BLUEBONNET": GOSUB 10000
190 REM ------------------------------------------------------------
200 REM       FRAME 3 - NEXT QUESTION SEQUENCE
210 REM
220 PRINT "THE LARGEST MUSCLE IN THE BODY IS THE"
230 ANSWER$ = "GLUTEUS MAXIMUS": GOSUB 10000
240 REM ------------------------------------------------------------
250 REM       (FRAMES FOR ADDITIONAL QUESTIONS)
260 REM
9000 REM ------------------------------------------------------------
9010 REM       FINAL FRAME - PERFORMANCE REPORT
9020 REM
9030 PRINT "YOU WERE CORRECT ON "C" QUESTION(S).": END
9040 REM ------------------------------------------------------------
9050 REM       THE POSITIONING AND INPUT SUBROUTINE
9060 REM
10000 VTAB 16: HTAB 12: FOR S = 1 TO LEN (ANSWER$): PRINT "-";: NEXT S
```

```
10010 VTAB 16: HTAB 9: INPUT "=> ";REPLY$: PRINT
10020 IF REPLY$ = ANSWER$ THEN 10050
10030 PRINT "THE CORRECT ANSWER IS "ANSWER$
10040 VTAB 20: HTAB 30: INPUT "RETURN =>";Z$: HOME : VTAB 12: RETURN
10050 C = C + 1: HOME : VTAB 12: HTAB 12: PRINT FDBK$(6 * RND (1) + 1)
10060 FOR P = 1 TO 1000: NEXT P: HOME : VTAB 12: RETURN
11000 REM ------------------------------------------------------------
11010 REM         DATA ELEMENTS FOR FEEDBACK
11020 REM
11030 DATA "RAZZLE-DAZZLE","HOT-DOGGIES","WONDERFUL"
11040 DATA "SIMPLY SWELL","OHH, GREAT","THAT'S THE WAY"
```

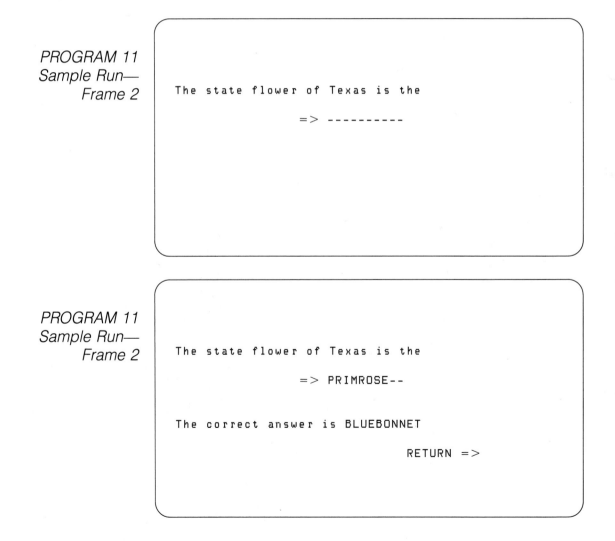

PROGRAM 11
Sample Run—
Frame 2

```
The state flower of Texas is the

            => ----------
```

PROGRAM 11
Sample Run—
Frame 2

```
The state flower of Texas is the

            => PRIMROSE--


The correct answer is BLUEBONNET

                        RETURN =>
```

6.5.2   PROGRAM 12: Linear Drill Using FOR-NEXT and DATA-READ

Linear drill programs also can be easily constructed with FOR-NEXT and DATA-READ statements. The DATA consist of question-answer pairs on any chosen topic that are READ as part of a FOR-NEXT question sequence. Arbitrarily, the example program also includes as many as two hints to be given for a missed question. The program may be used for drill on any topic by changing the PRINT statements in the title and introduction frames and the DATA statements accordingly.

RUN from disk and refer to the listing and run of PROGRAM 12.

LIST

```
10 REM        PROGRAM 12
20 REM
30 REM --------------------------------------------------------------
40 REM        FRAME 1 - TITLE AND NO. OF ITEMS ASSIGNMENT
50 REM
60 HOME : VTAB 12: HTAB 8
70 PRINT "S T A T E  C A P I T A L S"
80 FOR P = 1 TO 3000: NEXT P
90 READ ITEMS
100 REM -------------------------------------------------------------
110 REM        FRAME 2 - INTRODUCTION
120 REM
130 HOME : VTAB 4
140 PRINT "I WILL GIVE YOU "ITEMS" STATES..."
150 PRINT "YOU GIVE ME THE CAPITAL OF EACH..."
160 VTAB 20: HTAB 30: INPUT "RETURN =>";Z$
170 REM -------------------------------------------------------------
180 REM        LOOP FRAMES, STEP 1 - QUESTION FROM DATA; ANSWER CHECKED
190 REM
200 FOR I = 1 TO ITEMS
210 READ QUES$,ANS$,FSTHNT$,SECHNT$
220 HOME : VTAB 4: HTAB 8
230 PRINT : PRINT QUES$;: INPUT REPLY$
240 IF REPLY$ = ANS$ THEN C = C + 1: GOTO 340
250 REM -------------------------------------------------------------
260 REM        LOOP FRAMES, STEP 2 - FEEDBACK FOR MISSED QUESTIONS
270 REM
280 MISS = MISS + 1: PRINT
290 ON MISS GOTO 300,310,320
300 PRINT "FIRST HINT: ": PRINT FSTHNT$: GOTO 230
310 PRINT "SECOND HINT: ": PRINT SECHNT$: GOTO 230
320 PRINT "A CORRECT ANSWER IS: "ANS$
330 VTAB 20: HTAB 30: INPUT "RETURN =>";Z$
```

```
340 MISS = 0
350 NEXT I
360 REM --------------------------------------------------------------
370 REM       FINAL FRAME - PERFORMANCE REPORT
380 REM
390 HOME : VTAB 12: HTAB 8
400 PRINT "YOU ANSWERED "C" CORRECTLY!"
410 END
420 REM --------------------------------------------------------------
430 REM       DATA FOR ITEMS, QUESTIONS, ANSWERS, AND HINTS
440 REM
450 DATA 5
460 DATA "TEXAS","AUSTIN","IT'S IN CENTRAL TEXAS","AUS---"
470 DATA "NEW MEXICO","SANTA FE","THINK OF A RAILROAD","NOT SANTA
    CLAUS..."
480 DATA "OREGON","SALEM","WITCHES IN NEW ENGLAND","BARGAIN PRICES"
490 DATA "MISSISSIPPI","JACKSON","OFFSPRING OF A GIANT KILLER","JACK---"
500 DATA "NEVADA","CARSON CITY","HERE'S JOHNNY!","CAR--- CITY"
```

PROGRAM 12
Sample Run—
Loop Frames,
Steps 1–2

```
                    MISSISSIPPI? BILOXI

      First hint: OFFSPRING OF A GIANT KILLER

                 MISSISSIPPI? HATTIESBURG

      Second hint: JACK---

                 MISSISSIPPI? JACKSBURG

      The correct answer is JACKSON
                                    RETURN =>
```

6.5.3 PROGRAM 13:
Spelling Drill Using Random Selection

We have already seen some examples of standard drill programs in earlier chapters. Recall that PROGRAMs 5 and 5A presented routine drill on simple mathematical concepts. Each of these programs presented certain user options in terms of the number and numeric range of the problems. You were shown that it is often a simple matter to modify an existing program to present different material and how programs could be linked to a MENU of program options. A problem in a later chapter dealt with developing a spelling drill program.

PROGRAM 13 presents one possible solution to Problem 4 in Chapter 5, the spelling word drill. Again, note that the program may be used to present words of your choosing simply by changing the DATA statements accordingly. Thus, in a manner similar to the MENU of math programs, it would be possible to have a series of "spelling drill" programs containing words of varying difficulty and display rates available through a MENU of selections.

RUN from disk and refer to the listing and run of PROGRAM 13.

```
] LIST


10 REM        PROGRAM 13
20 REM
30 REM --------------------------------------------------------------
40 REM        FRAME 1, STEP 1 - TITLE
50 REM
60 HOME : VTAB 12: HTAB 10
70 PRINT "SPELLING WORD DRILL"
80 FOR P = 1 TO 2000: NEXT P
90 REM --------------------------------------------------------------
100 REM        FRAME 1, STEP 2 - READ NUMBER OF WORDS POSSIBLE
110 REM
120 READ SPELWRD
130 REM --------------------------------------------------------------
140 REM        FRAME 1, STEP 3 - ASSIGNMENTS; READ WORDS
150 REM
160 DIM WRD$(SPELWRD),MISSWRD$(SPELWRD),FLAG(SPELWRD):MISS = 0
170 FOR I = 1 TO SPELWRD: READ WRD$(I): NEXT I
180 REM --------------------------------------------------------------
190 REM        FRAME 2 - INTRODUCTION
200 REM
210 HOME : HTAB 12
220 PRINT "INTRODUCTION": PRINT : PRINT
230 PRINT "THIS PROGRAM WILL PRESENT WORDS FOR YOU": PRINT
240 PRINT "TO SPELL. YOU WILL GET TO SELECT THE": PRINT
250 PRINT "NUMBER OF WORDS TO SPELL AND HOW LONG": PRINT
260 PRINT "THE WORD IS DISPLAYED. IF YOU SPELL IT": PRINT
270 PRINT "CORRECTLY, THE NEXT WORD WILL BE": PRINT
280 PRINT "DISPLAYED. IF YOU MISS A WORD, THE": PRINT
290 PRINT "SAME WORD WILL BE DISPLAYED AGAIN."
300 VTAB 22: HTAB 30: INPUT "RETURN =>";Z$
310 REM --------------------------------------------------------------
320 REM        FRAME 3, STEP 1 - USER SELECTS NUMBER OF WORDS
330 REM
340 HOME : VTAB 6
350 PRINT "THERE ARE "SPELWRD" WORDS AVAILABLE.": PRINT
360 INPUT "HOW MANY WOULD YOU LIKE TO TRY? ";TRY: PRINT
```

```
370 IF TRY < 1 OR TRY > SPELWRD THEN 360
380 REM --------------------------------------------------------------
390 REM          FRAME 3, STEP 2 - USER SELECTS DISPLAY RATE
400 REM
410 PRINT "DO YOU WANT A DISPLAY RATE OF:"
420 PRINT TAB( 8)"1 - ONE SECOND"
430 PRINT TAB( 8)"2 - TWO SECONDS"
440 PRINT TAB( 8)"3 - THREE SECONDS"
450 INPUT "ENTER YOUR CHOICE (1-3) ";DISPLAY
460 IF DISPLAY < 1 OR DISPLAY > 3 THEN 450
470 REM --------------------------------------------------------------
480 REM          LOOP FRAMES, STEP 1 - RANDOMLY SELECT WORD
490 REM
500 FOR WRD = 1 TO TRY
510 RANWRD = INT (SPELWRD * RND (1) + 1)
520 IF FLAG(RANWRD) = 1 THEN 510
530 FLAG(RANWRD) = 1
540 REM --------------------------------------------------------------
550 REM          LOOP FRAMES, STEP 2 - DISPLAY WORD; GET USER RESPONSE
560 REM                                                          '
570 HOME : VTAB 12: HTAB 12
580 PRINT WRD$(RANWRD): FOR P = 1 TO (DISPLAY * 1000): NEXT P
590 HOME : VTAB 12
600 INPUT "YOUR SPELLING IS => ";SPELL$
610 REM --------------------------------------------------------------
620 REM          LOOP FRAMES, STEP 3 - IF CORRECT, ASK NEXT WORD
630 REM
640 IF SPELL$ = WRD$(RANWRD) THEN 690
650 REM --------------------------------------------------------------
660 REM          LOOP FRAMES, STEP 4 - OTHERWISE, ASSIGN RESPONSE; REPEAT WORD
670 REM
680 MISSWRD$(RANWRD) = SPELL$:MISS = MISS + 1: GOTO 570
690 NEXT WRD
700 REM --------------------------------------------------------------
710 REM          FRAME 4, STEP 1 - CHECK FOR PERFECT SCORE; GIVE FEEDBACK
720 REM
730 HOME : VTAB 12
740 PRINT "YOU HAD A TOTAL OF "MISS" MISSPELLING(S)": PRINT
750 IF MISS = 0 THEN PRINT "EXCELLENT! YOU GOT THEM ALL!": GOTO 850
760 REM --------------------------------------------------------------
770 REM          FRAME 4, STEP 2 - OTHERWISE, PRESENT LISTS
780 REM
790 PRINT TAB( 12)"PROBLEM WORDS": PRINT
800 PRINT "LAST MISSPELLING" TAB( 20)"CORRECT SPELLING": PRINT
810 FOR I = 1 TO SPELWRD
820 IF MISSWRD$(I) = "" THEN 840
830 PRINT MISSWRD$(I) TAB( 20)WRD$(I)
840 NEXT I
850 VTAB 22: HTAB 30: INPUT "RETURN =>";Z$
```

```
860 REM -------------------------------------------------------------
870 REM        FINAL FRAME - CLOSING COMMENT
880 REM
890 HOME : VTAB 12: HTAB 8
900 PRINT "YOU CAST A SPELL ON ME"
910 END
920 REM -------------------------------------------------------------
930 REM        DATA FOR NUMBER OF WORDS; SPELLING WORDS
940 REM
950 DATA 5
960 DATA "ALIGN","ALREADY","ALL RIGHT","ALLEVIATE","ALUMINUM"
```

PROGRAM 13
Sample Run—
Frame 3

```
There are 5 words available.

How many would you like to try? 4

Do you want a display rate of:
        1 - One second
        2 - Two seconds
        3 - Three seconds
Enter your choice (1-3)1
```

PROGRAM 13
Sample Run—
Frame 4

```
You had a total of 2 misspelling(s)

             PROBLEM WORDS

Last misspelling          Correct spelling

ALINE                     ALIGN
ALL READY                 ALREADY
```

6.5.4 PROGRAM 14:
Random Selection of Drill Questions

If questions are to be randomly selected, the list of questions and answers (and any hints) can be READ from DATA and assigned to one-dimensional arrays. PROGRAM 14 illustrates this technique. Again, as in PROGRAM 13, any incorrect response is assigned to a position in a "missed response" array. Missed questions, including the user's incorrect response and the anticipated correct response, are reviewed at the conclusion of the program.

RUN from disk and refer to the listing and run of PROGRAM 14.

```
] LIST


10 REM       PROGRAM 14
20 REM
30 REM ---------------------------------------------------------------
40 REM       FRAME 1 - TITLE
50 REM
60 HOME : VTAB 12
70 PRINT "RANDOM QUESTIONS WITH FEEDBACK & REVIEW"
80 FOR P = 1 TO 4000: NEXT P
90 REM ---------------------------------------------------------------
100 REM      DATA ASSIGNMENTS
110 REM
120 READ ITEMS
130 DIM QUES$(ITEMS),ANS$(ITEMS),HNT$(ITEMS),MISSED$(ITEMS)
140 DIM ASKED(ITEMS),RGHTFDBK$(5),WRNGFDBK$(5)
150 FOR A = 1 TO ITEMS: READ QUES$(A),ANS$(A),HNT$(A): NEXT A
160 FOR A= 1 TO 5: READ RGHTFDBK$(A),WRNGFDBK$(A): NEXT A
170 REM ---------------------------------------------------------------
180 REM      FRAME 2 - INTRODUCTION
190 REM
200 HOME: VTAB 2: HTAB 10: PRINT "TRIVIAL QUESTIONS"
210 VTAB 6: PRINT "SO YOU THINK YOU KNOW TRIVIA...WELL,"
220 PRINT : PRINT "THERE ARE "ITEMS" QUESTIONS AVAILABLE."
230 PRINT : INPUT "HOW MANY WOULD YOU LIKE? ";TRY
240 IF TRY < 1 OR TRY > ITEMS THEN 220
250 REM ---------------------------------------------------------------
260 REM       LOOP FRAMES, STEP 1 - POSITION; INITIALIZE MISS FLAG
270 REM
280 FOR Q = 1 TO TRY
290 HOME : VTAB 4:MISS = 0
300 REM ---------------------------------------------------------------
310 REM       LOOP FRAMES, STEP 2 - SELECT FEEDBACK AND QUESTION
320 REM
330 FDBK = INT (5 * RND (1) + 1)
```

```
340 RANQ = INT (ITEMS * RND (1) + 1)
350 IF ASKED(RANQ) = 1 THEN 340
360 ASKED(RANQ) = 1
370 PRINT : PRINT QUES$(RANQ);: INPUT REPLY$: PRINT
380 REM -------------------------------------------------------------
390 REM         LOOP FRAMES, STEP 3 - FEEDBACK BASED UPON REPLY & MISS VALUE
400 REM
410 IF REPLY$ = ANS$(RANQ) THEN 500
420 MISSED$(RANQ) = REPLY$
430 IF MISS = 1 THEN 450
440 MISS = 1: PRINT WRNGFDBK$(FDBK): PRINT HNT$(RANQ): GOTO 370
450 PRINT "THE CORRECT ANSWER IS "ANS$(RANQ)
460 VTAB 20: HTAB 30: INPUT "RETURN =>";R$: GOTO 540
470 REM -------------------------------------------------------------
480 REM         LOOP FRAMES, STEP 3 - PROCESSES FOR CORRECT ANSWER
490 REM
500 HOME : VTAB 12: HTAB 12: PRINT RGHTFDBK$(FDBK)"!"
510 FOR P = 1 TO 1000: NEXT P
520 IF MISS = 0 THEN FRSTCNT = FRSTCNT + 1
530 IF MISS = 1 THEN SCNDCNT = SCNDCNT + 1
540 NEXT Q
550 REM -------------------------------------------------------------
560 REM         NEXT FRAME - PERFORMANCE REPORT
570 REM
580 HOME : VTAB 4: HTAB 8: PRINT "HERE ARE YOUR SCORES:"
590 VTAB 6: PRINT "CORRECT ON FIRST TRY = "FRSTCNT: PRINT
600 PRINT "CORRECT ON SECOND TRY = "SCNDCNT: PRINT
610 PRINT "TOTAL CORRECT = "FRSTCNT + SCNDCNT: PRINT
620 IF FRSTCNT = TRY THEN PRINT "E X C E L L E N T !": GOTO 640
630 PRINT "HERE ARE QUESTIONS MISSED AT LEAST ONCE:"
640 VTAB 20: HTAB 30: INPUT "RETURN =>";R$
650 REM -------------------------------------------------------------
660 REM         LOOP FRAMES - REVIEW OF MISSED QUESTIONS
670 REM
680 FOR L = 1 TO ITEMS
690 IF MISSED$(L) = "" THEN 750
700 HOME : VTAB 4
710 PRINT "THE QUESTION WAS:": PRINT QUES$(L): PRINT
720 PRINT "YOUR ANSWER WAS:": PRINT MISSED$(L): PRINT
730 PRINT "THE CORRECT ANSWER IS:": PRINT ANS$(L)
740 VTAB 20: HTAB 30: INPUT "RETURN =>";R$
750 NEXT L
760 REM -------------------------------------------------------------
770 REM         FINAL FRAME - SCORE
780 REM
790 HOME : VTAB 12
800 SCRE = INT ((FRSTCNT * 100 / TRY) * 10) / 10
810 PRINT "YOUR 'FIRST TRY' SCORE IS "SCRE" PERCENT."
820 END
830 REM -------------------------------------------------------------
```

```
840 REM        DATA FOR THE NUMBER OF QUESTION ITEMS
850 REM
860 DATA 5
870 REM -------------------------------------------------------------------
880 REM        DATA FOR QUESTIONS, ANSWERS, AND HINTS
890 REM
900 DATA "THE LARGEST RIVER IN THE WORLD","AMAZON","BIG MOMMA!"
910 DATA "LAST NAME OF THE COMPOSER OF 'BOLERO'","RAVEL","SWEATERS CAN UN-"
920 DATA "WHAT IS THE NUMBER OF CRANIAL NERVES","12","A BAKER'S DOZEN - 1"
930 DATA "LAST NAME OF PLAYER WHO HIT 61 HOMERUNS","MARIS"
940 DATA "COLTS' MOTHERS ARE","THE PILGRIMS' YEAR","1620",",,,4,8,12,,,"
5000 REM -------------------------------------------------------------------
5010 REM        DATA FOR FIVE (5) CORRECT, INCORRECT FEEDBACK
5020 REM
5030 DATA "GRRREAT","NO,,,THINK OF THIS"
5040 DATA "FINE","HOLD IT","PERFECT","NO,,,NOT YET"
5050 DATA "HOT-DOG","LET ME HELP"
5060 DATA "MARVELOUS","THIS MAY HELP"
```

*PROGRAM 14
Sample Run—
Loop Frames,
Steps 1–2*

```
Last name of the composer of 'Bolero'?BACH

Let me help:
Sweaters can UN-

Last name of the composer of 'Bolero'?THREAD

The correct answer is RAVEL

                              RETURN =>
```

PROGRAM 14
Sample Run—
Loop Frames,
Review

```
THE QUESTION WAS:
Last name of the composer of 'Bolero'

YOUR ANSWER WAS:
THREAD

THE CORRECT ANSWER IS:
RAVEL


                              RETURN  =>
```

6.6 POSERS AND PROBLEMS

1. Following the display of the percentile rankings in PROGRAM 9, make modifications that will produce a display of the "count" of each score entered. That is, if four out of all the scores entered were 100 and two scores were 91, the program will display:

    ```
    Score = 100    Count = 4
    Score =  91    Count = 2
            •              •
            •              •
            •              •
          etc.           etc.
    ```

2. Modify PROGRAM 11 to present any five questions of your choosing.

3. Modify PROGRAM 13 to present spelling words of your choosing. Change the display-time options to 0.5, 1.0, and 1.5 seconds. Have both PROGRAM 13 and your program accessible through a MENU program.

4. Modify PROGRAM 14 to randomly select ten of fifteen possible questions with appropriate answers and hints of your choosing.

THINK ABOUT THIS . . .

. . . FOR FUN

. . . SERIOUSLY

In going over his books one day, a bookkeeper for a toy company noticed that the word "balloon" had two sets of double letters, one following the other. Someplace on this page there is a word that has three sets of double letters, one right after the other. Can you find it?

Should teachers have the ability to develop instructional computing materials for their own use in the classroom, or should most rely only on "commercially available" software?

Chapter 7
More Show and Tell: Tutorial, Simulation, and Testing Examples; Teacher Utility Programs

7.1 OBJECTIVES

For the successful completion of this chapter, you should be able to:

1. Describe the purpose and application of instructional computing programs that are:
   a. tutorial (dialog) (Section 7.2)
   b. simulation (Section 7.3)
   c. testing (Section 7.4)

2. Modify certain programs in this chapter to present information of your choosing.

7.2 TUTORIAL (DIALOG) APPLICATIONS

An extension of the drill-and-practice application allows for more feedback to the user whenever difficulty is indicated. This "tutorial dialog" could assist the user in locating the specific cause of errors, provide feedback more directly related to the user's response, or, if needed, branch to a separate section for detailed review.

From an instructional computing standpoint, programs of this type are often the most complicated to design, are time-consuming to develop, and generally go through many stages of testing and revision. The reason is that these programs (if carefully and thoroughly designed) must anticipate a variety of users' responses and treat them accordingly: Is the user's answer partly correct? Has the user indicated difficulty to the extent that a branch for review is needed? If the user stops in the middle of an interaction, will the program start again at that point? Should the program record the questions and responses for questions missed? Because of these and other extensive design, development, and evaluation considerations, thorough tutorial dialog programs are not widely available.

For these reasons, we will give here only two short example programs of this type. The first example will illustrate a problem in which the correct solution strategy is defined in a step-by-step process. The second will use the KEYWORD subroutine to respond more appropriately to anticipated responses. These examples illustrate some programming strategies for introducing more of a "dialog" into the interaction. They are by no means examples of instructional computing programs with extensive tutorial applications. However, they do show some of the techniques that may be used in developing programs of this type.

7.2.1 PROGRAM 15: Step-by-Step Dialog

A tutorial program can do more than just give hints when users are having difficulty with a given question. It can, to some degree, approach the type of dialog that occurs between a tutor and a student. As an example, consider a question related to the chemical concept of a mole. (*Don't panic!* It is a simple concept, as you will see.) By definition, a mole is a quantity of a chemical compound equal to the formula weight (FW) of that compound. Thus, for a given weight of a chemical compound, the number of moles is determined by the following formula:

$$\text{Moles} = \frac{\text{GM (grams)}}{\text{FW (gram–formula weight)}}$$

The key to developing a tutorial dialog is in defining a series of steps that lead to the correct solution. For this method (and many other similar applications), these steps are simply:

1. Was the correct formula used?

2. Were the correct values applied to the formula?

3. If Steps 1 and 2 are true, yet the user missed the question, then a "math error" must have occurred.

Tutorial programs of this nature may be written by refining any concept into a step-by-step approach for solution or explanation.

The following program illustrates a type of dialog that could occur in a tutorial instructional computing application. Note that the program makes use of the ABS (absolute) function to allow for a tolerance of ± 0.1 in the student's answers (see statements 400 and 610). Also be reminded that this is, in essence, a program fragment and does not include an introduction with examples, random selection of positive responses, use of counters for the number correct, and so on. These elements should always be incorporated into programs for actual use in an educational setting.

RUN from disk and refer to the listing and run of PROGRAM 15.

] LIST

```
10 REM        PROGRAM 15
20 REM
30 REM ----------------------------------------------------------------
40 REM        FRAME 1, STEP 1 - TITLE
50 REM
60 HOME : VTAB 12: HTAB 6
70 PRINT "CALCULATING THE NUMBER OF MOLES"
80 FOR P = 1 TO 2000: NEXT P
90 REM ----------------------------------------------------------------
100 REM        FRAME 1, STEP 2 - ASSIGNMENTS
110 REM
120 READ NMCPD
130 DIM CPD$(NMCPD),FW(NMCPD)
140 FOR I = 1 TO NMCPD: READ CPD$(I),FW(I): NEXT I
150 REM ----------------------------------------------------------------
160 REM        FRAME 2 - INTRODUCTION
170 REM
180 HOME : VTAB 4
190 PRINT "THIS PROGRAM WILL ALLOW YOU TO PRACTICE": PRINT
200 PRINT "CALCULATING THE NUMBER OF MOLES OF": PRINT
210 PRINT "A COMPOUND. I'LL TRY TO HELP YOU": PRINT
220 PRINT "WITH EACH STEP NEEDED IF YOU MAKE": PRINT
230 PRINT "ANY MISTAKE IN YOUR ANSWERS.": PRINT
240 PRINT "I'LL LET YOU PRACTICE AS MUCH AS": PRINT
250 PRINT "YOU WISH...": GOSUB 830
260 REM ----------------------------------------------------------------
270 REM        FRAME 3, STEP 1 - GET RANDOM VALUES; ASK QUESTION
280 REM
290 MISS = 0
300 GM = INT (10 * RND (1) + 1) * 20
310 X = INT (NMCPD * RND (1) + 1)
320 MOLES = GM / FW(X)
330 HOME : VTAB 6
340 PRINT "HOW MANY MOLES OF "CPD$(X)" ARE PRESENT": PRINT
```

```
350 PRINT "IN "GM" GRAMS OF THE COMPOUND?"
360 VTAB 10: HTAB 10: INPUT "=>";REPLY: PRINT
370 REM -----------------------------------------------------------------
380 REM        FRAME 3, STEP 2 - CHECK ANSWER USING ABS FUNCTION
390 REM
400 IF ABS (REPLY - MOLES) < = .1 THEN 720
410 REM -----------------------------------------------------------------
420 REM        FRAME 3, STEP 3 - IF SECOND MISS, GIVE ANSWER
430 REM
440 IF MISS = 0 THEN MISS = 1: GOTO 510
450 PRINT TAB( 4)"MOLES = GRAMS / GRAM-FORMULA WT.": PRINT
460 PRINT TAB( 10)"= "GM"/"FW(X): PRINT
470 PRINT TAB( 10)"= " INT (MOLES * 100) / 100: GOSUB 830: GOTO 740
480 REM -----------------------------------------------------------------
490 REM        FRAME 3, STEP 4 - ASK FIRST STAGE IN SOLUTION SEQUENCE
500 REM
510 PRINT "DID YOU DIVIDE THE GRAMS BY THE"
520 INPUT "GRAM-FORMULA WEIGHT (Y/N)? ";REPLY$: PRINT
530 IF LEFT$ (REPLY$,1) = "Y" THEN 580
540 PRINT TAB( 10) "WELL, YOU SHOULD!": GOSUB 820: GOTO 330
550 REM -----------------------------------------------------------------
560 REM        FRAME 3, STEP 5 - ASK SECOND STAGE IN SOLUTION SEQUENCE
570 REM
580 PRINT "GOOD...THAT IS CORRECT. WHAT VALUE DID"
590 INPUT "YOU USE FOR THE FORMULA WEIGHT? ";REPLY
600 PRINT
610 IF ABS (REPLY - FW(X)) < = .1 THEN 670
620 PRINT "AHA! THIS MAY BE YOUR PROBLEM. THE"
630 PRINT "CORRECT FORMULA WEIGHT IS "FW(X)"!": GOSUB 820: GOTO 330
640 REM -----------------------------------------------------------------
650 REM        FRAME 3, STEP 6 - CORRECT SEQUENCE TO HERE; MATH ERROR MADE
660 REM
670 PRINT "HMMM...THAT IS THE CORRECT VALUE."
680 PRINT "YOU MUST HAVE MADE AN ARITHMETIC ERROR.": GOSUB 820: GOTO 330
690 REM -----------------------------------------------------------------
700 REM        FRAME 4 - FEEDBACK FOR CORRECT; OPTION FOR ANOTHER
710 REM
720 HOME : VTAB 12: HTAB 10
730 PRINT "E X C E L L E N T !"
740 VTAB 24: HTAB 10
750 INPUT "WANT ANOTHER (Y/N)? ";REPLY$
760 IF LEFT$ (REPLY$,1) = "Y" THEN 290
770 HOME : VTAB 12: PRINT "REMEMBER, MAKE NO MOUNTAINS OUT OF MOLES"
780 END
790 REM -----------------------------------------------------------------
800 REM        FEEDBACK/DISPLAY HOLDING SUBROUTINE
810 REM
820 PRINT "LET ME PRESENT THE PROBLEM AGAIN."
830 VTAB 22: HTAB 30: INPUT "RETURN =>";Z$: RETURN
840 REM -----------------------------------------------------------------
```

```
850 REM        DATA FOR NUMBER OF COMPOUNDS, FORMULA, FORMULA WEIGHT
860 REM
870 DATA 3
880 DATA "KOH",56,"HF",20,"KI",166
```

PROGRAM 15
Sample Run—
Frame 3,
Steps 1–5

```
How many moles of KOH are present
in 90 grams of the compound?
          =>2.4
Did you divide the grams by the
gram-formula weight(Y/N)? Y

Good...that is correct. What value did
you use for the formula weight? 172

Aha! This may be your problem. The
correct formula weight is 56.
Let me present the problem again.

                              RETURN  =>
```

PROGRAM 15
Sample Run—
Frame 3,
Steps 1–6

```
How many moles of HF are present
in 60 grams of the compound?
          =>0.33
Did you divide the grams by the
formula weight(Y/N)? Y

Good...That is correct. What value did
you use for the formula weight? 20

Hmmm...That is the correct value.
You must have made an arithmetic error.
Let me present the problem again.

                              RETURN  =>
```

PROGRAM 15
Sample Run—
Frame 3,
Steps 1–3

```
How many moles of HF are present
in 60 grams of the compound?
          =>2.5
Moles  =  grams/gram-formula wt.

       =  60/20

       =  3

                          RETURN =>
```

7.2.2 PROGRAM 16: KEYWORD
Matching from DATA

Keywords or key phrases may also be defined as DATA statements for use with the Minimum Answer subroutine. PROGRAM 16 illustrates this technique. DATA elements contain a given question and three anticipated answers and a response for each. Although the example program contains trivial questions about the first president of our country, the program may be used for any topic by modifying the PRINT statements in Frames 1 and 2 and the DATA statements accordingly. However, again note that the design of the program requires three anticipated answers and responses for each question that is asked (see statements 920–1050).

RUN from disk and refer to the listing and run of PROGRAM 16.

```
] LIST


10 REM        PROGRAM 16
20 REM
30 REM --------------------------------------------------------------
40 REM        FRAME 1, STEP 1 - TITLE
50 REM
60 HOME : VTAB 12
70 HTAB 10: PRINT "OUR FIRST PRESIDENT"
80 FOR P = 1 TO 2000: NEXT P
90 REM --------------------------------------------------------------
100 REM       FRAME 1, STEP 2 - QUESTION, ANSWERS, FEEDBACK ASSIGNMENTS
110 REM
```

```
120 READ ITEMS
130 DIM Q$(ITEMS),A1$(ITEMS),F1$(ITEMS),A2$(ITEMS),F2$(ITEMS)
140 DIM A3$(ITEMS),F3$(ITEMS):C = 0
150 FOR I = 1 TO ITEMS
160 READ Q$(I),A1$(I),F1$(I),A2$(I),F2$(I),A3$(I),F3$(I)
170 NEXT I
180 REM --------------------------------------------------------------
190 REM          FRAME 2 - INTRODUCTION
200 REM
210 HOME : VTAB 2: HTAB 6
220 PRINT "THE FATHER OF OUR COUNTRY": PRINT : PRINT
230 PRINT "I WILL ASK YOU A FEW QUESTIONS ABOUT": PRINT
240 PRINT "OUR FIRST PRESIDENT. I WILL TRY TO": PRINT
250 PRINT "HELP YOU WITH ANY ANSWER THAT YOU": PRINT
260 PRINT "GIVE THAT IS NOT COMPLETE. ALSO,": PRINT
270 PRINT "I WILL PROVIDE THE FOLLOWING OPTIONS:": PRINT
280 PRINT "YOU MAY ENTER 'HINT' FOR A HINT,": PRINT
290 PRINT "OR 'ANSWER' IF YOU WANT THE CORRECT": PRINT
300 PRINT "ANSWER, OR 'STOP' IF YOU WISH TO": PRINT
310 PRINT "STOP AT ANY TIME BEFORE WE FINISH."
320 VTAB 23: HTAB 30: INPUT "RETURN =>";Z$
330 REM --------------------------------------------------------------
340 REM          LOOP FRAMES, STEP 1 - INITIALIZE; ASK QUESTION; GET REPLY
350 REM
360 FOR ASK = 1 TO ITEMS
370 MISS = 0
380 HOME : VTAB 12
390 PRINT Q$(ASK)
400 VTAB 14: HTAB 9: INPUT "=>";R$
410 REM --------------------------------------------------------------
420 REM          LOOP FRAMES, STEP 2 - CHECK FOR OPTIONAL ANSWER
430 REM
440 IF R$ = "HINT" THEN 600
450 IF R$ = "ANSWER" THEN MISS = 1: GOTO 590
460 IF R$ = "STOP" THEN 680
470 REM --------------------------------------------------------------
480 REM          LOOP FRAMES, STEP 3 - CHECK FOR ANTICIPATED ANSWERS
490 REM
500 A$ = A1$(ASK): GOSUB 740
510 IF FLAG = 1 THEN FDBK$ = F1$(ASK):C = C + 1: GOSUB 830: GOTO 640
520 A$ = A2$(ASK): GOSUB 740
530 IF FLAG = 1 THEN FDBK$ = F2$(ASK): GOSUB 830: GOTO 380
540 A$ = A3$(ASK): GOSUB 740
550 IF FLAG = 1 THEN FDBK$ = F3$(ASK): GOSUB 830: GOTO 380
560 REM --------------------------------------------------------------
570 REM          LOOP FRAMES, STEP 4 - NO MATCH; GIVE A HINT OR THE ANSWER
580 REM
590 IF MISS = 1 THEN FDBK$ = A1$(ASK) + " IS CORRECT.": GOSUB 830: GOTO
    640
600 MISS = 1
```

```
610 HNT$ = LEFT$ (A1$(ASK), LEN (A1$(ASK)) /2)
620 FDBK$ = "HERE'S A HINT: " + HNT$
630 GOSUB 830: GOTO 380
640 NEXT ASK
650 REM -----------------------------------------------------------
660 REM        FINAL FRAME - PERFORMANCE REPORT
670 REM
680 HOME : VTAB 12
690 PRINT "YOU CORRECTLY ANSWERED "C" QUESTION(S)."
700 END
710 REM -----------------------------------------------------------
720 REM        KEYWORD/PHRASE SUBROUTINE
730 REM
740 FLAG = 0
750 L = LEN (A$)
760 FOR I = 1 TO ( LEN (R$) - L + 1)
770 IF MID$ (R$,I,L) = A$ THEN FLAG = 1: RETURN
780 NEXT I
790 RETURN
800 REM -----------------------------------------------------------
810 REM        FEEDBACK SUBROUTINE
820 REM
830 VTAB 18: PRINT FDBK$
840 VTAB 22: HTAB 30: INPUT "RETURN =>";Z$: RETURN
850 REM -----------------------------------------------------------
860 REM        DATA FOR THE NUMBER OF QUESTIONS TO ASK
870 REM
880 DATA 3
890 REM -----------------------------------------------------------
900 REM        DATA FOR EACH QUESTION, ANTICIPATED ANSWERS, AND FEEDBACK
910 REM
920 DATA "THE FIRST PRESIDENT OF THE USA WAS"
930 DATA "GEORGE WASHINGTON","VERY GOOD, THAT IS HIS NAME."
940 DATA "WASHINGTON","THE LAST NAME IS OK, BUT TRY AGAIN."
950 DATA "GEORGE","I LIKE THAT FIRST NAME; WHAT'S HIS LAST?"
960 REM -----------------------------------------------------------
970 DATA "AS A YOUNG LAD, HE ONCE CHOPPED DOWN A"
980 DATA "CHERRY TREE","AH, YES, TO MAKE A PIE, NO DOUBT."
990 DATA "CHERRY","A CHERRY WHAT? PLEASE TRY AGAIN."
1000 DATA "TREE","WHAT KIND OF A TREE WAS IT?"
1010 REM -----------------------------------------------------------
1020 DATA "IN HIS LATER YEARS, HE LIVED AT"
1030 DATA "MOUNT VERNON","YES, A BEAUTIFUL HOME ON THE POTOMAC."
1040 DATA "MOUNT","MOUNT WHAT? PLEASE ANSWER AGAIN."
1050 DATA "VERNON","YOU ARE MISSING THE FIRST PART."
```

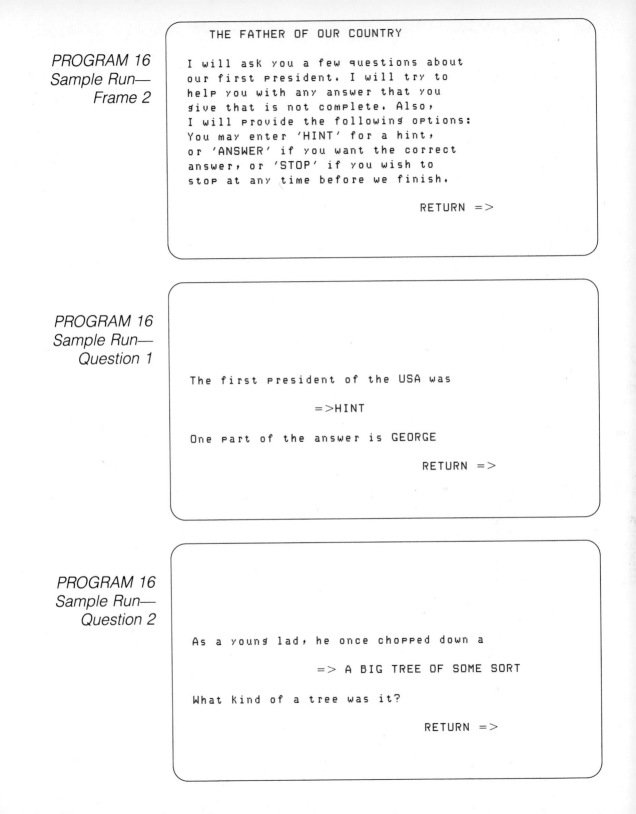

PROGRAM 16
Sample Run—
Frame 2

```
        THE FATHER OF OUR COUNTRY

I will ask you a few questions about
our first president. I will try to
help you with any answer that you
give that is not complete. Also,
I will provide the following options:
You may enter 'HINT' for a hint,
or 'ANSWER' if you want the correct
answer, or 'STOP' if you wish to
stop at any time before we finish.

                        RETURN =>
```

PROGRAM 16
Sample Run—
Question 1

```
The first president of the USA was

            =>HINT

One part of the answer is GEORGE

                        RETURN =>
```

PROGRAM 16
Sample Run—
Question 2

```
As a young lad, he once chopped down a

             => A BIG TREE OF SOME SORT

What kind of a tree was it?

                        RETURN =>
```

PROGRAM 16
Sample Run—
Question 2

```
As  a  young  lad,  he  once  chopped  down  a

                =>CHERRY  BUSH

A  cherry  what?  Please  answer  again.

                                    RETURN  =>
```

PROGRAM 16
Sample Run—
Question 2
Correct

```
As  a  young  lad,  he  once  chopped  down  a

        =>A  GREAT  BIG  OL'  CHERRY  TREE  WITH  HIS  AXE

Ah,  yes,  to  make  a  pie,  no  doubt.

                                    RETURN  =>
```

7.3 SIMULATION APPLICATIONS

Usually, simulation applications in instructional computing are used when it is important to understand a given concept, but one or more of the following situations may apply:

1. There are time, space, and/or equipment limitations.

2. The real process might place the user in a perilous situation.

3. Review and/or practice would be beneficial prior to performing the actual experiment or process.

Simulations in instructional computing are based on models, most of which are mathematical in origin. In general, these programs allow a user to manipulate parameters and perhaps discover the effect of those manipulations. One popular application is in population dynamics: What happens to the population over a certain span of years if both the birth and death rates decrease and the female/male birth ratio increases? Another application is in environmental studies: What happens to the water oxygen content if untreated raw sewage is dumped into a slow-moving stream? A fast-moving river? What is the effect of performing primary treatment? Secondary treatment? How does temperature affect the foregoing results?

Again, the example programs to be discussed are not extensive simulations; they do illustrate the concept of basing the design on some defined model.

7.3.1 PROGRAM 17: Dealing a Bridge Hand

As might be expected, one model that is very easy to simulate is a deck of 52 cards. Manipulations, however, are limited to "shuffling" the deck, then observing the deal. A simulated deck may be considered as a two-dimensional array of 13 rows (card values) and 4 columns (suits). Two random-number generators can pick (deal) a given row and column, respectively, defining a position in the array. Since the random row also defines the card value (ace, king, etc.) and the random column defines the suit (spades, hearts, etc.), it is simple to PRINT the card "dealt" (flagged). The position in the array is flagged so that any dealt card will not be redealt until the deck has been "shuffled" (by reinitializing the array).

PROGRAM 17 simulates dealing a bridge hand (13 cards) and then arranging the hand by suit. This "arranging the hand by suit" introduces a very simple example of a common programming strategy: *sorting* (see statements 560–670). That is, let the program order a given list in either increasing or decreasing value. In the example here, the list is sorted by suit values (1–4) by simply checking each "suit" in the two-dimensional array and PRINTing the value of each card that was "dealt."

However, there are more sophisticated sorting routines. The one shown next sorts 100 or fewer numbers greater than zero from a one-dimensional array [N(J)] into increasing numeric order.

```
1000 REM = = = = =BEGIN SORT= = = = =
1010 FOR J = 1 TO 100
1020     D = N(J)
1130         FOR K = J - 1 TO 1 STEP -1
1040             IF N(K) < D THEN 1080
1050             N(K + 1) = N(K)
1060         NEXT K
1070     K = 0
1080     N(K + 1) = D
```

```
1090 NEXT J
1100 REM = = = = =END OF SORT= = = = =
1110 FOR I = 1 TO 100
1120    IF N(I) = 0 THEN 1140
1130    PRINT N(I)
1140 NEXT I
```

How could this sorting routine be modified so that it would alphabetize a list of names that have been INPUT into an array, L$(), as:

LAST NAME(space)FIRST NAME

then print out the sorted (alphabetized) list? (*Note:* An "A" is considered less than a "B," which is less than a "C," and so on.) Program A731 on the text diskette gives one possible solution.

RUN from disk and refer to the listing and run of PROGRAM 17.

] LIST

```
10 REM          PROGRAM 17
20 REM
30 REM -----------------------------------------------------------------
40 REM          FRAME 1, STEP 1 - TITLE
50 REM
60 HOME : VTAB 12: HTAB 8
70 PRINT "A SIMULATED BRIDGE HAND"
80 FOR P = 1 TO 2000: NEXT P
90 REM -----------------------------------------------------------------
100 REM         FRAME 1, STEP 2 - ASSIGNMENTS
110 REM
120 DIM DECK(13,4),CARD$(13),SUIT$(4):HAN = 0
130 FOR I = 1 TO 13: READ CARD$(I): NEXT I
140 FOR I = 1 TO 4: READ SUIT$(I): NEXT I
150 REM -----------------------------------------------------------------
160 REM         FRAME 2 - INTRODUCTION
170 REM
180 HOME : VTAB 6
190 PRINT "THIS PROGRAM WILL SIMULATE DEALING 13": PRINT
200 PRINT "CARDS FOR A BRIDGE HAND. YOU WILL": PRINT
210 PRINT "BE SHOWN HOW THE CARDS WERE DEALT,": PRINT
220 PRINT "THEN THE HAND WILL BE ARRANGED AND": PRINT
230 PRINT "YOU WILL BE ASKED TO COUNT THE": PRINT
240 PRINT "NUMBER OF 'HONOR POINTS' IN THE HAND."
250 VTAB 22: HTAB 30: INPUT "RETURN=>";Z$
260 REM -----------------------------------------------------------------
270 REM         FRAME 3, STEP 1 - SHUFFLE THE DECK
280 REM
```

```
290 FOR CARD = 1 TO 13
300 FOR SUIT = 1 TO 4
310 DECK(CARD,SUIT) = 0
320 NEXT SUIT
330 NEXT CARD
340 REM ----------------------------------------------------------------
350 REM         FRAME 3, STEP 2 - DEAL 13 UNIQUE CARDS
360 REM
370 HNRPTS = 0:HAN = HAN + 1
380 HOME : VTAB 2: HTAB 6
390 PRINT "HERE'S HOW HAND "HAN" WAS DEALT:": PRINT
400 FOR DEAL = 1 TO 13
410 CARD = INT (13 * RND (1) + 1)
420 SUIT = INT (4 * RND (1) + 1)
430 IF DECK(CARD,SUIT) = 1 THEN 410
440 DECK(CARD,SUIT) = 1
450 PRINT TAB( 8)CARD$(CARD) TAB( 13)" OF "SUIT$(SUIT)
460 REM ----------------------------------------------------------------
470 REM         FRAME 3, STEP 3 - COUNT THE HONOR POINTS
480 REM
490 IF CARD = 1 THEN HNRPTS = HNRPTS + 4
500 IF CARD = 2 THEN HNRPTS = HNRPTS + 3
510 IF CARD = 3 THEN HNRPTS = HNRPTS + 2
520 IF CARD = 4 THEN HNRPTS = HNRPTS + 1
530 NEXT DEAL
540 VTAB 22
550 PRINT "PRESS ANY KEY AND I'LL ARRANGE THE HAND";: GET Z$
560 REM ----------------------------------------------------------------
570 REM         FRAME 4, STEP 1 - ARRANGE THE HAND BY SUIT
580 REM
590 HOME : HTAB 6
600 PRINT "HAND "HAN" ARRANGED BY SUIT": PRINT
610 FOR SUIT = 1 TO 4
620 FOR CARD = 1 TO 13
630 IF DECK(CARD,SUIT) = 0 THEN 650
640 PRINT TAB( 8)CARD$(CARD) TAB( 13)" OF "SUIT$(SUIT)
650 NEXT CARD
660 PRINT
670 NEXT SUIT
680 REM ----------------------------------------------------------------
690 REM         FRAME 4, STEP 2 - ASK FOR THE NUMBER OF HONOR POINTS
700 REM
710 PRINT : INPUT "HOW MANY HONOR POINTS DO YOU COUNT? ";HP: PRINT
720 IF HP = HNRPTS THEN PRINT TAB( 6)"THAT'S WHAT I COUNT!": GOTO 740
730 PRINT TAB( 6)"I COUNT "HNRPTS" HONOR POINTS!"
740 VTAB 24: HTAB 30: INPUT "RETURN =>";Z$
750 REM ----------------------------------------------------------------
760 REM         FRAME 5 - OPTION FOR ANOTHER HAND
770 REM
780 HOME : VTAB 12
```

```
790 INPUT "WOULD YOU LIKE ANOTHER HAND DEALT? ";Z$
800 IF LEFT$ (Z$,1) = "Y" THEN 290
810 HOME : VTAB 12: HTAB 6
820 PRINT "MAY ALL YOUR SLAMS BE GRAND!"
830 END
840 REM -------------------------------------------------------------
850 REM        DATA FOR CARD AND SUIT VALUES
860 REM
870 DATA "ACE","KING","QUEEN","JACK","TEN","NINE","EIGHT","SEVEN"
880 DATA "SIX","FIVE","FOUR","TREY","DEUCE"
890 REM -------------------------------------------------------------
900 DATA "SPADES","HEARTS","DIAMONDS","CLUBS"
```

*PROGRAM 17
Sample Run—
Frame 3, Step 2*

```
            HERE'S HOW HAND 1 WAS DEALT
                 Ten     of Clubs
                 Five    of Spades
                 Five    of Diamonds
                 Queen   of Clubs
                 Eight   of Hearts
                 Deuce   of Hearts
                 Queen   of Hearts
                 King    of Diamonds
                 Jack    of Spades
                 Seven   of Hearts
                 Ten     of Spades
                 Eight   of Diamonds
                 Ten     of Hearts
        PRESS ANY KEY AND I'LL ARRANGE THE HAND
```

*PROGRAM 17
Sample Run—
Frame 4, Step 1*

```
            HAND 1 ARRANGED BY SUIT
                 Jack    of Spades
                 Ten     of Spades
                 Five    of Spades
                 Queen   of Hearts
                 Ten     of Hearts
                 Eight   of Hearts
                 Seven   of Hearts
                 Deuce   of Hearts
                 King    of Diamonds
                 Eight   of Diamonds
                 Five    of Diamonds
                 Queen   of Clubs
                 Ten     of Clubs
        HOW MANY HONOR POINTS DO YOU COUNT? 8
```

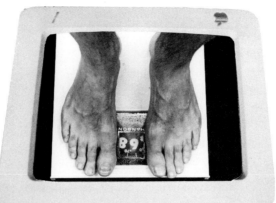

A program won't tell you what you do weigh, but it can recommend an "ideal" weight.

7.3.2 PROGRAM 18: Caloric Intake and Ideal Weight

Diet and the maintenance of proper body weight are popular concerns in our society. It is well known that by careful control of caloric intake and a good exercise program, weight can be lost or gained and then maintained at an "ideal" level.

PROGRAM 18 allows manipulation of a limited daily menu of food items and exercise activity factors to examine the effect on weight. Its use here is primarily to illustrate basing a simulation on some defined model. If a reasonable model has been defined, it may be possible to simulate that model with a computer program.

As an example, we will examine the model for this program, state a programming "problem," then outline the design procedures to simulate the model and solve the problem.

The Model

- An "ideal" weight is a base weight plus a weight increment for each inch over 5 feet in height.

- The base weight for a female is 100 pounds.

- The base weight for a male is 106 pounds.

- The weight increment for a female is 5 pounds for each inch over 5 feet in height.

- The weight increment for a male is 6 pounds for each inch over 5 feet in height.

- The caloric intake needed to maintain an ideal weight is:

    Ideal weight × Exercise activity factor

- Exercise activity factors are:

  12, for little or no exercise activity

  15, for moderate exercise activity

  18, for high exercise activity

- A pound of fat is equivalent to 3500 calories.

- Weight lost or gained over a 7-day period is:

$$\frac{(\text{Caloric intake} - \text{Calories needed}) \times 7}{3500}$$

- A list of foods and their caloric equivalents is included.

The Problem

Design a program that will present a hypothetical breakfast menu. Items from the menu are to be selected one at a time. For each item selected, the number of calories for that item will be displayed beside the food item. This sequence is to be repeated for lunch and dinner menus. The total calorie counts for a given meal and the day are to be displayed with each menu.

After the day's menus are given, information on sex, height, and exercise activity is to be obtained. The user's ideal weight and daily caloric intake are then displayed. The user's projected weight loss or gain over a 7-day period (assuming consistent daily caloric consumption) is then calculated and displayed. Finally, the user has the option to repeat the simulation.

The Design

Frame 1.   Title and variable assignments.

Frame 2.   Introduction.

SUBROUTINE FRAMES FOR MENUS

Frame 4.   Additional information requested.

Frame 5, Step 1.   Get user's sex.

Frame 5, Step 2.   Assign base weight and increment.

Frame 6, Step 1.   Get user's height.

Frame 6, Step 2.   Calculate ideal weight.

Frame 7, Step 1.   Get user's exercise activity.

Frame 7, Step 2.   Assign exercise activity factor.

Frame 7, Step 3.   Calculate calories for ideal weight.

Frame 8.   Display ideal weight and daily calories.

Frame 9, Step 1.   Calculate weight loss or gain.

Frame 9, Step 2.   Display results.

Frame 10.   Option to repeat simulation.

Final Frame.   Closing comments.

THE SUBROUTINE

Frame 1, Step 1.   Initialize; READ meal DATA.

Frame 1, Step 2.   Display menu and selected calories.

Frame 1, Step 3.   Get selection; flag item; sum calories.

Frame 1, Step 4.   Repeat Step 2 until RETURN.

Carefully examine the listing of PROGRAM 18 to see how these design procedures are translated into BASIC code.

RUN from disk and refer to the listing and run of PROGRAM 18.

```
] LIST


10 REM        PROGRAM 18
20 REM
30 REM -----------------------------------------------------------------
40 REM        FRAME 1 - TITLE AND ASSIGNMENTS
50 REM
60 HOME : VTAB 10
70 PRINT "A SIMULATED DAILY CALORIC INTAKE AND"
80 PRINT : PRINT " ITS EFFECT ON YOUR IDEAL WEIGHT"
90 FOR P = 1 TO 4000: NEXT P
100 DIM CALRIES(15),FOOD$(15),FLAGFOOD(15)
110 REM -----------------------------------------------------------------
120 REM        FRAME 2 - INTRODUCTION
130 REM
140 HOME : VTAB 2
150 PRINT "YOU WILL BE PRESENTED A MENU FOR BREAK-"
160 PRINT : PRINT "FAST, LUNCH, AND DINNER. SELECT AS MANY"
170 PRINT : PRINT "ITEMS FROM EACH MENU AS YOU WISH. AFTER"
180 PRINT : PRINT "YOUR DAILY MENU HAS BEEN COMPLETED, YOU"
190 PRINT : PRINT "WILL RECEIVE A SUMMARY OF YOUR CALORIC"
200 PRINT : PRINT "INTAKE AND ITS EFFECT ON YOUR IDEAL WT."
210 VTAB 20; HTAB 30: INPUT "RETURN =>";Z$
220 REM -----------------------------------------------------------------
230 REM        SUBROUTINE FRAMES - PRESENT BREAKFAST MENU
240 REM
250 GOSUB 2000
260 REM -----------------------------------------------------------------
```

```
270 REM       SUBROUTINE FRAMES - PRESENT LUNCH MENU
280 REM
290 GOSUB 2000
300 REM --------------------------------------------------------------
310 REM       SUBROUTINE FRAMES - PRESENT DINNER MENU
320 REM
330 GOSUB 2000
340 REM --------------------------------------------------------------
350 REM       FRAME 4 - BEGIN SEQUENCE FOR ADDITIONAL INFO
360 REM
370 HOME : VTAB 12
380 PRINT "NOW, SOME PERSONAL DATA IS NEEDED..."
390 FOR P = 1 TO 3000: NEXT P
400 REM --------------------------------------------------------------
410 REM       FRAME 5, STEP 1 - GET SEX INFORMATION
420 REM
430 HOME : VTAB 8
440 PRINT "ARE YOU:": PRINT
450 PRINT "   1. FEMALE"
460 PRINT "   2. MALE": PRINT
470 INPUT "ENTER 1 OR 2 ";SEX
480 IF SEX < 1 OR SEX > 2 THEN 470
490 REM --------------------------------------------------------------
500 REM       FRAME 5, STEP 2 - ASSIGN BASE WEIGHT AND INCREMENT
510 REM
520 IF SEX = 1 THEN BASEWT = 100:WTINCRMNT = 5
530 IF SEX = 2 THEN BASEWT = 106:WTINCRMNT = 6
540 REM --------------------------------------------------------------
550 REM       FRAME 6, STEP 1 - GET HEIGHT INFORMATION
560 REM
570 HOME : VTAB 12
580 INPUT "WHAT IS YOUR HEIGHT IN INCHES? ";HEIGHT
590 IF HEIGHT > 47 AND HEIGHT < 85 THEN 640
600 PRINT TAB( 10)"* OUT OF RANGE *": GOTO 580
610 REM --------------------------------------------------------------
620 REM       FRAME 6, STEP 2 - CALCULATE IDEAL WEIGHT
630 REM
640 IDEALWT = ((HEIGHT - 60) * WTINCRMNT) + BASEWT
650 REM --------------------------------------------------------------
660 REM       FRAME 7, STEP 1 - GET EXERCISE ACTIVITY INFORMATION
670 REM
680 HOME : VTAB 6
690 PRINT "DO YOU CONSIDER YOURSELF:": PRINT
700 PRINT "   1. SEDENTARY (LITTLE EXERCISE)"
710 PRINT "   2. MODERATELY ACTIVE"
720 PRINT "   3. VERY ACTIVE": PRINT
730 INPUT "ENTER 1, 2, OR 3 ";EXERCISE
740 IF EXERCISE < 1 OR EXERCISE > 3 THEN 730
750 REM --------------------------------------------------------------
760 REM       FRAME 7, STEP 2 - ASSIGN ACTIVITY FACTOR
```

```
770 REM
780 IF EXERCISE = 1 THEN ACTFACTR = 12
790 IF EXERCISE = 2 THEN ACTFACTR = 15
800 IF EXERCISE = 3 THEN ACTFACTR = 18
810 REM -------------------------------------------------------------
820 REM          FRAME 7, STEP 3 - CALCULATE CALORIES NEEDED TO MAINTAIN WT
830 REM
840 NEEDEDCALS = IDEALWT * ACTFACTR
850 REM -------------------------------------------------------------
860 REM          FRAME 8 - DISPLAY INITIAL RESULTS
870 REM
880 HOME : VTAB 4: HTAB 8
890 PRINT "SUMMARY OF DATA": PRINT
900 PRINT "YOUR IDEAL WEIGHT IS "IDEALWT" POUNDS.": PRINT
910 PRINT "TO MAINTAIN THAT WEIGHT YOU NEED"
920 PRINT NEEDEDCALS" CALORIES PER DAY.": PRINT
930 PRINT "YOUR DAILY CALORIC INTAKE BASED UPON"
940 PRINT "THE LIMITED MENU IS "SUMCAL" CALORIES.": PRINT
950 VTAB 20: HTAB 30: INPUT "RETURN =>";Z$
960 REM -------------------------------------------------------------
970 REM          FRAME 9, STEP 1 - CALCULATE WEIGHT LOSS/GAIN
980 REM
990 HOME : VTAB 4
1000 LBS = INT ((((SUMCAL - NEEDEDCALS) * 7) / 3500) * 10) / 10
1010 REM -------------------------------------------------------------
1020 REM          FRAME 9, STEP 2 - DISPLAY RESULTS
1030 REM
1040 PRINT : PRINT "IF YOU ARE CONSISTENT IN THIS CALORIC"
1050 PRINT : PRINT "INTAKE, YOUR WEIGHT DIFFERENTIAL WILL"
1060 PRINT : PRINT "BE APPROXIMATELY "LBS" POUNDS/WEEK."
1070 VTAB 20: HTAB 30: INPUT "RETURN =>";Z$
1080 REM -------------------------------------------------------------
1090 REM          FRAME 10 - OPTION TO REPEAT THE SIMULATION
1100 REM
1110 HOME : VTAB 12
1120 INPUT "DO YOU WISH ANOTHER ANALYSIS? ";AGAIN$
1130 IF LEFT$ (AGAIN$,1) = "Y" THEN SUMCAL = 0: RESTORE : GOTO 220
1140 REM -------------------------------------------------------------
1150 REM          FINAL FRAME - CLOSING COMMENT
1160 REM
1170 HOME : VTAB 12
1180 PRINT "MAY YOUR BODY BE BEAUTIFUL..."
1190 FOR P = 1 TO 4000: NEXT P: HOME
1200 END
1960 REM
1970 REM -------------------------------------------------------------
1980 REM          SUBROUTINE FRAMES, STEP 1 - INITIALIZE; READ MEAL DATA
1990 REM
2000 FOR I = 1 TO 15:FLAGFOOD(I) = 0: NEXT I: MEALCNT = 0
2010 READ MEAL$,ITEMS
```

```
2020 FOR I = 1 TO ITEMS: READ FOOD$(I),CALRIES(I): NEXT I
2030 REM -------------------------------------------------------------
2040 REM        SUBROUTINE FRAMES, STEP 2 - DISPLAY MENU AND SELECTED
     CALORIES
2050 REM
2060 HOME : PRINT TAB( 14)MEAL$: PRINT
2070 PRINT "MEAL CALORIES = "MEALCNT TAB( 22)"DAY CALORIES = "SUMCAL
2080 PRINT : PRINT TAB( 8)"FOOD"; TAB( 28);"CALORIES"
2090 FOR I = 1 TO ITEMS
2100 PRINT I" - "FOOD$(I);
2110 IF FLAGFOOD(I) = 1 THEN PRINT TAB( 32)CALRIES(I);
2120 PRINT
2130 NEXT I
2140 PRINT I" - GO TO NEXT MEAL MENU OR SECTION"
2150 REM -------------------------------------------------------------
2160 REM        SUBROUTINE FRAMES, STEP 3 - GET CHOICE; FLAG ITEM; SUM
     CALORIES
2170 REM
2180 PRINT : PRINT "YOUR CHOICE IS (1 TO "I")";
2190 INPUT CHOICE
2200 IF CHOICE < 1 OR CHOICE > I THEN 2180
2210 IF CHOICE = I THEN RETURN
2220 FLAGFOOD(CHOICE) = 1
2230 MEALCNT = MEALCNT + CALRIES(CHOICE)
2240 SUMCAL = SUMCAL + CALRIES(CHOICE)
2250 REM -------------------------------------------------------------
2260 REM        SUBROUTINE FRAMES, STEP 4 - REPEAT SAME MEAL MENU
2270 REM
2280 GOTO 2060
4000 REM -------------------------------------------------------------
4010 REM        DATA FOR BREAKFAST - MEAL; ITEMS; FOOD; CALORIES
4020 REM
4030 DATA "BREAKFAST",11
4040 DATA "BACON OR SAUSAGE",200,"CEREAL WITH MILK/SUGAR",300
4050 DATA "COFFEE (BLACK)",5,"COFFEE (WITH SUGAR)",50
4060 DATA "EGGS (2)",100,"MILK",125
4070 DATA "ORANGE JUICE",60,"PANCAKES",225
4080 DATA "SWEET ROLL",250,"TOAST",75,"WAFFLES",550
4090 REM -------------------------------------------------------------
4100 REM        DATA FOR LUNCH - MEAL; ITEMS; FOOD; CALORIES
4110 REM
4120 DATA "LUNCH",12
4130 DATA "BEER",125,"BEFORE LUNCH DRINK",115
4140 DATA "CHEESEBURGER",310,"COLA",144
4150 DATA "COTTAGE CHEESE",110,"CRACKERS",75
4160 DATA "FRENCH FRIES",400,"HAMBURGER",260
4170 DATA "MILK",125,"TUNA FISH",50
4180 DATA "VEGETABLE OR FRUIT SALAD",75
4190 DATA "ZUCCHINI SOUP (YUK)",200
4200 REM -------------------------------------------------------------
```

```
4210 REM        DATA FOR DINNER - MEAL; ITEMS; FOOD; CALORIES
4220 REM
4230 DATA "DINNER",11
4240 DATA "APPLE (OF COURSE) PIE",300
4250 DATA "BAKED POTATO",250,"BEFORE DINNER DRINK",115
4260 DATA "BEEF STEAK",560,"BEETS",40
4270 DATA "DOZEN RAW OYSTERS",240,"FISH",400
4280 DATA "MACARONI",85,"PEAS",115
4290 DATA "TOSSED SALAD",75,"T.V. DINNER",500
```

PROGRAM 18
Sample Run—
Frame 2

```
You will be presented a menu for break-

fast, lunch, and dinner. Select as many

items from each menu as you wish. After

your daily menu has been completed, you

will receive a summary of your caloric

intake and its effect on your ideal weight.


                                    RETURN =>
```

PROGRAM 18
Sample Run—
Dinner
Subroutine

```
                        DINNER
MEAL CALORIES = 365            DAY CALORIES = 1865
FOOD                           CALORIES
 1 - Apple (of course) Pie
 2 - Baked Potato              250
 3 - Before Dinner Drink       115
 4 - Beef Steak
 5 - Beets
 6 - Dozen Raw Oysters
 7 - Fish
 8 - Macaroni
 9 - Peas
10 - Tossed Salad
11 - T.V. Dinner
12 - Go to Next Menu or Section
        Your choice is (1 - 13) ? 4
```

PROGRAM 18
Sample Run—
Frame 8

```
              SUMMARY OF DATA

Your ideal weight is 166 pounds.

To maintain that weight you need
2495 calories per day.

Your daily caloric intake based upon
the limited menu is 2460 calories.




                         RETURN  =>
```

PROGRAM 18
Sample Run—
Frame 9

```
If you are consistent in this caloric

intake, your weight differential will

be approximately 0 pounds/week.




                         RETURN  =>
```

7.4 TESTING APPLICATIONS

Testing is another application similar to drill-and-practice. A question is asked, user response is entered, feedback may or may not be given, and, at some point, the user's performance is indicated.

7.4.1 PROGRAM 19: Name the Seven Dwarfs

PROGRAM 19 is a short example of a testing program. This particular program tests the naming of the seven dwarfs of Snow White fame. Names are READ into a one-dimensional array, and then a question loop asks for one of those names. An internal loop searches the list of names for a match. If a match occurs, it is checked for being previously named (flagged). At the conclusion of the program, the complete list is shown and any names in the list not given by the user are starred (*****). Note the use of the one-dimensional array FLAG() as a flag that prevents double credit for the same name being entered twice. The same flag is also used to "star" those names not entered when the test was taken (see statements 330 and 460).

Although this program tests on naming dwarfs, the program itself may be used as a general test program. By simply changing the title PRINT and the DATA statements accordingly, the program could test naming from *any* chosen list.

RUN from disk and refer to the listing and run of PROGRAM 19.

```
] LIST


10 REM        PROGRAM 19
20 REM
30 REM -----------------------------------------------------------------
40 REM        FRAME 1 - TITLE
50 REM
60 HOME : VTAB 12: HTAB 5
70 PRINT "SNOW WHITE AND THE 7 DWARFS"
80 FOR P = 1 TO 3000: NEXT P
90 REM -----------------------------------------------------------------
100 REM        DATA ASSIGNMENTS
110 REM
120 READ ITEMS
130 DIM NAME$(ITEMS),FLAG(ITEMS)
140 FOR I = 1 TO ITEMS: READ NAME$(I): NEXT I
150 REM -----------------------------------------------------------------
160 REM        FRAME 2 - INTRODUCTION
170 REM
180 HOME : VTAB 12
190 PRINT "LET'S SEE IF YOU CAN NAME THEM..."
200 VTAB 20: HTAB 30: INPUT "RETURN =>";Z$
210 REM -----------------------------------------------------------------
220 REM        LOOP FRAMES, STEP 1 - GET A NAME INPUT
230 REM
240 FOR I = 1 TO ITEMS
250 HOME : VTAB 12
260 PRINT "ANSWER NUMBER "I" IS";
270 INPUT REPLY$: PRINT
280 REM -----------------------------------------------------------------
290 REM        LOOP FRAMES, STEP 2 - CHECK LIST VIA LOOP FOR A MATCH
300 REM
```

```
310 FOR CHECK = 1 TO ITEMS
320 IF REPLY$ < > NAME$(CHECK) THEN 360
330 IF FLAG(CHECK) = 0 THEN C = C + 1:FLAG(CHECK) = 1: GOTO 380
340 PRINT "THAT'S BEEN NAMED PREVIOUSLY!"
350 VTAB 20: HTAB 30: INPUT "RETURN =>";Z$: GOTO 380
360 NEXT CHECK
370 PRINT "THAT IS NOT IN MY LIST!": VTAB 20: HTAB 30: INPUT "RETURN
    =>";Z$
380 NEXT I
390 REM --------------------------------------------------------------
400 REM        FINAL FRAME - SHOW LIST AND PERFORMANCE
410 REM
420 HOME
430 PRINT TAB( 10)"THE COMPLETE LIST IS:": PRINT
440 FOR I = 1 TO ITEMS
450 PRINT TAB( 12)NAME$(I);
460 IF FLAG(I) = 0 THEN PRINT " *****";
470 PRINT
480 NEXT I
490 PRINT
500 IF C < > ITEMS THEN PRINT TAB( 10)"(ITEMS MISSED ARE STARRED)"
510 PRINT
520 SCRE = INT (((C * 100) / ITEMS) * 10) / 10
530 PRINT TAB( 10)"YOUR SCORE IS "SCRE" PERCENT."
540 END
550 REM --------------------------------------------------------------
560 REM        DATA FOR NUMBER OF ITEMS AND NAMES IN LIST
570 REM
580 DATA 7
590 DATA "BASHFUL","DOC","DOPEY","GRUMPY"
600 DATA "HAPPY","SLEEPY","SNEEZY"
```

PROGRAM 19
Sample Run—
Loop Frames,
Steps 1–2

```
Answer number 3 is? GROUCHY

That is not in my list!

                               RETURN =>
--------------------------------------------------

Answer number 4 is? DOC

That's been named previously!

                               RETURN =>
```

```
THE COMPLETE LIST IS:

BASHFUL *****
DOC
DOPEY
GRUMPY *****
HAPPY
SLEEPY
SNEEZY *****

(ITEMS MISSED ARE STARRED)

Your score is 57.1 percent.
```

7.4.2 PROGRAM 20: Multiple-Choice Questions with Feedback

PROGRAM 20 is one example of generating multiple-choice questions. This example, however, goes beyond simply saying *"correct"* or *"incorrect"* following selection of a choice. An appropriate response is given for each possible choice. Thus, the user can also gain information from an incorrect choice selection.

PRINT statement(s) ask a given question and DATA statements provide the choices and their appropriate responses in the program. The number of possible choices and the correct choice by number are assigned to NUMCHOICES and RGHTCHOICE, respectively. A GOSUB then transfers execution to a subroutine that displays the choices and evaluates the user's input. This sequence of PRINT(s) (for the question), DATA (for each choice and its response), NUM-CHOICES = (the number of possible choices), RGHTCHOICE = (the correct choice), and GOSUB 10000 may be repeated for an indefinite number of multiple-choice questions in the program.

RUN from disk and refer to the listing and run of PROGRAM 20.

```
] LIST


10 REM       PROGRAM 20
20 REM
30 REM  ----------------------------------------------------------------
40 REM       FRAME 1 - TITLE
```

```
50 REM
60 HOME : VTAB 12: HTAB 4
70 PRINT "LINEAR MULTIPLE-CHOICE EXAMPLES"
80 FOR P = 1 TO 3000: NEXT P: HOME
90 DIM CHOICE$(5),FEEDBK$(5)
100 REM -----------------------------------------------------------------
110 REM       FRAME 2 - QUESTION 1 SEQUENCE
120 REM
130 PRINT "WHICH OF THE FOLLOWING IS AN"
140 PRINT "EXAMPLE OF A COMPUTER OUTPUT"
150 PRINT "DEVICE?"
160 DATA "CPU","NO, THAT'S THE CENTRAL PROCESSING UNIT"
170 DATA "A PRINTER","YES, BUT THERE IS A BETTER CHOICE"
180 DATA "THE TERMINAL KEYBOARD","THAT'S AN INPUT DEVICE"
190 DATA "A MONITOR SCREEN","YES, BUT SO IS A PRINTER"
200 DATA "BOTH 2, AND 4, ABOVE","YES, THAT'S THE BEST ANSWER"
210 NUMCHOICES = 5:RGHTCHOICE = 5: GOSUB 10000
220 REM -----------------------------------------------------------------
230 REM       FRAME 3 - QUESTION 2 SEQUENCE
240 REM
250 PRINT "THE LARGEST RIVER IN THE WORLD IS THE"
260 DATA "AMAZON","THAT IS THE CORRECT CHOICE"
270 DATA "NILE","NO, THAT'S THE L O N G E S T RIVER"
280 DATA "MISSISSIPPI","THAT'S THE LARGEST IN THE USA"
290 NUMCHOICES = 3:RGHTCHOICE = 1: GOSUB 10000
300 REM -----------------------------------------------------------------
310 REM       (FRAMES FOR ADDITIONAL QUESTION SEQUENCES)
320 REM
9910 REM -----------------------------------------------------------------
9920 REM       FINAL FRAME - PERFORMANCE REPORT
9930 REM
9940 HOME : VTAB 12: HTAB 5
9950 PRINT "YOU ANSWERED "C" CORRECTLY."
9960 END
9970 REM -----------------------------------------------------------------
9980 REM        THE INPUT SUBROUTINE
9990 REM
10000 PRINT : FOR I = 1 TO NUMCHOICES
10010 READ CHOICE$(I),FEEDBK$(I): PRINT I" - "CHOICE$(I)
10020 NEXT I: PRINT
10030 PRINT "YOUR CHOICE IS (1-"NUMCHOICES")";: INPUT REPLY: PRINT
10040 IF REPLY < 1 OR REPLY > NUMCHOICES THEN 10030
10050 PRINT CHOICE$(REPLY): PRINT FEEDBK$(REPLY)"."
10060 PRINT : IF REPLY = RGHTCHOICE THEN C = C + 1: GOTO 10090
10070 PRINT "THE CORRECT CHOICE IS "RGHTCHOICE":"
10080 PRINT CHOICE$(RGHTCHOICE)
10090 VTAB 20: HTAB 30: INPUT "RETURN =>";Z$
10100 HOME : RETURN
```

PROGRAM 20
Sample Run—
Frame 2

```
Which of the following is an
example of a computer output
device?

1 - CPU
2 - A printer
3 - The terminal keyboard
4 - A monitor screen
5 - Both 2 and 4 above

Your choice is (1 - 5)?4
A monitor screen
Yes, but so is a printer.

The correct choice is 5:
Both 2 and 4 above          RETURN =>
```

PROGRAM 20
Sample Run—
Frame 3

```
The largest river in the world is the

1 - Amazon
2 - Nile
3 - Mississippi

Your choice is (1 - 3)?1
Amazon
That is the correct choice.




                            RETURN =>
```

7.5 TEACHER UTILITY PROGRAMS USING TEXT FILES

To this point in the book, we have presented many programs that may be easily modified to present content of your choosing. Generally, this involves LOADing a given program, modifying PRINT and DATA statements, then SAV(E)ing the program using the same or a unique name, depending on your preference.

Now we will present four sets of program pairs that may be used directly for record storing and retrieval applications. One of the programs, GRADE-BOOK, requires modification of DATA statements for actual use; the others "stand alone," that is, they may be used with *no* modification.

Each of these programs uses *text files* for storing information on the disk. With one exception, these files are named by you, the user, during the execution of a given program. Thus, as you will see, you might use a file named PERIOD1 to store information about your first-period class, PERIOD2 for your second-period class, and so on. The text file names that are created will be preceded by a "T" when a CATALOG of the disk is displayed.

In the simplest sense, text files contain information in a form similar to DATA statements in a program. However, the information in text files may be modified automatically in program execution. DATA statements, on the other hand, would have to be reentered and SAVEd.

7.5.1 GRADEBOOK and NEW SEMESTER Programs

The GRADEBOOK program allows as many as 20 numeric scores, for as many as 200 students, to be recorded. Options include entering scores, retrieving scores and their average, editing scores, dropping the lowest score, and producing a printed output of the class roll, scores and averages, and the class average.

DATA statements, beginning at line 1370, containing the NUMBER of students and their NAMES must be added to the program. If a separate GRADEBOOK is desired for each class, SAVE using a unique name after adding the appropriate DATA for each class. It is important to remember that commas must *not* be used with student names.

The NEW SEMESTER program allows you to initialize a new text file or "erase" scores in an existing text file at the beginning of a new semester or term (or at any time, for that matter).

Naming the gradebook program(s) and associated text files in a logical sense is important. Use names that have meaning to you. For example, the gradebook program containing the number and names of students for one class might be CLASS1 and its associated text file might be C1, and so on. A written record of the names you use should be kept. The version of GRADEBOOK on the disk contains five hypothetical students. Its associated text file is named G1. Run this version to see the options provided by the program, add some scores, edit, and so on, then run NEW SEMESTER to become familiar with its options and actions.

RUN from disk and refer to the listing and run of GRADEBOOK and NEW SEMESTER.

```
] LIST


10 REM     GRADEBOOK PROGRAM
20 REM
30 REM  -----------------------------------------------------------
40 REM     FRAME 1 - TITLE AND ASSIGNMENTS
```

```
50 REM
60 HOME : VTAB 12: HTAB 4
70 PRINT "C L A S S   S C O R E   K E E P I N G"
80 FOR P = 1 TO 3000: NEXT P
90 DIM STUDNT$(200),RCRD(200),SCRE(200,20)
100 REM -------------------------------------------------------------
110 REM         FRAME 2, STEP 1 - RECORD FILE NAME TO ACCESS
120 REM
130 HOME : VTAB 10
140 INPUT "ENTER THE NAME OF THE RECORD FILE ";F$:PRINT
150 PRINT "THE NAME YOU ENTERED IS "F$: PRINT
160 HTAB 8: INPUT "IS THIS CORRECT? ";Z$
170 IF LEFT$ (Z$,1) < > "Y" THEN 130
180 REM -------------------------------------------------------------
190 REM         FRAME 2, STEP 2 - ASSIGN NUMBER AND NAME OF STUDENTS
200 REM
210 READ ROLL
220 FOR I = 1 TO ROLL: READ STUDNT$(I): NEXT I
230 REM -------------------------------------------------------------
240 REM         FRAME 2, STEP 3 - FILE READING SEQUENCE
250 REM
260 D$ = CHR$ (4)
270 PRINT D$"OPEN "F$
280 PRINT D$"READ "F$
290 FOR I = 1 TO ROLL: INPUT RCRD(I)
300 FOR J = 1 TO RCRD(I): INPUT SCRE(I,J): NEXT J
310 NEXT I
320 PRINT D$"CLOSE "F$
330 REM -------------------------------------------------------------
340 REM         FRAME 3 - GRADE BOOK OPTIONS
350 REM
360 HME : VTAB 8: HTAB 4
370 PRINT "DO YOU WANT TO:": PRINT
380 PRINT "1. RETRIEVE SCORES"
390 PRINT "2. ENTER NEW SCORES"
400 INPUT "3. STOP (ENTER 1-3)? ";CHOICE
410 IF CHOICE < 1 OR CHOICE > 3 THEN 360
420 IF CHOICE = 3 THEN 840
430 REM -------------------------------------------------------------
440 REM         FRAME 4, STEP 1 - GET STUDENT NAME SOUGHT
450 REM
460 HOME : VTAB 12
470 INPUT "STUDENT'S NAME (OR STOP)? ";STUDNT$
480 IF STUDNT$ = "STOP" THEN 360
490 FOR I = 1 TO ROLL
500 IF STUDNT$ = STUDNT$(I) AND CHOICE = 1 THEN 570
510 IF STUDNT$ = STUDNT$(I) AND CHOICE = 2 THEN 770
520 NEXT I
530 PRINT STUDNT$" IS NOT ON FILE.": GOTO 470
540 REM -------------------------------------------------------------
550 REM         FRAME 4, STEP 2 - OUTPUT RECORDS FOR THE STUDENT
```

```
560 REM
570 IF RCRD(I) = 0 THEN PRINT STUDNT$" HAS NO SCORES.": GOTO 470
580 PRINT : PRINT "SCORES FOR "STUDNT$":"
590 FOR J = 1 TO RCRD(I)
600 PRINT SCRE(I,J)" ";:SUM = SUM + SCRE(I,J)
610 NEXT J
620 PRINT : PRINT "AVERAGE: " INT ((SUM / RCRD(I)) * 100) / 100:SUM = 0
630 REM -----------------------------------------------------------------
640 REM         FRAME 4, STEP 3 - EDITING OPTION AND SEQUENCE
650 REM
660 PRINT : INPUT "DO YOU WISH TO EDIT? ";Z$
670 IF LEFT$ (Z$,1) < > "Y" THEN 470
680 FOR J = 1 TO RCRD(I)
690 PRINT "EDIT THIS SCORE: "SCRE(I,J);: INPUT Z$
700 IF LEFT$ (Z$,1) < > "Y" THEN 720
710 PRINT "SCORE SHOULD BE: ";: INPUT SCRE(I,J)
720 NEXT J
730 GOTO 580
740 REM -----------------------------------------------------------------
750 REM         FRAME 5 - PLACE THE SCORE IN THE NEXT ARRAY POSITION
760 REM
770 HOME : VTAB 12: PRINT "NEXT SCORE FOR "STUDNT$;
780 RCRD(I) = RCRD(I) + 1:ENTRIES = ENTRIES + 1
790 INPUT SCRE(I,RCRD(I)):TESTSUM = TESTSUM + SCRE(I,RCRD(I))
800 GOTO 470
810 REM -----------------------------------------------------------------
820 REM         FRAME 6, STEP 1 - OUTPUT OPTIONS
830 REM
840 HOME : VTAB 12
850 INPUT "WANT TO DROP THE LOWEST SCORE? ";DROP$: PRINT
860 IF LEFT$ (DROP$,1) < > "Y" THEN 880
870 INPUT "H I G H E S T POSSIBLE GRADE IS? ";HI: PRINT
880 INPUT "WANT A PRINTER COPY? ";P$
890 IF LEFT$ (P$,1) = "Y" THEN PRINT D$"PR#1"
900 REM -----------------------------------------------------------------
910 REM         FRAME 6, STEP 2 - OUTPUT ALL IN THE GRADEBOOK
920 REM
930 FOR I = 1 TO ROLL
940 IF RCRD(I) = 0 THEN PRINT STUDNT$(I)" HAS NO SCORES": GOTO 1010
950 PRINT STUDNT$(I): PRINT "SCORES:";
960 FOR J = 1 TO RCRD(I)
970 PRINT SCRE(I,J)" ";:SUM = SUM + SCRE(I,J):CLASSUM = CLASSUM +
    SCRE(I,J)
980 NEXT J
990 PRINT : PRINT "AVERAGE IS: " INT ((SUM / RCRD(I)) * 100) / 100
1000 IF LEFT$ (DROP$,1) = "Y" THEN GOSUB 1250
1010 PRINT "//////////////":SUM = 0:COUNT = COUNT + RCRD(I)
1020 NEXT I
1030 PRINT : IF ENTRIES = 0 THEN 1050
1040 PRINT "SESSION ENTRIES AVERAGE: " INT ((TESTSUM / ENTRIES) * 100) /
    100
```

```
1050 PRINT "THE CLASS AVERAGE IS "; INT ((CLASSUM / COUNT) * 100) / 100
1060 IF P$ = "Y" THEN PRINT D$"PR#0"
1070 REM -----------------------------------------------------------------
1080 REM        FRAME 6, STEP 3 - FILE WRITING SEQUENCE
1090 REM
1100 PRINT D$"OPEN "F$
1110 PRINT D$"WRITE "F$
1120 FOR I = 1 TO ROLL: PRINT RCRD(I)
1130 FOR J = 1 TO RCRD(I): PRINT SCRE(I,J): NEXT J
1140 NEXT I
1150 PRINT D$"CLOSE "F$
1160 REM -----------------------------------------------------------------
1170 REM        FRAME 6, STEP 4 - CONCLUSION
1180 REM
1190 PRINT
1200 PRINT "*** THE GRADE BOOK IS CLOSED ***"
1210 END
1220 REM -----------------------------------------------------------------
1230 REM        SUBROUTINE FOR DROPPING LOWEST GRADE
1240 REM
1250 IF RCRD(I) = < 1 THEN RETURN
1260 LO = HI
1270 FOR J = 1 TO RCRD(I)
1280 IF SCRE(I,J) < LO THEN LO = SCRE(I,J)
1290 NEXT J
1300 SUM = SUM - LO:CLASSUM = CLASSUM - LO:COUNT = COUNT - 1
1310 PRINT "DROPPING SCORE "LO
1320 PRINT "AVERAGE IS NOW " INT ((SUM / (RCRD(I) - 1)) * 100) / 100
1330 RETURN
1340 REM -----------------------------------------------------------------
1350 REM        DATA FOR THE NUMBER AND EACH NAME ON THE CLASS ROLL
1360 REM
1370 DATA 5
1380 DATA "ABLE","BAKER","CAIN A.","CAIN R.","OMEGA"
```

GRADEBOOK
Sample Run—
Frame 3

```
            Do you want to:

   1. Retrieve Scores
   2. Enter New Scores
   3. Stop (Enter 1 - 3)? 1
```

GRADEBOOK
Sample Run—
Frame 4,
Steps 1–3

```
Student's name (or STOP)? ABLE

Scores for ABLE:
100 80 90
Average: 80

Do you wish to edit? N
```

] LIST


```
10 REM        NEW SEMESTER PROGRAM
20 REM
30 REM ---------------------------------------------------------------------
40 REM        FRAME 1 - TITLE
50 REM
60 HOME : VTAB 12: HTAB 2
70 PRINT "A NEW SEMESTER FOR THE GRADE BOOK"
80 FOR P = 1 TO 3000: NEXT P
90 REM ---------------------------------------------------------------------
100 REM        FRAME 2 - INTRODUCTION
110 REM
120 HOME : VTAB 4
130 PRINT "THIS PROGRAM WILL *ERASE* ALL SCORES IN": PRINT
140 PRINT "THE FILE YOU SPECIFY USED IN CONJUNC-": PRINT
150 PRINT "TION WITH THE APPROPRIATE GRADEBOOK": PRINT
160 PRINT "PROGRAM, SPACE WILL BE RESERVED": PRINT
170 PRINT "FOR 200 STUDENTS."
180 PRINT : INPUT "DO YOU REALLY WANT TO DO THIS? ";Z$
190 IF LEFT$ (Z$,1) < > "Y" THEN 470
200 REM ---------------------------------------------------------------------
210 REM        FRAME 3 - FILE NAME TO INITIALIZE
220 REM
230 HOME : VTAB 12
240 INPUT "WHAT IS THE NAME OF THE FILE? ";F$: PRINT
250 PRINT "THE NAME YOU ENTERED IS "F$: PRINT
260 HTAB 8: INPUT "IS THIS CORRECT? ";Z$
270 IF LEFT$ (Z$,1) < > "Y" THEN 230
280 REM ---------------------------------------------------------------------
290 REM        FRAME 4 - FILE INITIALIZING SEQUENCE
300 REM
```

```
310 HOME : VTAB 12: HTAB 8
320 PRINT "INITIALIZING THE FILE..."
330 D$ = CHR$ (4)
340 PRINT D$"OPEN "F$: PRINT D$"DELETE "F$
350 PRINT D$"OPEN "F$
360 PRINT D$"WRITE "F$
370 SCRE = 0
380 FOR I = 1 TO 400
390 PRINT SCRE
400 NEXT I
410 PRINT D$"CLOSE "F$
420 REM ------------------------------------------------------------------
430 REM        FRAME 5 - CONCLUSION
440 REM
450 HOME : VTAB 12: HTAB 4
460 PRINT "FILE '"F$"' IS NOW INITIALIZED."
470 END
```

NEW SEMESTER
Sample Run—
Frame 2

```
This program will *ERASE* all scores in

the file you specify used in conjunction

with the appropriate GRADEBOOK

program. Space will be reserved

for 200 students.

DO YOU REALLY WANT TO DO THIS? Y
```

NEW SEMESTER
Sample Run—
Frame 3

```
What is the name of the file? C1

The name you entered is C1

     Is this correct? Y
```

7.5.2 FILEWRITE and FILEREAD Programs

The FILEWRITE program allows you to enter a student's name, a test name, and the score for that student on that test. As many as 200 names and scores may be entered during any one run of the program. Again, you may specify the text file name to which the information is to be written. Thus, unique names such as PERIOD1, PERIOD2, and so on may be used. Of course, these names should be different from the text file names you use with GRADEBOOK. Again, you should keep written records of the names you use.

The FILEREAD program allows you to retrieve information either by student name or test name from the specified text file. An average of the scores is displayed and an option to edit names or scores is provided. Thus, you may retrieve *all* scores for either a given student *or* a given test using FILEREAD.

These programs may be used directly without any modification.

Note: The disk contains a text file named S1 containing sample information that may be accessed using FILEREAD. (Use QUIZ 1 in a search by test name.)

RUN from disk and refer to the listing and run of FILEWRITE and FILEREAD.

```
] LIST


10 REM        FILEWRITE PROGRAM
20 REM
30 REM --------------------------------------------------------------
40 REM        FRAME 1 - TITLE AND ASSIGNMENTS
50 REM
60 HOME : VTAB 12: HTAB 12
70 PRINT "RECORD KEEPING:": PRINT
80 PRINT TAB( 2)"STUDENT NAME, TEST NAME, AND SCORE"
90 FOR P = 1 TO 4000: NEXT P
100 DIM STUDNT$(200),TSTNAME$(200),SCRE(200)
110 REM --------------------------------------------------------------
120 REM        FRAME 2 - INTRODUCTION
130 REM
140 HOME : VTAB 4
150 PRINT "UP TO 200 STUDENT NAMES, TEST NAMES,": PRINT
160 PRINT "AND SCORES MAY BE ENTERED DURING ONE": PRINT
170 PRINT "'RUN' OF THIS PROGRAM."
180 VTAB 20: HTAB 30: INPUT "RETURN =>";Z$
190 REM --------------------------------------------------------------
200 REM        FRAME 3 - TEXT FILE NAME FOR STORING INFORMATION
210 REM
220 HOME : VTAB 10
230 PRINT "WHAT IS THE NAME OF THE FILE TO WHICH": PRINT
240 PRINT "YOU WILL ADD INFORMATION?": PRINT
250 INPUT "(MAY BE A NEW OR EXISTING FILE) ";F$: PRINT
260 PRINT "THE NAME YOU ENTERED IS "F$: PRINT
```

```
270 HTAB 8: INPUT "IS THIS CORRECT? ";Z$: IF LEFT$ (Z$,1) < > "Y" THEN
    220
280 REM -----------------------------------------------------------------
290 REM        FRAME 4 - INFORMATION TO BE FILED
300 REM
310 HOME
320 FOR I = 1 TO 200
330 INPUT "STUDENT NAME (OR STOP)? ";STUDNT$(I)
340 IF STUDNT$(I) = "STOP" THEN 390
350 INPUT "TEST NAME? ";TSTNAME$(I)
360 INPUT "SCORE? ";SCRE(I)
370 PRINT
380 NEXT I
390 ENTRIES = I - 1
400 REM -----------------------------------------------------------------
410 REM        FRAME 5 - FILE WRITING SEQUENCE
420 REM
430 HOME : VTAB 12: HTAB 4
440 PRINT "UPDATING RECORDS IN FILE "F$
450 D$ = CHR$ (4)
460 PRINT D$"OPEN "F$
470 PRINT D$"APPEND "F$
480 PRINT D$"WRITE "F$
490 FOR I = 1 TO ENTRIES
500 PRINT STUDNT$(I)
510 PRINT TSTNAME$(I)
520 PRINT SCRE(I)
530 NEXT I
540 PRINT D$"CLOSE "F$
550 REM -----------------------------------------------------------------
560 REM        FRAME 6 - CONCLUSION
570 REM
580 HOME : VTAB 12: HTAB 6: PRINT "FILE RECORDS HAVE BEEN ADDED."
590 END
```

FILEWRITE
Sample Run—
Frame 2

> Up to 200 student names, test names,
>
> and scores may be entered during one
>
> 'RUN' of this program.
>
>   RETURN =>

FILEWRITE
Sample Run—
Frame 3

```
What is the name of the file to which

you will add information?

(May be a new or existing file) S1

The name you entered is S1

        Is this correct? Y
```

FILEWRITE
Sample Run—
Frame 4

```
Student name (or STOP)? JACK HORNER
Test name? QUIZ 1
Score? 70

Student name (or STOP)? SUE BANKER
Test name ? QUIZ 1
Score ? 90
        .
        .
        .
Student name (or STOP)? STOP
```

```
] LIST


10 REM       FILEREAD PROGRAM
20 REM
30 REM ------------------------------------------------------------------
40 REM       FRAME 1 - TITLE AND ASSIGNMENTS
50 REM
60 HOME : VTAB 12: HTAB 12
70 PRINT "RECORD RETRIEVAL": PRINT
80 PRINT TAB( 2)"STUDENT NAME, TEST NAME, AND SCORE"
90 FOR P = 1 TO 4000: NEXT P
100 DIM STUDNT$(200),TSTNAME$(200),SCRE(200):FLAG = 0:LINE = 0
110 REM ------------------------------------------------------------------
120 REM       FRAME 2 - TEXT FILE NAME FOR RETRIEVING INFO
```

```
130 REM
140 HOME : VTAB 10
150 PRINT "WHAT IS THE NAME OF THE FILE FROM WHICH": PRINT
160 INPUT "YOU WISH TO RETRIEVE INFORMATION? ";F$: PRINT
170 PRINT "THE NAME YOU ENTERED IS "F$: PRINT
180 HTAB 8: INPUT "IS THIS CORRECT? ";Z$
190 IF LEFT$ (Z$,1) < > "Y" THEN 140
200 REM -------------------------------------------------------------------
210 REM        FRAME 3 - FILE READING SEQUENCE
220 REM
230 D$ = CHR$ (4)
240 PRINT D$"OPEN "F$
250 PRINT D$"READ "F$
260 ONERR GOTO 300
270 FOR RECRD = 1 TO 200
280 INPUT STUDNT$(RECRD): INPUT TSTNAME$(RECRD): INPUT SCRE(RECRD)
290 NEXT RECRD
300 ENTRIES = RECRD - 1
310 PRINT D$"CLOSE "F$
320 REM -------------------------------------------------------------------
330 REM        FRAME 4 - SEARCH OPTIONS
340 REM
350 HOME : VTAB 4: HTAB 10:LINE = 0
360 PRINT "FILE SEARCH": PRINT
370 PRINT "DO YOU WISH TO SEARCH BY:"
380 PRINT
390 PRINT "      1. STUDENT NAME"
400 PRINT "      2. TEST NAME"
410 PRINT
420 INPUT "ENTER 1. OR 2. ";CHOICE
430 IF CHOICE = 1 THEN SRCH$ = "STUDENT"
440 IF CHOICE = 2 THEN SRCH$ = "TEST"
450 IF CHOICE < 1 OR CHOICE > 2 THEN 420
460 REM -------------------------------------------------------------------
470 REM        FRAME 5, STEP 1 - SEARCH PROCEDURE
480 REM
490 PRINT : PRINT SRCH$" NAME SOUGHT IS";: INPUT NAME$
500 HOME :SUM = 0:CNT = 0
510 PRINT "RECORD #" TAB( 10)"STUDENT" TAB( 26)"TEST" TAB( 35)"SCORE"
520 FOR P = 1 TO 39: PRINT "-";: NEXT P: PRINT
530 FOR I = 1 TO ENTRIES
540 IF NAME$ < > STUDNT$(I) AND NAME$ < > TSTNAME$(I) THEN 580
550 PRINT TAB( 5)I TAB( 10)STUDENT$(I) TAB( 26)TSTNAME$(I) TAB( 36)SCRE(I)
560 SUM = SUM + SCRE(I):CNT = CNT + 1:LINE = LINE + 1
570 IF LINE = 20 THEN VTAB 23: HTAB 30: INPUT "MORE =>";Z$:LINE = 0
580 NEXT I
590 IF CNT = 0 THEN PRINT "NO RECORDS FOUND FOR "NAME$: GOTO 870
600 PRINT : PRINT TAB( 10)"AVERAGE SCORE IS " INT ((SUM / CNT) * 10) / 10
610 PRINT
620 REM -------------------------------------------------------------------
```

```
630 REM        FRAME 5, STEP 2 - OPTION TO EDIT
640 REM
650 INPUT "DO YOU WISH TO EDIT ANY RECORD? ";Z$
660 IF LEFT$ (Z$,1) < > "Y" THEN 860
670 INPUT "RECORD NUMBER TO EDIT IS? ";RECRD:FLAG = 1
680 IF RECRD < 1 OR RECRD > ENTRIES THEN PRINT "* OUT OF RANGE *": GOTO
    670
690 REM ----------------------------------------------------------------
700 REM        FRAME 6 - EDITING OPTIONS/PROCEDURE
710 REM
720 HOME : HTAB 10
730 PRINT "RECORD # "RECRD
740 PRINT : PRINT "STUDENT = "STUDNT$(RECRD)
750 INPUT "EDIT? ";Z$: IF LEFT$ (Z$,1) < > "Y" THEN 770
760 INPUT "REVISED STUDENT NAME IS? ";STUDNT$(RECRD)
770 PRINT : PRINT "TEST NAME = "TSTNAME$(RECRD)
780 INPUT "EDIT? ";Z$: IF LEFT$ (Z$,1) < > "Y" THEN 800
790 INPUT "REVISED TEST NAME IS? ";TSTNAME$(RECRD)
800 PRINT : PRINT "SCORE = "SCRE(RECRD)
810 INPUT "EDIT? ";Z$: IF LEFT$ (Z$,1) < > "Y" THEN 500
820 INPUT "REVISED SCORE IS? ";SCRE(RECRD): GOTO 500
830 REM ----------------------------------------------------------------
840 REM        FRAME 7 - OPTION FOR ANOTHER SEARCH
850 REM
860 HOME : VTAB 12: HTAB 12
870 PRINT : INPUT "WANT ANOTHER SEARCH? ";Z$
880 IF LEFT$ (Z$,1) = "Y" THEN 350
890 REM ----------------------------------------------------------------
900 REM        FRAME 8 - UPDATE OF RECORDS IF EDITED
910 REM
920 IF FLAG = 0 THEN 1040
930 HOME : VTAB 12: HTAB 4
940 PRINT "UPDATING RECORDS IN FILE "F$
950 PRINT D$"OPEN "F$
960 PRINT D$"WRITE "F$
970 FOR I = 1 TO ENTRIES
980 PRINT STUDNT$(I): PRINT TSTNAME$(I): PRINT SCRE(I)
990 NEXT I
1000 PRINT D$"CLOSE "F$
1010 REM ----------------------------------------------------------------
1020 REM        FRAME 9 - CONCLUSION
1030 REM
1040 HOME : VTAB 12: HTAB 12
1050 PRINT "*** D O N E ***"
1060 END
```

FILEREAD
Sample Run—
Frame 2

```
What is the name of the file from which

you wish to retrieve information? S1

The name you entered is S1

    Is this correct? Y
```

FILEREAD
Sample Run—
Frame 4

```
                    File Search


        Do you wish to search by:

                1. Student name
                2. Test name

            Enter 1, or 2, 1
```

FILEREAD
Sample Run—
Frame 5

```
RECORD#      STUDENT     TEST     SCORE
---------------------------------------
   6         SUE BANKER  QUIZ 1     90
   17        SUE BANKER  QUIZ 2    100
   43        SUE BANKER  QUIZ 3     50
             Average score is 80

Do you wish to edit any record? N
```

Teachers find microcomputer programs very useful in keeping records and student performance evaluations.

7.5.3 BIBLWRITE and BIBLREAD Programs

Often teachers keep card files containing reference information on such items as journal articles, books, audiovisual materials, and so on. The BIBLWRITE program allows you to enter information of this type. The program prompts for the writer's name, the reference title, a brief abstract, and three descriptors that may be used later in retrieving information. (These descriptors may be considered as consistent "keywords" you would use with a given reference. Thus, you might use the descriptor DRILL, for example, for all references related to the use of drill programs in your area of interest.)

The BIBLREAD program allows you to either retrieve information by the writer's name or a descriptor or view the complete list of references on file. All references found in a given search are sorted alphabetically by writers' names.

Both BIBLWRITE and BIBLREAD use the text file BIBLIO on the disk. This file has one reference item stored as an example. (The descriptors are BASIC, CAI, and TEACH.)

Both programs may be used directly without modification.

RUN from disk and refer to the listing and run of BIBLWRITE and BIBLREAD.

```
] LIST


10 REM       BIBLWRITE PROGRAM
20 REM
```

```
30 REM --------------------------------------------------------------
40 REM         FRAME 1 - TITLE AND ASSIGNMENTS
50 REM
60 HOME : VTAB 12: HTAB 4
70 PRINT "BIBLIOGRAPHY FILE RECORD KEEPING"
80 FOR P= 1 TO 4000: NEXT P
90 DIM AUTHR$(50),TITLE$(50),ABSTRACT$(50),D1$(50),D2$(50),D3$(50)
100 REM --------------------------------------------------------------
110 REM         FRAME 2 - INTRODUCTION
120 REM
130 HOME : VTAB 8
140 PRINT "AS MANY AS 50 REFERENCES EACH WITH": PRINT
150 PRINT "3 DESCRIPTORS MAY BE ENTERED DURING": PRINT
160 PRINT "ANY ONE RUN OF THIS PROGRAM, THE": PRINT
170 PRINT "FILE RECORDS MAY BE SEARCHED WITH": PRINT
180 PRINT "THE PROGRAM 'BIBLREAD'."
190 VTAB 20: HTAB 30: INPUT "RETURN =>";Z$
200 REM --------------------------------------------------------------
210 REM         FRAME 3 - INPUT BIBLIOGRAPHIC INFORMATION
220 REM
230 HOME
240 FOR ITEM = 1 TO 50: PRINT
250 PRINT TAB( 8)"* USE NO COMMAS *": PRINT
260 PRINT "AUTHOR (LAST <SPACE> FIRST NAME OR STOP)"
270 INPUT "=> ";AUTHR$(ITEM): PRINT
280 IF AUTHR$(ITEM) = "STOP" THEN 410
290 PRINT "TITLE"
300 INPUT "=> ";TITLE$(ITEM): PRINT
310 PRINT "ABSTRACT (5 LINES MAXIMUM)"
320 INPUT "=> ";ABSTRACT$(ITEM): PRINT
330 IF ABSTRACT$(ITEM) = "" THEN ABSTRACT$(ITEM) = "NONE GIVEN"
340 INPUT "FIRST DESCRIPTOR => ";D1$(ITEM)
350 IF D1$(ITEM) = "" THEN D1$(ITEM) = "NONE GIVEN"
360 INPUT "SECOND DESCRIPTOR => ";D2$(ITEM)
370 IF D2$(ITEM) = "" THEN D2$(ITEM) = D1$(ITEM)
380 INPUT "THIRD DESCRIPTOR => ";D3$(ITEM)
390 IF D3$(ITEM) = "" THEN D3$(ITEM) = D1$(ITEM)
400 NEXT ITEM
410 ENTRIES = ITEM - 1
420 REM --------------------------------------------------------------
430 REM         FRAME 4 - FILE WRITING SEQUENCE
440 REM
450 HOME : VTAB 12: HTAB 4
460 PRINT "UPDATING BIBLIOGRAPHY FILE..."
470 D$ = CHR$ (4)
480 PRINT D$"OPEN BIBLIO"
490 PRINT D$"APPEND BIBLIO"
500 PRINT D$"WRITE BIBLIO"
510 FOR I = 1 TO ENTRIES
520 PRINT AUTHR$(I): PRINT TITLE$(I): PRINT ABSTRACT$(I)
```

```
 0 PRINT D1$(I): PRINT D2$(I): PRINT D3$(I)
 40 NEXT I
550 PRINT D$"CLOSE BIBLIO"
560 REM ------------------------------------------------------------
570 REM        FRAME 5 - CONCLUSION
580 REM
590 HOME : VTAB 12: HTAB 4
600 PRINT "BIBLIOGRAPHY FILE HAS BEEN UPDATED"
610 END
```

BIBLWRITE
Sample Run—
Frame 3

```
Author (last <space> first name or STOP)
=> TWAIN MARK

Title
=> TOM SAWYER

Abstract (5 lines maximum)
THE LIFE AND TIMES OF A YOUNG LAD
GROWING UP IN MISSOURI

First descriptor => CHILDHOOD
Second descriptor => ADVENTURE
Third descriptor => FENCES
```

] LIST

```
10 REM        BIBLREAD PROGRAM
20 REM
30 REM ------------------------------------------------------------
40 REM        FRAME 1 - TITLE AND ASSIGNMENTS
50 REM
60 HOME : VTAB 12: HTAB 4
70 PRINT "BIBLIOGRAPHIC FILE SEARCHING"
80 FOR P = 1 TO 3000: NEXT P
90 DIM AUTHR$(500),TITLE$(500),ABTRACT$(500)
100 REM
110 REM        FRAME 2 - SEARCH OPTIONS
120 REM
130 HOME : VTAB 4: HTAB 6:MTCH = 0
140 PRINT "REFERENCE SEARCH": PRINT
150 PRINT "DO YOU WISH TO SEARCH BY:"
160 PRINT
170 PRINT "      1. AUTHOR NAME"
180 PRINT "      2. DESCRIPTOR"
190 PRINT "      3. COMPLETE LIST"
```

```
200 PRINT
210 INPUT "YOUR CHOICE IS (1-3)? ";CHOICE
220 IF CHOICE < 1 OR CHOICE > 3 THEN 210
230 IF CHOICE = 1 THEN INSRT$ = "AUTHOR (LAST FIRST)"
240 IF CHOICE = 2 THEN INSRT$ = "DESCRIPTOR"
250 IF CHOICE = 3 THEN SRCH$ = "COMPLETE LIST": GOTO 300
260 PRINT : PRINT INSRT$" SOUGHT IS ";: INPUT "=> ";SRCH$
270 REM -------------------------------------------------------------
280 REM         FRAME 3, STEP 1 - FILE READING SEQUENCE
290 REM
300 HOME : VTAB 12: HTAB 10
310 PRINT "SEARCHING FILE..."
320 D$ = CHR$ (4)
330 PRINT D$"OPEN BIBLIO"
340 PRINT D$"READ BIBLIO"
350 ONERR GOTO 460
360 INPUT AUTHR$: INPUT TITLE$: INPUT ABTRACT$
370 INPUT D1$: INPUT D2$: INPUT D3$
380 REM -------------------------------------------------------------
390 REM         FRAME 3, STEP 2 - CHECK FOR A MATCH
400 REM
410 IF CHOICE = 3 THEN 430
420 IF SRCH$ < > AUTHR$ AND SRCH$ < > D1$ AND SRCH$ < > D2$ AND
    SRCH$ < > D3$ THEN 360
430 MTCH = MTCH + 1
440 AUTHR$(MTCH) = AUTHR$:TITLE$(MTCH) = TITLE$:ABTRACT$(MTCH) =
    ABTRACT$
450 GOTO 360
460 PRINT D$"CLOSE BIBLIO"
470 REM -------------------------------------------------------------
480 REM         FRAME 4 - OUTPUT SEQUENCE INCLUDING MATCH SORTING
490 REM
500 HOME : VTAB 12
510 IF MTCH = 0 THEN PRINT "NONE FOUND FOR "SRCH$: PRINT : GOTO 670
520 PRINT "NOW SORTING BY AUTHOR..."
530 GOSUB 780
540 REM -------------------------------------------------------------
550 REM         FRAME 5 - OUTPUT OF SORTED MATCHES
560 REM
570 FOR I = 1 TO MTCH
580 HOME : HTAB 8: PRINT "RECORDS FOUND FOR "SRCH$: PRINT
590 PRINT AUTHR$(I): PRINT : PRINT TITLE$(I): PRINT : PRINT ABTRACT$(I)
600 PRINT "////////////////"
610 VTAB 20: HTAB 30: INPUT "RETURN =>";Z$
620 NEXT I
630 REM -------------------------------------------------------------
640 REM         FRAME 6 - OPTION FOR ANOTHER SEARCH
650 REM
660 HOME : VTAB 12: HTAB 4
```

```
670 INPUT "WANT ANOTHER SEARCH? ";Z$
680 IF LEFT$ (Z$,1) = "Y" THEN 130
690 REM -----------------------------------------------------------------
700 REM          FRAME 7 - CONCLUSION
710 REM
720 HOME : VTAB 12: HTAB 8
730 PRINT "* SEARCH COMPLETED *"
740 END
750 REM -----------------------------------------------------------------
760 REM          THE SORTING SUBROUTINE
770 REM
780 FOR J = 1 TO MTCH
790 ARTHTEM$ = AUTHR$(J):TITLTEM$ = TITLE$(J):ABTRTEM$ = ABTRACT$(J)
800 FOR K = J - 1 TO 1 STEP - 1
810 IF AUTHR$(K) < = ARTHTEM$ THEN 870
820 AUTHR$(K + 1) = AUTHR$(K)
830 TITLE$(K + 1) = TITLE$(K)
840 ABTRACT$(K + 1) = ABTRACT$(K)
850 NEXT K
860 K = 0
870 AUTHR$(K + 1) = ARTHTEM$
880 TITLE$(K + 1) = TITLTEM$
890 ABTRACT$(K + 1) = ABTRTEM$
900 NEXT J: RETURN
```

BIBLREAD
Sample Run—
Frame 2

```
                    Reference Search

    Do you wish to search by:

            1. Author name
            2. Descriptor
            3. Get the complete list


    Your choice is (1-3)? 2

    Descriptor sought is => ADVENTURE
```

BIBLREAD
Sample Run—
Frame 5

```
                    Records found for ADVENTURE

      TWAIN MARK


      TOM SAWYER


      THE LIFE AND TIMES OF A YOUNG LAD
      GROWING UP IN MISSOURI
      /////////////////


                            RETURN =>
```

7.5.4   RAF CREATION and RAF USE Programs

These programs make use of random access text files for storing and retrieving *any* information of your choosing. The RAF CREATION program is used to create a file that contains information about a given random access text file and the first record entry in that file. You are given the choice of naming the information file and the random access file (again, use logical, but unique names); the title to be displayed when the file is accessed (e.g., MY LITTLE BLACK BOOK); the length of the record; the number of items in a given record (e.g., three—a person's name, address, and phone number); and a title for each item (e.g., NAME, ADDRESS, PHONE). Random access files require that the length of a record be specified. You may consider this as the maximum number of characters you would need for the total number of items you choose. For example, a length of 100 would probably be sufficient for a record containing a person's name, address, and phone number.

The RAF USE program allows you to retrieve information from a given random access file. You must remember the name you gave the "information" file when you created the first record using RAF CREATION. Again, keep a written record of the names. RAF USE allows you to retrieve information by record number or by the complete list, edit records, or add records at your option.

The disk contains a text file named R1 that illustrates RAF USE. Run RAF USE, specifying this file name as the information file, to examine the options provided. Then start creating files of your own choosing.

Note: The items in a given record are all string variable values. Numeric data may be stored as strings and then converted to actual numeric values by use of the VAL (string) function (see Appendix B). The RAF USE program would have to be modified to incorporate this function if, for example, you wished to store student scores and do any computation using these scores.

RUN from disk and refer to the listing and run of RAF CREATION and RAF USE.

] LIST

```
10 REM       RAF CREATION
20 REM
30 REM  --------------------------------------------------------------
40 REM        FRAME 1 - INTRODUCTION
50 REM
60 HOME : HTAB 4
70 PRINT "RANDOM ACCESS FILE INITIALIZATION": PRINT : PRINT
80 PRINT "THIS PROGRAM WILL INITIALIZE THE RANDOM": PRINT
90 PRINT "ACCESS FILE YOU CHOOSE, ANY PREVIOUSLY": PRINT
100 PRINT "STORED INFORMATION IN THE FILE YOU": PRINT
110 PRINT "NAME WILL BE PERMANENTLY (I.E., FOREVER)": FLASH : HTAB 10
120 PRINT "E R A S E D": NORMAL : PRINT
130 INPUT "DO YOU WANT TO CONTINUE WITH THIS? ";Z$
140 IF LEFT$ (Z$,1) < > "Y" THEN 770
150 REM  --------------------------------------------------------------
160 REM        FRAME 2 - SEQUENTIAL FILE NAME FOR STORING RAF INFO
170 REM
180 HOME : VTAB 4
190 PRINT "WHAT NAME DO YOU WISH FOR THE FILE"
200 PRINT "THAT WILL STORE INFORMATION ABOUT THE"
210 INPUT "RANDOM ACCESS FILE? ";SEQFILE$
220 REM  --------------------------------------------------------------
230 REM        FRAME 3 - RANDOM ACCESS FILE NAME AND TITLE TO USE
240 REM
250 HOME : VTAB 4
260 PRINT "WHAT NAME DO YOU WISH TO GIVE THE"
270 INPUT "RANDOM ACCESS FILE? ";RANFILE$
280 VTAB 12: PRINT "WHAT TITLE DO YOU WISH DISPLAYED"
290 INPUT "IN PROGRAM EXECUTION? ";TITLE$
300 REM  --------------------------------------------------------------
310 REM        FRAME 4 - RECORD INFORMATION FOR THE RAF
320 REM
330 HOME : VTAB 6
340 INPUT "WHAT IS THE RECORD LENGTH (1-256)? ";L
350 VTAB 10: INPUT "HOW MANY ITEMS ARE IN EACH RECORD? ";N
360 DIM DT$(N),I$(N)
370 REM  --------------------------------------------------------------
380 REM        FRAME 5 - TITLES FOR EACH ITEM IN A RECORD
390 REM
400 HOME : HTAB 12: PRINT "ITEM TITLES": PRINT
410 FOR I = 1 TO N
420 PRINT "DESCRIPTIVE TITLE FOR ITEM "I
430 INPUT DT$(I): PRINT
440 NEXT I
```

```
450 REM -------------------------------------------------------------------
460 REM       FRAME 6 - GET INFORMATION FOR FIRST RECORD IN THE RAF
470 REM
480 HOME : HTAB 4: PRINT "ENTRIES FOR RECORD 1": PRINT
490 FOR I = 1 TO N
500 PRINT DT$(I)":"
510 INPUT I$(I): PRINT
520 NEXT I
530 REM -------------------------------------------------------------------
540 REM       FRAME 7 - DELETE OLD, THEN CREATE FIRST RECORD FOR NEW RAF
550 REM
560 HOME : VTAB 12: HTAB 4: PRINT "CREATING RECORD 1 IN "RANFILE$:R = 1
570 D$ = CHR$ (4): PRINT D$"OPEN "RANFILE$", L256"
580 PRINT D$"DELETE "RANFILE$
590 PRINT D$"OPEN "RANFILE$", L"L
600 PRINT D$"WRITE "RANFILE$", R"R
610 FOR I = 1 TO N
620 PRINT I$(I)
630 NEXT I
640 PRINT D$"CLOSE "RANFILE$
650 REM -------------------------------------------------------------------
660 REM       FRAME 8 - WRITE RAF INFO TO SEQUENTIAL FILE
670 REM
680 HOME : VTAB 12: HTAB 4: PRINT "CREATING SEQUENTIAL FILE "SEQFILE$
690 PRINT D$"OPEN "SEQFILE$
700 PRINT D$"WRITE "SEQFILE$
710 PRINT RANFILE$: PRINT TITLE$
720 PRINT L: PRINT R: PRINT N
730 FOR I = 1 TO N
740 PRINT DT$(I)
750 NEXT I
760 PRINT D$"CLOSE "SEQFILE$
770 HOME : VTAB 12: HTAB 12: PRINT "DONE..."
780 END
```

RAF CREATION
Sample Run—
Frames 2–4

```
What name do you wish for the file
that will store information about the
random access file? R1
-----------------------------------------
What name do you wish to give the
     random access file? RAFEXAMPLE

What title do you wish displayed
in program execution? EXAMPLE OF RANDOM FILES
-----------------------------------------
What is the record length? 100

How many items are in each record? 3
```

*RAF CREATION
Sample Run—
Frame 5*

```
                      ITEM TITLES

    Descriptive title for Item 1
    NAME

    Descriptive title for Item 2
    ADDRESS

    Descriptive title for Item 3
    PHONE
```

*RAF CREATION
Sample Run—
Frame 6*

```
                 ENTRIES FOR RECORD 1

    NAME:
    JACK AND JILL

    ADDRESS:
    SOMEWHERE ON THE HILL

    PHONE:
    UNLISTED
```

```
] LIST


10 REM       RAF USE
20 REM
30 REM ---------------------------------------------------------------
40 REM       FRAME 1, STEP 1 - DEFINE VARIABLES FOR FILE USE
50 REM
60 D$ = CHR$ (4):OP$ = D$ + "OPEN ":CL$ = D$ + "CLOSE "
70 RD$ = D$ + "READ ":WR$ = D$ + "WRITE "
80 REM ---------------------------------------------------------------
90 REM       FRAME 1, STEP 2 - RETRIEVE RAF INFO FROM SEQUENTIAL FILE
100 REM
110 HOME : VTAB 2: HTAB 8
```

```
120 PRINT "RANDOM ACCESS FILE USE": VTAB 12
130 PRINT "WHAT IS THE NAME OF THE SEQUENTIAL FILE"
140 INPUT "CONTAINING THE RAF INFORMATION? ";SEQFILE$
150 PRINT OP$SEQFILE$
160 PRINT RD$SEQFILE$
170 INPUT RANFILE$: INPUT TITLE$
180 INPUT L: INPUT R: INPUT N
190 DIM DT$(N),I$(N)
200 FOR I = 1 TO N
210 INPUT DT$(I)
220 NEXT I
230 PRINT CL$SEQFILE$
240 PRINT D$"PR#0"
250 REM -----------------------------------------------------------------
260 REM       FRAME 2 - FILE ACCESS OPTIONS
270 REM
280 HOME : PRINT "INFORMATION FILE" TAB( 20)"RANDOM ACCESS FILE"
290 INVERSE " PRINT SEQFILE$: VTAB 2: HTAB 20: PRINT RANFILE$: NORMAL
300 PRINT : PRINT "RECORD LENGTH: "L
310 PRINT "CURRENT NUMBER OF RECORDS: "R
320 PRINT : PRINT TAB( 8)TITLE$: PRINT
330 VTAB 10: HTAB 4: PRINT "DO YOU WANT TO: ": PRINT
340 HTAB 8: PRINT "1. RETRIEVE INFORMATION"
350 HTAB 8: PRINT "2. EDIT A RECORD"
360 HTAB 8: PRINT "3. ADD A RECORD"
370 HTAB 8: PRINT "4. STOP"
380 PRINT : HTAB 4
390 INPUT "ENTER YOUR CHOICE => ";C
400 IF C < 1 OR C > 4 THEN 380
410 ON C GOTO 450,750,860,1050
420 REM -----------------------------------------------------------------
430 REM       FRAME 3, STEP 1 - PRESENT RETRIEVAL OPTIONS
440 REM
450 HOME : VTAB 10: HTAB 6: PRINT "DO YOU WANT:"
460 HTAB 10: PRINT "1. ALL RECORDS"
470 HTAB 10: PRINT "2. A SPECIFIC RECORD"
480 HTAB 6: INPUT "ENTER 1 OR 2 ";C
490 IF C < 1 OR C > 2 THEN 480
500 IF C = 2 THEN 660
510 REM -----------------------------------------------------------------
520 REM       FRAME 3, STEP 2 - RETRIEVE ALL RECORDS
530 REM
540 HOME : VTAB 12
550 INPUT "DO YOU WANT TO USE THE PRINTER? ";P$
560 IF LEFT$ (P$,1) = "Y" THEN PRINT D$"PR#1"
570 PRINT OP$RANFILE$", L"L
580 HOME : FOR I = 1 TO R
590 GOSUB 1200
600 NEXT I
610 GOSUB 1310
```

```
620 GOTO 240
630 REM ------------------------------------------------------------------
640 REM        FRAME 3, STEP 3 - RETRIEVE A SINGLE RECORD
650 REM
660 HOME : VTAB 12
670 INPUT "ENTER THE RECORD ID NUMBER ";I
680 IF I < 1 OR I > R THEN PRINT TAB( 10)"***OUT OF RANGE***": GOTO 670
690 HOME : GOSUB 1190
700 GOSUB 1310
710 GOTO 240
720 REM ------------------------------------------------------------------
730 REM        FRAME 4, STEP 1 - RECORD TO EDIT
740 REM
750 HOME : VTAB 12
760 INPUT "RECORD ID TO EDIT (OR ZERO TO STOP) ";I
770 IF I = 0 THEN HOME : GOTO 240
780 IF I < 1 OR I > R THEN PRINT TAB( 10)"***OUT OF RANGE***": GOTO 760
790 HOME : PRINT " C U R R E N T   I N F O R M A T I O N"
800 PRINT
810 GOSUB 1190
820 PRINT CL$RANFILE$
830 REM ------------------------------------------------------------------
840 REM        FRAME 4, STEP 2 - EDIT AND/OR ADDING RECORD
850 REM
860 PRINT : PRINT : IF C = 3 THEN R = R + 1:I = R:FLAG = 1: HOME
870 FOR J = 1 TO N
880 PRINT "NEW "DT$(J)" (OR RETURN)"
890 INPUT E$: IF E$ < > "" THEN I$(J) = E$: PRINT
900 NEXT J
910 PRINT OP$RANFILE$", L"L
920 PRINT WR$RANFILE$", R"I
930 FOR J = 1 TO N
940 PRINT I$(J)
950 NEXT J
960 PRINT CL$RANFILE$
970 IF C < > 3 THEN 750
980 HOME : VTAB 12: HTAB 10
990 INPUT "ADD ANOTHER? ";Z$
1000 IF LEFT$ (Z$,1) = "Y" THEN 860
1010 GOTO 240
1020 REM ------------------------------------------------------------------
1030 REM        FRAME 5 - UPDATE OF SEQUENTIAL FILE INFO IF NEEDED
1040 REM
1050 HOME : VTAB 12: HTAB 18: PRINT "DONE...": PRINT : HTAB 8
1060 IF FLAG = 0 THEN PRINT "(NO ADDITIONS MADE TO RECORDS)": GOTO 1150
1070 PRINT OP$SEQFILE$
1080 PRINT WR$SEQFILE$
1090 PRINT RANFILE$: PRINT TITLE$
1100 PRINT L: PRINT R: PRINT N
1110 FOR J = 1 TO N
```

```
1120 PRINT DT$(J)
1130 NEXT J
1140 PRINT CL$SEQFILE$
1150 END
1160 REM ---------------------------------------------------------------
1170 REM          RECORD RETRIEVAL SUBROUTINE
1180 REM
1190 PRINT OP$RANFILE$", L"L
1200 PRINT RD$RANFILE$", R"I
1210 PRINT "RECORD NUMBER: "I
1220 FOR J = 1 TO N
1230 INPUT I$(J)
1240 PRINT DT$(J)": "I$(J)
1250 NEXT J
1260 PRINT "================"
1270 RETURN
1280 REM ---------------------------------------------------------------
1290 REM          FILE CLOSING SUBROUTINE
1300 REM
1310 PRINT CL$RANFILE$: PRINT
1320 VTAB 22: HTAB 30: INPUT "RETURN =>";Z$: HOME
1330 RETURN
```

RAF USE
Sample Run—
Frame 2

```
INFORMATION FILE              RANDOM ACCESS FILE
R1                            RAFEXAMPLE

RECORD LENGTH: 100
CURRENT NUMBER OF RECORDS: 1

        EXAMPLE OF RANDOM FILES

     Do you want to:
          1. Retrieve Information
          2. Edit a Record
          3. Add a Record
          4. STOP
     Enter your choice => 1
```

7.6 POSERS AND PROBLEMS

1. Modify PROGRAM 16 to present five sequential questions on any topic of your choosing.

2. Modify PROGRAM 18 to present a varying number of food items of your choosing for each menu.

3. Modify PROGRAM 19 to test naming from any list of items of your choosing.

4. Modify PROGRAM 20 to present ten multiple-choice questions of your choosing, each with at least three, but no more than five, possible choices.

*5. Modify PROGRAMs 19 and 20 so that the user's name, program name, and user's score are written to a text file that may be searched with the FILEREAD program. *Hint:* Examine Frame 5 in the FILEWRITE program. But remember, you will be writing only *one* student name, *one* program name, and *one* score to a text file that you must identify.

*6. Identify an area in your particular field of interest in which an instructional computing program could be written for each of the five applications described in Chapters 6 and 7. *Briefly* outline each program by describing in a short paragraph its area, content, and application.

*7. Select one of the topics you identified in Problem 6 and outline the program in a frame-by-frame, step-by-step design.

"What is the use of a book," thought Alice,
"without pictures or conversations?"
—LEWIS CARROLL

THINK ABOUT THIS . . .

. . . FOR FUN

*A single English word can be formed from
these letters. What is it? Use all the letters:
PNLLEEEESSSSS.*

. . . SERIOUSLY

*Is it possible that graphics do not always en-
hance instructional computing materials?*

Chapter 8
One Picture
Is Worth
Ten Thousand Words

8.1 OBJECTIVES

For the successful completion of this chapter, you should be able to:

1. Explain and give an example of how to specify a point on a graphics screen (Section 8.2).

2. Define the purpose and give at least one example of the low-resolution graphics statements GR, COLOR, PLOT, HLIN, VLIN, and TEXT (Section 8.3).

3. Define the purpose and give at least one example of the high-resolution graphics statements HGR, HCOLOR, and HPLOT (Section 8.4).

4. Design, enter, and RUN a BASIC program of your own choosing using low-resolution graphics.

5. Design, enter, and RUN a BASIC program of your own choosing using high-resolution graphics.

8.2 WHAT ARE GRAPHICS?

Throughout history, progress has been the result of people's ability to understand complex concepts. Visual tools such as drawings, photographs, films, and videotapes provide the medium for making complex concepts understandable to the masses. With the development of the computer and its ability to analyze vast amounts of data rapidly, its use as a tool for portraying visual information (graphics) naturally evolved.

A computer graphic is somewhat like a printed map. Both are two-dimensional surfaces with a vertical direction and a horizontal direction. Just as any point on a map may be identified by its horizontal and vertical coordinates (latitude and longitude), any point on a computer's graphics screen can be specified by measuring its vertical and horizontal distance from the upper left corner.

The horizontal distance scale is called the x-axis; the vertical distance scale is called the y-axis. Figure 8.1 shows the Apple low-resolution graphics screen with the x-axis across the top of the screen and the y-axis down the left side of the screen. When the position of a point is specified, the distance on the x-axis is specified first, followed by the distance on the y-axis (the *x- and y-coordi-*

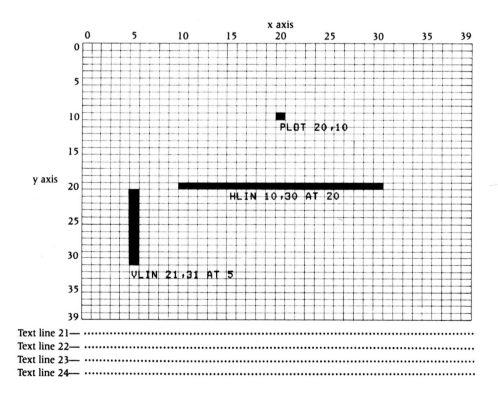

Figure 8.1
Low-resolution
graphics screen
(GR).

nates of the point). For example, 20,10 specifies the point 20 units to the right in the x-direction and 10 units down in the y-direction. Similarly, the corners of the Apple low-resolution graphics screen are specified by 0,0 (upper left), 39,0 (upper right), 39,39 (lower right), and 0,39 (lower left).

8.3 STATEMENTS FOR LOW-RESOLUTION GRAPHICS

8.3.1   Statement GR

Purpose   The GR statement is used to initialize the low-resolution graphics screen in a program. When it is executed, the computer monitor will change from text to low-resolution graphics and the screen will be cleared to black. As pictured in Figure 8.1, the low-resolution screen contains 160 points (0 to 39 by 0 to 39). In addition, four text lines are available at the bottom of the screen for instructions, questions, and comments.

8.3.2   Statement COLOR

Purpose   The COLOR statement sets the color for subsequent graphics statements. Once the color has been set, all graphics drawn on the screen will be of that color until another COLOR statement is executed. Sixteen colors are available. Each color is represented by a number from 0 to 15:

```
COLOR  =  0        (black)
COLOR  =  1        (magenta)
COLOR  =  2        (dark blue)
COLOR  =  3        (purple)
COLOR  =  4        (dark green)
COLOR  =  5        (grey)
COLOR  =  6        (medium blue)
COLOR  =  7        (light blue)
COLOR  =  8        (brown)
COLOR  =  9        (orange)
COLOR  =  10       (grey)
COLOR  =  11       (pink)
COLOR  =  12       (green)
COLOR  =  13       (yellow)
COLOR  =  14       (aqua)
COLOR  =  15       (white)
```

8.3.3 Statement PLOT

Purpose The PLOT statement will place a rectangular "brick" on the screen at the x- and y-coordinates specified in the statement. The color of the brick will be the color specified by the most recently executed COLOR statement.

Example PLOT 20,10

(A brick will be PLOTted at a point 20 units to the right on the x-axis and 10 units down on the y-axis. See Figure 8.1.)
    Enter the following program and RUN it:

```
10 REM ----------------------------------------------------
20 REM         STEP 1 - INITIALIZE LOW-RESOLUTION SCREEN
30 REM
40 HOME : GR
50 REM ----------------------------------------------------
60 REM         STEP 2 - START THE LOOP; SET VALUE FOR COLOR
70 REM
80 FOR I = 1 TO 15
90 COLOR = I
100 REM ----------------------------------------------------
110 REM         STEP 3 - CHOOSE RANDOM X- AND Y-COORDINATES
120 REM
130 X = INT(RND(1) * 40)
140 Y = INT(RND(1) * 40)
150 REM ----------------------------------------------------
160 REM         STEP 4 - PLOT BRICK ON SCREEN; END LOOP
170 REM
180 PLOT X,Y
190 NEXT I
200 END
```

What happened? If entered correctly, fifteen bricks of different colors were PLOTted on the screen.

8.3.4 Statement HLIN

Purpose The HLIN statement draws a horizontal line on the screen from a specified starting point on the x-axis to a specified ending point on the x-axis. The line is located at a specified point on the y-axis. The color of the line will be the color indicated by the most recently executed COLOR statement.

Example HLIN 10,30 AT 20

(A horizontal line will be drawn from the 10th to the 30th unit on the x-axis at the 20th unit down on the y-axis. See Figure 8.1.)

8.3.5   Statement VLIN

Purpose The VLIN statement draws a vertical line on the screen from a specified starting point on the y-axis to a specified ending point on the y-axis. The line is located at a specified point on the x-axis. The color of the line will be the color indicated by the most recently executed COLOR statement.

Example `VLIN 21,31 AT 5`

(A vertical line will be drawn from the 21st to the 31st unit on the y-axis at the 5th unit to the right on the x-axis. See Figure 8.1.)

8.3.6   Statement TEXT

Purpose The TEXT statement returns the computer's monitor to a full text screen (twenty-four lines of forty characters). If this statement is not included at the end of a program using graphics, the graphic screen will remain on the monitor. TEXT may also be typed as an individual command to return to the full text screen.

8.3.7   PROGRAM 21: Random Colored Lines

The five low-resolution graphics statements GR, COLOR, PLOT, HLIN, and VLIN provide the basis for adding diagrams, charts, and illustrations to instructional computing materials. PROGRAM 21 demonstrates the use of these statements to generate unique graphics by drawing 100 random horizontal and 100 random vertical lines on the screen. Step by step, the design of this program is:

Step 1.   Clear the screen and initialize the low-resolution graphics screen.

Step 2.   Set the COLOR to light blue. Fill in the background by drawing horizontal lines completely across the screen.

Step 3.   Begin a loop that executes 100 times.

Step 4.   Choose a random color for the next line. Check to see if it matches the background color (7). If so, choose another color.

Step 5.   Jump to the subroutine that randomly selects the line's length and location. Then draw the next vertical line.

Step 6.   Choose another random color and check to make sure that it doesn't match the background color.

Step 7.   Jump to the subroutine that randomly selects the line's length and location. Then draw the next horizontal line.

Step 8.   Complete the loop that draws the random lines.

Since PROGRAM 21 is dynamic, it must be RUN to be appreciated. The actions on the screen cannot be sufficiently illustrated by words or pictures in this text.

RUN from disk and refer to the listing of PROGRAM 21.

```
] LIST


10 REM        PROGRAM 21
20 REM
30 REM  ------------------------------------------------------------
40 REM        STEP 1 - INITIALIZE LOW-RESOLUTION GRAPHICS SCREEN
50 REM
60 HOME
70 GR
80 REM  ------------------------------------------------------------
90 REM        STEP 2 - PAINT BACKGROUND TO LIGHT BLUE
100 REM
110 COLOR= 7
120 FOR I = 0 TO 39
130 HLIN 0,39 AT I
140 NEXT I
150 REM  ------------------------------------------------------------
160 REM        STEP 3 - BEGIN LOOP
170 REM
180 FOR I = 1 TO 100
190 REM  ------------------------------------------------------------
200 REM        STEP 4 - CHOOSE RANDOM COLOR FOR LINE
210 REM
220 X = INT ( RND (1) * 16)
230 IF X = 7 THEN 220
240 COLOR= X
250 REM  ------------------------------------------------------------
260 REM        STEP 5 - PLOT VERTICAL LINE
270 REM
280 GOSUB 500
290 VLIN A,B AT C
300 REM  ------------------------------------------------------------
310 REM        STEP 6 - CHOOSE ANOTHER RANDOM COLOR
320 REM
330 X = INT ( RND (1) * 16)
340 IF X = 7 THEN 330
350 COLOR= X
360 REM  ------------------------------------------------------------
370 REM        STEP 7 - PLOT HORIZONTAL LINE
380 REM
390 GOSUB 500
400 HLIN A,B AT C
410 REM  ------------------------------------------------------------
```

```
420 REM        STEP 8 - CONTINUE LOOP OR END PROGRAM
430 REM
440 NEXT I
450 PRINT : INPUT "PRESS RETURN TO CLEAR SCREEN";Z$
460 TEXT : HOME : END
470 REM --------------------------------------------------------------
480 REM        SUBROUTINE TO CHOOSE LENGTH AND LOCATION OF LINE
490 REM
500 A = INT ( RND (1) * 40)
510 B = INT ( RND (1) * 40)
520 C = INT ( RND (1) * 40)
530 RETURN
```

8.4 STATEMENTS FOR HIGH-RESOLUTION GRAPHICS

The Apple II microcomputer has two levels of graphics available: low-resolution graphics, as previously discussed, and high-resolution graphics. High-resolution graphics, as the name implies, have greater detail, or more resolution. However, something must be sacrificed for this feature—the variety of colors.

The high-resolution screen is illustrated in Figure 8.2. A point on the screen is specified in the same fashion as on the low-resolution screen, by giving the x-axis position first, followed by the y-axis position. However, the axes have considerably more units: The x-axis contains 280 units (0 through 279) and the y-axis contains 160 (0 through 159). Four text lines are available at the bottom of the screen for instructions, questions, and comments.

Instead of having sixteen colors available, only six are allowed: black, white, green, blue, orange, and violet. These colors will vary in hue depending on the type of television or monitor being used.

8.4.1 Statement HGR

Purpose   The HGR statement is used to initialize the high-resolution graphics screen in a program. When it is executed, the computer monitor will change from text to high-resolution graphics and the screen will be cleared to black. As pictured in Figure 8.2, the high-resolution screen initialized with the HGR statement contains 44,800 points (0 to 279 by 0 to 159).

8.4.2 Statement HCOLOR

Purpose   The HCOLOR statement sets the color for subsequent graphics statements. Once the color has been set, all graphics drawn on the screen will be of that color until another HCOLOR statement is executed. Six colors are available. Each color is represented by a number from 0 to 7 (black and white are each represented by two codes):

```
HCOLOR = 0    (black)
HCOLOR = 1    (green)
HCOLOR = 2    (violet)
HCOLOR = 3    (white)
HCOLOR = 4    (black)
HCOLOR = 5    (orange)
HCOLOR = 6    (blue)
HCOLOR = 7    (white)
```

8.4.3   Statement HPLOT

Purpose   HPLOT will place a dot on the screen at the x- and y-coordinates specified in the statement. The color of the dot will be the color specified by the most recently executed COLOR statement.

Example   `HPLOT 95,101`

(Plots a dot on the high-resolution screen 95 units to the right on the x-axis and 101 units down on the y-axis. See Figure 8.2.)

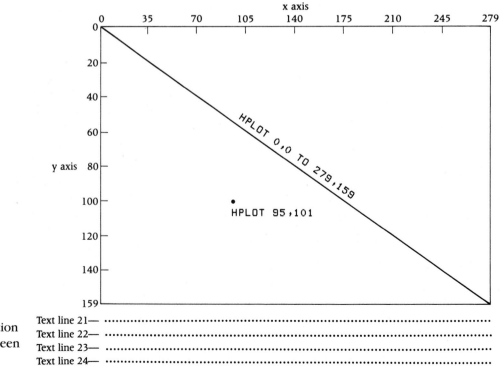

Figure 8.2
High-resolution
graphics screen
(HGR).

Text line 21— ···
Text line 22— ···
Text line 23— ···
Text line 24— ···

The HPLOT statement can also be used to draw a line from one point on the screen to another.

Example
```
10 HGR
20 HCOLOR = 3
30 HPLOT 0,0 TO 279,159
40 END
```

(Draws a diagonal white line from the upper left corner to the lower right corner of the screen. See Figure 8.2.)

HPLOT can also be used to draw a line from the last point plotted to the x- and y-coordinates specified.

Example
```
10 HGR
20 HCOLOR = 3
30 HPLOT 0,0
40 HPLOT TO 279,0
50 HPLOT TO 279,159
60 HPLOT TO 0,159
70 HPLOT TO 0,0
80 END
```

(Draws a white border completely around the high-resolution screen.)

A series of lines can be specified in a single HPLOT statement. The following example will have the same result as the previous example (a border around the graphics screen); however, it is done in one statement.

Computer assignments that require students working in groups of two or three can foster communication skills and improved comprehension.

Example
```
10 HGR
20 HCOLOR = 3
30 HPLOT 0,0 TO 279,0 TO 279,159 TO 0,159 TO 0,0
40 END
```

8.4.4 Statement VTAB

Purpose
The VTAB statement tabs to the line number specified so that text can be PRINTed on that line. Both the low-resolution and high-resolution graphics screens have four text lines available. These lines are the 21st, 22nd, 23rd, and 24th lines on the text screen. VTAB 21 in statement 80 of the following program allows statement 240 to PRINT on line 21 and statement 250 to PRINT on line 22.

Example
Enter the following high-resolution graphics program and RUN it:

```
10 REM --------------------------------------------------
20 REM        STEP 1 - INITIALIZE THE HIGH-RES SCREEN
30 REM
40 HOME : HGR
50 REM --------------------------------------------------
60 REM        STEP 2 - BEGIN LOOP
70 REM
80 FOR I = 1 TO 100
90 REM --------------------------------------------------
100 REM       STEP 3 - CHOOSE COLOR & X- AND Y- COORD.
110 REM
120 HCOLOR = INT(RND(1) * 8)
130 X = INT(RND(1) * 280)
140 Y = INT(RND(1) * 160)
150 REM --------------------------------------------------
160 REM       STEP 4 - PLOT THE POINT AND END THE LOOP
170 REM
180 HPLOT X,Y
190 NEXT I
200 REM --------------------------------------------------
210 REM       STEP 5 - VTAB TO LINE 21 AND PRINT MESSAGE
220 REM
230 VTAB 21
240 PRINT "THE STARS AT NIGHT...ARE BIG AND BRIGHT"
250 PRINT " DEEP IN THE HEART OF TEXAS.";
260 END
```

Brilliant! One hundred random points (stars) were plotted on the screen.

8.5 INCORPORATING HIGH-RESOLUTION GRAPHICS INTO INSTRUCTIONAL COMPUTING MATERIALS

When developing instructional computing materials that contain graphics, some special planning is necessary. In addition to the normal designing of the program, the graphic screens used in the program should be sketched or plotted on graph paper. Longer tutorial programs may require a *storyboard* to be prepared. This is a series of sketches of the graphics with the related textual information or questions included.

When designing the program, the graphics are most easily done in subroutines that can be called as needed in the program. The subroutines can easily be tested by typing RUN and the starting line number of the subroutine. (For example, RUN 800 would execute the subroutine beginning at line 800.)

8.5.1 PROGRAM 22: Shape-Recognition Drill

PROGRAM 22 is a drill-and-practice program that displays a shape on the screen for the student to identify. Four shapes are used: circle, rectangle, square, and triangle. The program randomly presents five questions, presents the shape in random sizes, and keeps track of the student's score. The frame-by-frame, step-by-step design of this program is:

Frame 1.   Print instructions to the student.

Loop Frames, Step 1.   Initialize the high-resolution graphics screen.

Loop Frames, Step 2.   Print answer choices at the bottom of the screen.

Loop Frames, Step 3.   Choose a random number representing one of the four shapes and branch to the appropriate subroutine.

Final Frame.   Report the student's performance.

Square, triangle, rectangle, and circle subroutines:

Step 1.   Choose a random height and width for the shape and calculate the starting position to draw the shape.

Step 2.   Plot the shape centered on the screen.

Step 3.   Ask the student to identify the shape and input the student's answer.

Step 4.   Check the answer and jump to either the correct answer subroutine or the incorrect answer subroutine.

Correct answer subroutine:

Step 1. Display that the answer is correct.

Step 2. Add 1 to the total number of correct answers.

Incorrect answer subroutine:

Step 1. Display that the answer is incorrect.

RUN from disk and refer to the listing and run of PROGRAM 22.

] LIST

```
10 REM        PROGRAM 22
20 REM
30 REM -----------------------------------------------------------------
40 REM        FRAME 1 - PRINT INSTRUCTIONS TO STUDENTS
50 REM
60 HOME : VTAB 4
70 PRINT "I AM GOING TO SHOW YOU 5 SHAPES.": PRINT
80 PRINT "YOU TELL ME WHAT KIND OF SHAPE IT IS."
90 PRINT : PRINT
100 VTAB 22: HTAB 30: INPUT "RETURN =>";Z$
110 C = 0
120 REM -----------------------------------------------------------------
130 REM        LOOP FRAMES, STEP 1 - BEGIN THE LOOP; INITIALIZE SCREEN
140 REM
150 FOR I = 1 TO 5
160 HOME
170 HGR
180 HCOLOR= 3
190 REM -----------------------------------------------------------------
200 REM        LOOP FRAMES, STEP 2 - PRINT ANSWER CHOICES
210 REM
220 VTAB 22
230 PRINT "C= CIRCLE R=RECTANGLE S=SQUARE T=TRIANGLE": PRINT
240 REM -----------------------------------------------------------------
250 REM        LOOP FRAMES, STEP 3 - CHOOSE SHAPE; BRANCH TO SUBROUTINE
260 REM
270 Z = INT ( RND (1) * 4 + 1)
280 ON Z GOSUB 400,620,830,1050
290 NEXT I
300 REM -----------------------------------------------------------------
310 REM        FINAL FRAME - PERFORMANCE REPORT
320 REM
330 HOME : TEXT
340 PRINT "YOU GOT "C" SHAPES CORRECT!": PRINT
```

```
350 PRINT "SO LONG FOR NOW."
360 END
370 REM ------------------------------------------------------------
380 REM        SQUARE, STEP 1 - CHOOSE HEIGHT, WIDTH, AND STARTING POINT
390 REM
400 H = INT ( RND (1) * 61 + 10)
410 W = H * 1.20
420 Y = 80 - H / 2
430 X = 140 - W / 2
440 REM ------------------------------------------------------------
450 REM        SQUARE, STEP 2 - DRAW THE SQUARE
460 REM
470 HPLOT X,Y TO X + W,Y TO X + W,Y + H TO X,Y + H TO X,Y
480 HPLOT X - 1,Y - 1 TO X + W + 1,Y - 1 TO X + W + 1,Y + H + 1 TO
    X - 1, Y + H + 1 TO X - 1,Y - 1
490 REM ------------------------------------------------------------
500 REM        SQUARE, STEP 3 - ASK FOR ANSWER AND INPUT IT
510 REM
520 INPUT "WHICH SHAPE IS IT? ";ANS$
530 REM ------------------------------------------------------------
540 REM        SQUARE, STEP 4 - CHECK FOR CORRECT ANSWER AND BRANCH
550 REM
560 IF ANS$ = "S" THEN GOSUB 1300
570 IF ANS$ < > "S" THEN GOSUB 1400
580 RETURN
590 REM ------------------------------------------------------------
600 REM        TRIANGLE, STEP 1 - CHOOSE HEIGHT, WIDTH, & STARTING POINT
610 REM
620 H = INT ( RND (1) * 61 + 10)
630 W = H * .7
640 Y = 80 - H / 2
650 X = 140
660 REM ------------------------------------------------------------
670 REM        TRIANGLE, STEP 2 - DRAW THE TRIANGLE
680 REM
690 HPLOT X,Y TO X + W,Y + H TO X - W,Y + H TO X,Y
700 REM ------------------------------------------------------------
710 REM        TRIANGLE, STEP 3 - ASK FOR ANSWER AND INPUT IT
720 REM
730 INPUT "WHICH SHAPE IS IT? ";ANS$
740 REM ------------------------------------------------------------
750 REM        TRIANGLE, STEP 4 - CHECK FOR CORRECT ANSWER AND BRANCH
760 REM
770 IF ANS$ = "T" THEN GOSUB 1300
780 IF ANS$ < > "T" THEN GOSUB 1400
790 RETURN
800 REM ------------------------------------------------------------
810 REM        RECTANGLE, STEP 1 - CHOOSE HEIGHT, WIDTH, & STARTING POINT
820 REM
830 H = INT ( RND (1) * 61 + 10)
```

```
840 W = H * 2
850 Y = 80 - H / 2
860 X = 140 - W / 2
870 REM --------------------------------------------------------------------
880 REM          RECTANGLE, STEP 2 - DRAW THE RECTANGLE
890 REM
900 HPLOT X,Y TO X + W,Y TO X + W,Y + H TO X,Y + H TO X,Y
910 HPLOT X - 1,Y - 1 TO X + W + 1,Y - 1 TO X + W + 1,Y + H + 1 TO
    X - 1, Y + H + 1 TO X - 1,Y - 1
920 REM --------------------------------------------------------------------
930 REM          RECTANGLE, STEP 3 - ASK FOR ANSWER AND INPUT IT
940 REM
950 INPUT "WHICH SHAPE IS IT? ";ANS$
960 REM --------------------------------------------------------------------
970 REM          RECTANGLE, STEP 4 - CHECK FOR CORRECT ANSWER AND BRANCH
980 REM
990 IF ANS$ = "R" THEN GOSUB 1300
1000 IF ANS$ < > "R" THEN GOSUB 1400
1010 RETURN
1020 REM --------------------------------------------------------------------
1030 REM          CIRCLE, STEP 1 - CHOOSE RADIUS AND STARTING POINT
1040 REM
1050 H = INT ( RND (1) * 61 + 10)
1060 X = COS ( -3.14) * H * 1.2 + 140
1070 Y = SIN ( -3.14) * H + 80
1080 REM --------------------------------------------------------------------
1090 REM          CIRCLE, STEP 2 - DRAW THE CIRCLE
1100 REM
1110 HPLOT X,Y
1120 FOR J = -3.15 TO 3.15 STEP .1
1130 X = COS (J) * H * 1.2 + 140
1140 Y = SIN (J) * H + 80
1150 HPLOT TO X,Y
1160 NEXT J
1170 REM --------------------------------------------------------------------
1180 REM          CIRCLE, STEP 3 - ASK FOR ANSWER AND INPUT IT
1190 REM
1200 INPUT "WHICH SHAPE IS IT? ";ANS$
1210 REM --------------------------------------------------------------------
1220 REM          CIRCLE, STEP 4 - CHECK FOR CORRECT ANSWER AND BRANCH
1230 REM
1240 IF ANS$ = "C" THEN GOSUB 1300
1250 IF ANS$ < > "C" THEN GOSUB 1400
1260 RETURN
1270 REM --------------------------------------------------------------------
1280 REM          CORRECT ANSWER, STEP 1 - PRINT RESPONSE
1290 REM
1300 PRINT : PRINT "YOU ARE CORRECT!"
1310 REM --------------------------------------------------------------------
1320 REM          CORRECT ANSWER, STEP 2 - ADD 1 TO TOTAL CORRECT
```

```
1330 REM
1340 C = C + 1
1350 FOR P = 1 TO 1000: NEXT P
1360 RETURN
1370 REM --------------------------------------------------------------
1380 REM        INCORRECT ANSWER, STEP 1 - PRINT RESPONSE
1390 REM
1400 PRINT : PRINT "SORRY, TRY ANOTHER."
1410 FOR P = 1 TO 1000: NEXT P
1420 RETURN
```

8.6 SOME NOTES ABOUT USING COLOR

The graphic statements in this chapter can be employed to "add a little color" to instructional computing materials. However, there are both positive and negative factors to be considered when using color:

1. Color can increase attention.

2. Color can increase motivation.

3. Color is less fatiguing to the eye than black-and-white text.

4. If color is used for highlighting concepts, it must be used consistently throughout the program.

5. Limit the number of colors used at one time to four.

6. Use highly saturated (bold) colors.

7. Consider color stereotypes. (Stop signs must be red.)

8. The greater the contrast between two colors (e.g., complementary colors), the greater the visual impact.

9. Remember that 10% of all males and 5% of all females are color-blind.

10. *Most important:* If you emphasize everything, nothing on the screen will stand out!

8.7 POSERS AND PROBLEMS

1. Correct any errors in the following statements:

```
10 GR
20 COLOR = 10
30 HPLOT 10,10 TO 100,100
40 END
```

2. Modify PROGRAM 21 to draw random squares, rather than random lines, of random colors on the low-resolution graphics screen.

3. What would result from the execution of the following statements?

```
10 HGR
20 HCOLOR = 2
30 FOR Y = 0 TO 159
40 HPLOT 0,Y TO 279,Y
50 NEXT Y
60 END
```

4. Write a low-resolution graphics program that displays sixteen bars of different colors. (This program can be used as a test pattern to adjust the color on the television or monitor).

5. Write a low-resolution graphics program that displays a checkerboard or gingham pattern (your choice of colors) on the screen.

6. Write a high-resolution graphics program that plots the function X = SQR(Y) * 20 (vary Y from 0 to 159).

PART TWO

AN INTRODUCTION TO THE DESIGN AND DEVELOPMENT OF INSTRUCTIONAL COMPUTING MATERIALS

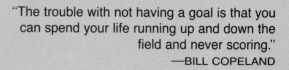

"The trouble with not having a goal is that you can spend your life running up and down the field and never scoring."
—BILL COPELAND

"It takes less time to do a thing right than to explain why you did it wrong."
—H. W. LONGFELLOW

"And what is writ is writ. Would it worthier!"
—LORD BYRON

"Garbage in, garbage out."
—ANON.

"A thing of beauty is a joy forever."
—JOHN KEATS

THINK ABOUT THIS . . .

. . . FOR FUN

Using each number only once, arrange the figures 0,1,2,3,4,5,6,7,8,9 so that their sum is 100.

. . . SERIOUSLY

What characteristics may be identified with educationally valid instructional computing materials?

Chapter 9
What Are Your Intentions?

9.1 OBJECTIVES

For the successful completion of this chapter, you should be able to:

1. Identify the steps of a "systems approach" to the design of instructional computing materials (Section 9.3).

2. Identify an area of personal interest within which to apply instructional computing.

3. Outline a rationale, a set of quantitative performance objectives, and a sequence of instruction for a unit of instructional computing materials (Sections 9.3.1–9.3.3).

9.2 DESIGNING INSTRUCTIONAL COMPUTING MATERIALS

A working knowledge of BASIC (or any programming language) provides only a very small step toward the actual development of educationally valid instructional computing materials. In fact, such materials have been designed by educators with *no* computing experience whatsoever! In these cases, the completed design is given to a computer programmer (who often knows very little about the specific academic area) for translation into an executable computer program. The executable program is tested, refined, and eventually put to use in the classroom. Thus, the key to the development of valid educational materials rests initially with their *design*.

The entire design and development process can be improved if both the author and the programmer have something more than a casual awareness of the other's area of expertise. However, it is not often that the author and programmer are one and the same person, with expertise in both programming and a given academic area. Very few educators have high proficiency in programming techniques and strategies. Likewise, few programmers know the intricacies of learning theory, instructional design, teaching methodology, and so on.

Pilot testing is an important step in the systems approach to developing instructional computing materials.

The wide acceptance and use of microcomputers in education is bringing about a gradual change in this, however. More and more, both in-service and preservice teachers are gaining knowledge in computer literacy and instructional computing uses. With this knowledge will come improved materials and improved use of this medium of instructional technology that, literally, is at our fingertips.

Design! It is not too unusual for someone to have the feeling that they have never designed anything! However, if they have ever wanted anything, anything at all, that was eventually obtained through their efforts, they have experienced the design process! This process, then, is really something common to most people, and it has at least one fringe benefit: It makes us think logically and creatively. That is, the procedure—from identification of an objective to its attainment—becomes a series of steps.

Often, this logical procedure is called an *algorithm,* and, in fact, it *is* a logical series of steps that must be followed in designing *any* effective package of instructional materials. This process, however, is amplified greatly in designing and developing interactive instructional computing materials. There are several reasons for this amplification; the primary ones are that instructional computing requires immediate feedback and active participation by the user. The design of an instructional program—for better or worse—rapidly becomes apparent to a user through its interactive nature.

9.3 THE SYSTEMS APPROACH

The design stage of instructional computing materials is one part of a process that is used extensively in the overall development of educational materials. Although this process is known by several names, and the steps may differ slightly among versions, it may be summarized as follows:

1. statement of the rationale for use

2. statement of quantitative performance objectives

3. definition of the instructional sequence

4. program construction

5. debugging

6. pilot testing

7. revision

8. use in the classroom

9. revision

10. evaluation

Instructional
computing materials
should be designed
with careful attention
to the learner's
objectives and the
sequence of
instruction.

These ten steps comprise the process often called *a systems approach to instructional design.* However, since it does involve a logical approach, another name might be, "A Common-Sense Approach to Instructional Design."

The first three steps constitute the design stage and will be discussed in this chapter. The following seven steps will be discussed in Chapter 10. Note that, although all of these steps are important, the contents of each are determined solely by the author(s) of the instructional computing materials. In other words, the steps and general procedures for each can be outlined in this book, but the reason for any given instructional computing lesson—what it does and how it does it—can only be determined by its author(s).

9.3.1 The Rationale

Assume that an area of interest has been identified for the design and development of a unit of instructional computing material. Can reasons be stated why this particular area of interest should be taught in the first place? Can reasons be stated why a computer should be used? In other words, the rationale is the answer to *why: Why* teach this academic concept, and *why* use the computer as an adjunct to the instructional process? If the *why* cannot be answered in both instances, the design stage should be terminated and another area of interest identified.

The following examples of rationales are taken directly from instructional computing units developed by various teachers. Note how brief or how thorough such a rationale may be. The first example is very brief:

The purpose of this learning module (unit) is to enrich the student's personal communication skills, provide a background knowledge for future study in business and economics, and provide a beginning knowledge base of terminology for application in the selected career area. Terminology is essential for communicating in a specialized technological society. This module provides a beginning for building a vocabulary base in business, management, and economics.

The second, slightly longer rationale is very specific:

Correct association of compound names with molecular formulas is a necessary skill for continuing successfully in a chemistry course. The names and formulas for compounds are used interchangeably throughout most chemical literature. Mastery of chemistry textbook reading material requires the correct identification of compound names and formulas. In the chemistry laboratory, names and formulas are also used interchangeably in labeling containers and in written laboratory procedures. A serious error could result in the laboratory if a student incorrectly identified a compound used in the experiment.

The computer can serve as an effective tool for the student who is learning to identify the names and molecular formulas of compounds because: 1) it allows the student to work at his/her individual pace, 2) it provides immediate feedback to the student after each answer is given, 3) it may randomly generate different questions so that the student has a variety of practice, 4) it scores the student at the end of the drill providing an estimation of progress, and, 5) it may be adapted for use in both drill exercises and testing.

The third example is as specific as the second and is slightly more expansive:

Preservice educational preparation for nursing in a coronary care unit generally focuses on dysrhythmia recognition. Given various electrocardiographic tracings, the learner is expected to label the patterns by origin and conduction of impulse, rate, and probable clinical sequela. She/he is rarely provided opportunity to project and evaluate nursing actions based on recognition of the dysrhythmia. Consequently, these decision making skills are usually learned "on the job" under tutelage of a more experienced nurse practitioner. The trainee's learning depends, then, on numerous variables—the experienced nurse's willingness to teach, clinical situations which "happen" to be present, critical time factors which may or may not permit the trainee opportunity to project appropriate actions before action is required, and numerous other equally uncontrollable factors. Preservice teaching methods can, and should, be developed which facilitate the trainee's acquisition of decision making/judgment skills in environments created deliberately for learning; learning within the setting of a coronary care unit is best reserved for only those abilities that cannot be synthesized in any other environment.

Simulation is one possibly effective preservice teaching technique to facilitate acquisition of decision making/judgment skills. Simulation teaching strategies have been noted to enable the student to: 1) actively participate in learning, 2) integrate theoretical concepts to simulated life situations, 3) desensitize oneself against threatening situations, 4) be presented with identical "hands-on experiences" as those presented fellow learners, 5) experience some of the doubts, competencies, difficulties, and anxieties that would be experienced in actual clinical settings, and, 6) respond in a safe standardized context free of concern about harming the patient or pleasing a tutor.

What are the advantages of using the computer in designing these simulated experiences? First, the selection and sequencing of problems can be randomized independent of instructor or learner choice at the moment—a situation more closely approximating the "randomness" of the actual clinical setting. Second, the learner can be provided with immediate feedback on decisions made. Third, since computers are interactive, the student's response has a measurable effect on the material as it is presented. Fourth, the learner can choose the time for instruction, times when faculty may or may not be available. Fifth, the instructor can reconstruct precisely the sequence in which the student responds to the simulated clinical situation, diagnose errors in approach, and pinpoint reinforcement and help.

In summary, the rationale underlying this unit rests on three premises: 1) A need for preservice acquisition of decision making/judgment skills exists. 2) Simulated experiences can assist in acquisition of these needed skills. 3) Use of the computer enhances the student's independence, assists instructor diagnosis of learning difficulties, and facilitates the process of simulating clinical situations.

9.3.2   Quantitative Performance Objectives

Users will be interacting with your programs. Do they know what is expected of them before, during, and after this interaction? Before a user sits down at a computer terminal, information should be provided that at least outlines the prerequisites for interaction, what the interaction will deal with, and, *specifically,* what constitutes a successful interaction. For what goals should the user strive, and how will it be determined if these goals are attained?

Continuing with our examples from the previous section, a statement of quantitative objectives might be as brief as:

General: Given a basic list of business terms, the student will develop a working knowledge of basic business terms. The student will demonstrate this ability by completing successfully the instructional computing units focusing on terminology mastery.

Specific: Given a set of terminology, the student will complete the instructional computing unit with 90% or better accuracy on a 20-word list.

The second example is succinct and equally brief:

1. The student will be able to state the name of a compound when given its molecular formula with 80% accuracy.

2. The student will be able to state the molecular formula of a compound when given its name with 80% accuracy.

The third example is longer but also quite specific:

Given a cardiac rhythm strip, the student will identify the pattern by site of origin and rhythm with 100% accuracy.

Given a cardiac rhythm strip, the student will identify an appropriate sequence of nursing actions from among the following four alternatives: obtain more data, execute a standing order, call the physician, or continue close observation.

Given a decision to call the physician, the student will indicate the information to be shared, omitting no pertinent data.

Given a decision to obtain more data, the student will ask for data pertinent to formulating a subsequent action-decision.

Given feedback regarding a questionable action-decision, the student will re-evaluate the decision and indicate with 100% accuracy if the decision was appropriate.

For a thorough and enlightening description of defining instructional objectives, the reader is referred to the classic text in this field, *Preparing Instructional Objectives* by R. F. Mager (Fearon Publications, Palo Alto, CA, 1962).

9.3.3 The Instructional Sequence

This step in design is probably the most difficult for tutorial dialog programs and the least difficult for linear (nonbranching) programs. Obviously, the instructional sequence is in part determined by the type of instructional computing use (problem solving, drill, simulation, etc.) to be applied. This in turn is determined by the rationale, objectives, and interactive tasks defined for the unit. Regardless of the type of use, this step should include, as a minimum, answers to such questions as:

1. Should review material or other information specifically related to the unit be provided prior to actual interaction? If so, what is this information and how will it be provided? What information or examples will be provided by the program itself? Is the program a required or supplemental learning activity?

2. What student control options should be included? Stop at will? Skip problems or sections? Receive answers to questions without an actual attempt at answering? Will help or hints be provided by the program?

3. Will specific content questions be included in the interaction? Are they presented linearly or at random? Will questions be related to model or problem-solving parameters? What model or formula is used? What parameters are needed?

4. What are the anticipated correct answers to requested input? What response(s) will be given? Are ranges possible in the input?

5. What are the anticipated incorrect answers to requested input? What response(s) will be given?

6. What will the program do if neither an anticipated correct nor incorrect answer is matched? Give a hint? Give the answer? How many "misses" will be allowed?

7. Will a "menu" of programs be presented? May the user select at will, or will performance or other criteria determine the sequence?

8. Will branching to review sections be provided for students having difficulty? What will determine that a branch is needed?

9. What constitutes the user's "score"? How is it determined?

10. How will the performance report be presented to the student? Will areas of strength and/or weakness be identified?

Answers to these—and perhaps many other questions, depending on the design—must be outlined on paper prior to translation of the defined sequence into a computer programming language.

Most importantly, as the program is being designed, outline each sequential step necessary as the program progresses from the opening to the closing "frame" of display. Think through the total sequence of events necessary to impart the concept(s) of the program. Follow this same sequence in a step-by-step manner in the program code. This will ease not only the production of the design but also the translation from paper to actual program. It also provides the added advantage of giving your program good "structure," rather than skipping wantonly from section to section in the program in a "spaghettilike" fashion.

9.4 POSERS AND PROBLEMS

1. Outline on paper the rationale, quantitative objective(s), and sequence of instruction for a short unit of instructional computing in an area of your interest.

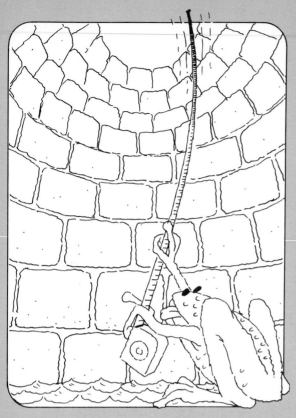

"The young do not know enough to be prudent and therefore they attempt the impossible—and achieve it, generation after generation."
—PEARL S. BUCK

"The next-best thing to knowing something is knowing where to find it."
—THE ENSIGN

"Them as has, gits."
—UNKNOWN

THINK ABOUT THIS . . .

. . . FOR FUN

A bullfrog is at the bottom of a 30-foot well, trying to escape. Every time he jumps up 3 feet, he falls back 2. How many jumps will it require for him to escape?

. . . SERIOUSLY

Should our society become a computer-literate society? If so, how could this be accomplished?

Chapter 10
Developmental Processes

10.1 OBJECTIVES

For the successful completion of this chapter, you should be able to:

1. Identify the processes involved in the developmental steps of the systems approach to instructional design (Section 10.2).

2. Identify the twelve guidelines for the design and development of instructional computing materials (Section 10.3).

3. Identify ten guidelines for evaluating software (Section 10.4).

4. Using information discussed in Chapters 1–10, design and develop instructional computing units.

10.2 THE SYSTEMS APPROACH (CONTINUED)

The design of instructional computing materials constitutes the first three steps of the systems approach. These steps are essentially mental, paper-and-pencil processes. Once the rationale, objectives, and instructional sequence have been defined, the remaining steps of the development process—the coding, debugging, testing, refinement, and use and evaluation of the materials—may be started.

The total process, from rationale to evaluation, for an original set of instructional computing materials may require 50 to 250 person-hours for each hour of user interaction at a terminal. This would include development of any accompanying materials, such as user and instructor manuals. Of course, if model programs are simply adapted to a user's specific needs, the time required for development is significantly reduced.

10.2.1 Program Construction

Actually, this step is still a mental, paper-and-pencil process for the most part. It primarily involves translation of the instructional sequence into computer program statements. This is the first of the systematic steps in which some degree of programming expertise is required from either the design author or the programmer. Programming techniques and strategies must be used in transferring the design concepts from paper to executable program code. This step may range from the trivial task of adapting a model program to the extremely involved, time-consuming process of translating an original, detailed design into program code.

10.2.2 Debugging

Once the code has been written, entered, and saved, execution of the program is attempted. Chances are, the program will not run. Problems, commonly called *bugs* in computerese, may be present. These may be anything from simple syntax errors (omitting quotes, misspelling statements, etc.) to technical or conceptual errors (incorrect use of a formula, right answer not accepted, omitting counters, branching at the wrong point, etc.). *Debugging* (extermination of the errors) is done to the point that program execution is satisfactory from the author's viewpoint.

10.2.3 Pilot Testing

Pilot testing of the program is performed next. Generally, this is done with the aid of teaching colleagues and a few volunteer students to test the program on an individual basis. It is recommended that the author literally "look over their shoulders" as they run the program, since it is a rare case in which something unanticipated *does not* occur. These events may be as trivial as the user typing in an anticipated answer, followed by an unanticipated period (.) that the program cannot handle. Alternately, a major discussion of the conceptual and/or instructional strategy may be involved. Of course, the main point of pilot testing is *feedback* to the author regarding the design and content of the program.

10.2.4   Revision

It is common for instructional computing materials to be frequently revised. However, the majority of revisions occur after pilot testing. These revisions are usually fairly minor in nature, involving redefining anticipated answers, improving responses, making cosmetic improvement to the display, and so on. However, the revisions could be as major as returning to the design stage for refinement of the program or, in extreme cases, discarding the program. (If the design steps are thought out carefully, this probably will not occur!) Note that the pilot testing and revision steps are cyclic and may be repeated several times prior to actual classroom use of the program.

10.2.5   Use in the Classroom; Further Revision

Use of instructional computing materials in the classroom is, obviously, directly related to the design of the materials. This use may be supplemental for those students needing review or assistance on a given concept; it may be a required segment of a set of "learning activities"; it may be a prerequisite simulation of a real experiment prior to entering the laboratory; it may be used as both a drill and a testing procedure; and so on.

Why use the computer as an adjunct to the instructional process? You must answer this question when using the systems approach to instructional design.

Regardless of the particular application, it is safe to anticipate minor revision of the materials, if for no other reason than that the number of users testing the materials will have increased. Again, it is unlikely that the materials will *ever* get to the point where no additional revisions (however minor) are needed. Thus, use in the classroom and revision are cyclic and may continue as long as the materials are a part of the given instructional process.

10.2.6 Evaluation

Evaluation of instructional computing materials may be divided into two categories. The first is *analysis,* to determine if the users are indeed attaining the defined objectives. This analysis may vary, depending on the design of the materials, but it is often based on pretest and posttest results. If negative results are indicated, a return to Step 1 of the systems approach may be appropriate.

The second evaluation is that of the *concept* of using instructional computing materials. Did this approach prove suitable as an instructional medium? Analysis of this comes in part from evaluation of the materials in terms of meeting defined objectives. Further evaluation may be based on both user and colleague feedback via attitudinal questionnaires, overall user performance, and, although it lacks quantitative measurement, the author's intuitive feelings.

Note: Research since the late 1960s has consistently indicated that the *concept* of the use of supplemental instructional computing materials is educationally valid. In general, the success or failure of any given instructional computing program rests heavily on the design steps previously discussed. Although it should go without saying, the importance of thoughtful design merits emphasis one final time. If, in particular, the rationale, objectives, and instructional sequence are very carefully defined, the chances for successful use of the materials are greatly enhanced. In other words, think it through, folks!

10.3 GUIDELINES FOR DESIGN AND DEVELOPMENT

10.3.1 Consider BASIC

A variety of programming languages may be used in developing instructional computing materials. A variety of "authoring" languages and systems also exists. However, to this point in time, BASIC is the most common language found on microcomputers. Although there are some disadvantages to using BASIC as an instructional computing language (primarily in translating instructional sequence into program code), they are minor when compared with the relative ease of acquiring a working knowledge of the language, its universal nature, and its transportability. These elements, along with the possibility that a working knowledge of a programming language allows creativity in development, make BASIC worthy of consideration.

10.3.2 Modularize the Units

It is good practice when writing any computer program to keep it as modular (concise by topic) as possible. For example, if a given concept includes a series of subconcepts, it is better to have one program for each subconcept, rather than one long program for the total concept. Programs are not only easier to design on this basis but are also easier to debug and revise. Modularization also allows for better "pacing" through an instructional sequence, identification of areas of weakness or strength for a given user, and easier evaluation of a lesson.

10.3.3 Follow a Systems Approach

It is very important that both the author and user of a program know the why, what, how, and effect of using instructional computing materials. Following a systems approach in the design and development of the materials is a means by which this may be accomplished. Above all else, remember that any unit of instruction must be carefully planned and designed "on paper" prior to writing the program code.

10.3.4 State Quantitative Objectives

Although this is one of the steps in the systems approach to instructional design, it merits reiteration. Ensure that users of instructional computing materials know specifically the *extent* and *effect* of a successful interaction with the materials. This means that measurement of the objectives *must* be possible.

10.3.5 Put in Personality

Be kind to the users of your materials. Have a variety of positive reinforcers. Avoid the use of any negative feedback to the user; rather, make your responses to incorrect answers indicate that you are there "in spirit" to assist the user, and then proceed to do so. Include enough humor to solicit a smile or two from the user, but avoid the use of "cute" statements and repetitive responses. Also avoid the use of "fad" responses; they go out of style quickly. Remember that although graphics have appeal, can impart information, can increase motivation, and so on, a "smiling face" that takes 5 to 10 seconds to be displayed will eventually become boring if given after *every* correct answer.

10.3.6 Consider Gluteal Limits

Another advantage of modularization is that the user will not be sitting at a terminal for lengthy periods. A good rule of rear is to limit the interaction to 30 minutes or less.

10.3.7   Avoid Lengthy Text

Do not make programs "page turners"! It is expensive and boring. One of the key elements in successful instructional computing is that the user be an active learner. If detailed information, figures, tables, and so on are required, have these available as supplemental materials prior to or during the interaction. In designing the program, consider it a series of "frames" of display, each providing information, giving examples, asking questions, giving feedback, presenting options, and so on. If possible, have the user *active* in each frame.

10.3.8   Branch

Another key to success is the individualization that may be provided by branching. If appropriate, the program should have the capability to allow users to review additional material, skip areas if competence is indicated, and/or stop the interaction at will, based on user need or performance. In any event, never construct a program so that the user is trapped in a routine with no means of escape. Always provide some means by which the user may continue. For example, give the answer after a certain number of incorrect responses, or provide other options.

10.3.9   Design for Supplemental Use

For better or worse, the major use of instructional computing is as a supplement or adjunct to traditional instruction. There are *few* courses that are taught by computer alone. Design units that will ease those areas that are routine to the instructional process or that can be best done by instructional computing techniques. Remember, it takes *teachers* to impart personality, lead discussions, and explain abstract concepts.

10.3.10   Document

Your work in the design and development of materials represents much time, effort, and thought. Thus, if possible, have your programs designed by frames and documented with REMark statements. Develop student and teacher guides when appropriate. This will facilitate not only local use of your materials, but also their potential use elsewhere.

10.3.11   Review the Literature

Have others done what you are doing? Is their approach different from yours? Are you "reinventing the wheel"? Before you invest the effort required to design and develop materials, you should know what has gone on before. Likewise, if your work is unique and successful, consider publishing a description of what you have done. There are a variety of journals and other publications oriented to instructional computing. Others interested in instructional computing should have the opportunity to become aware of your efforts.

10.3.12 Recognize the Capabilities of the Computer

Perhaps foremost, never forget that, to this point in the realm of instructional computing, computers are an incredibly fast, accurate, and useful *tool.* They can only do what they have been programmed to do. That means that *people* are providing the instructions. Thus, computer programs are only as good or bad in their actions as they have been designed to be by the people who provided the instructions.

Instructional computing materials have been used successfully in problem solving, drill, testing, simulation, and, to a lesser degree, tutorial applications. In general, these are applications in which speed and accuracy are important in improving the instructional process.

10.4 EVALUATION OF SOFTWARE (YOUR OWN AND THAT OF OTHERS)

It is estimated that there are at least 6,000 educational computer programs available in the United States. As you can imagine, some are good, some are poor, and some are in between. In order to begin to review software with a critical eye, some reference point is needed. Following are ten essentials that should be considered as the minimum criteria for software evaluation.

10.4.1 Utilizes Unique Capabilities of the Computer

Software should utilize the unique capabilities of the computer. If use of the computer as an adjunct to the instructional process cannot be justified, then why use it? Ask yourself: What does this software do on the computer that cannot be done in some other manner that is just as effective or efficient?

10.4.2 Pedagogically Sound

Software should be pedagogically sound. Is the program based on a learning or instructional theory that is appropriate to the subject matter and cognitive level of the student? Is the program itself pedagogically correct?

10.4.3 Current and Up-To-Date

Software should reflect current and valid curricula. Is the the curriculum content of the software consistent with the curriculum content of the classroom? Does it meet the defined goals of the school or district program?

10.4.4 Error-Free

Software should be free of any errors. Are there technical programming errors? Does the program have errors in spelling, grammar, or content? How extensively has the software been validated? Where? How? By whom?

10.4.5 Provides a Positive Learning Experience

Software should provide a positive learning experience. Is reinforcement immediate and positive? Many programs make the mistake of rewarding failure with "cute" graphics or sounds. Students may intentionally fail in order to see the results. On the other hand, programs should not have any "humiliating" elements, such as sour-sounding tones, for incorrect responses. Software should never contain insulting references to the student's progress, such as "Dummy," or sexual, racial, or religious slurs.

10.4.6 Easy to Use

Software should be easy to use. Are the instructions clear, concise, and consistent? Can the instructions be remembered easily, or can they be recalled if forgotten? Is the operational skill level consistent with the age of the student user? Does the student know the purpose and objectives of the software?

10.4.7 Allows Teacher Modification

Software should allow for teacher modification. Can the teacher select the number or content of questions to be presented? Can the teacher modify the length or instructional sequence of the learning session? Teacher "control" of such options may be an important consideration in some circumstances.

10.4.8 Motivates the Learner

Software should motivate the learner. Its design should be such that frame displays are pleasing, objectives and content are clear, and the learner is an active participant and does not become bored or tired.

10.4.9 Provides Supplemental Materials

Software should provide supplemental written materials. Are there written instructions for the software? Is there a teacher's guide describing the objectives, alternate activities, cross-references, instructional strategies, and evaluation techniques? Are there worksheets, handouts, exercises, tests, and so on?

10.4.10 Provides Backup

Software should provide backup capability. Educational software is costly and can be easily damaged. Are backup copies of the software available? If the software is from a commercial source, can a backup copy be obtained at a reasonable cost? What options does the vendor provide if each student in the class needs a copy of the software? Remember, however, that copyright laws must be respected at all levels.

10.5 THE FUTURE OF INSTRUCTIONAL COMPUTING

Where will instructional computing be in the future? More and better of the same? Faster and cheaper computing? Computers in every home and school? Libraries of validated instructional computing materials? Use in practically every academic discipline? Some of these elements are already being seen. However, it is difficult to accurately predict this future, for the limits are determined by something unpredictable and unlimited: *imagination.*

Appendix A
How to Use the Apple II Series Microcomputer

A.1 THE APPLE II FAMILY OF COMPUTERS

The Apple II microcomputer was first introduced in 1977 and has become one of the most popular computers used in education. Among the reasons for this popularity are its flexibility and expandability. An Apple owner can begin with a modest investment and gradually upgrade the system as his or her interest and budget allow.

Over the past 8 years, the Apple II has seen many changes. The original Apple II included only 16K of RAM memory and a 40-column screen with uppercase characters only. This changed when the Apple II+ was introduced in 1979 with 48K of memory, expandable to 64K. In 1981, the Apple IIe came on the scene with 64K of memory, expandable to 128K; uppercase and lowercase characters; and an optional 80-column screen. All of these features, 128K, 80 columns, and uppercase and lowercase characters, were combined into a portable computer, the Apple IIc, in 1984. This model also includes a built-in disk drive, a printer interface, and a communications interface for about one-third the cost of an Apple II system in 1977.

The variety of Apple II models and components makes it difficult to describe all the possible combinations. Therefore, this text will limit the discussion to the typical system found in schools:

1. Apple IIe with 64K of RAM.

2. 80-column card and monitor.

3. Floppy disk drive.

4. Dot matrix printer.

A.1.1 The "Core" of the Apple

From the exterior, the Apple resembles a typewriter with a keyboard but no place to put the paper. Inside the case of the Apple are the integrated circuits known as *IC's* or *chips* that make it operate. Figure A.1 illustrates the "core" of the Apple IIe.

Figure A.1
The "core" of the
Apple IIe.
(Photograph by
Carey Van Loon)

The functional work unit is the microprocessor chip, which is located centrally in the computer. Surrounding the microprocessor are memory chips, peripheral slots, and other electronics necessary for the operation of the Apple.

Two types of memory are found in most microcomputers. ROM, **R**ead-**O**nly **M**emory, has programs already stored in it by the manufacturer. These programs may be read but not changed in any way. They are permanent and are never lost, even when the power is turned off. In contrast, RAM, **R**andom **A**ccess **M**emory, is read-and-write memory. It may be read or changed (written to). When the power is turned off, anything stored in RAM is erased.

In the Apple II+, the Apple IIe, and the Apple IIc, ROM contains the programs that make the computer operate (the *operating system*) and the Applesoft language interpreter. The latter will convert Applesoft BASIC statements and commands to meaningful codes to which the microprocessor can react.

In the Apple II, the predecessor of the Apple II+, ROM contained the operating system and the Integer BASIC language. If you wish to use such a system with this text you will need either the Applesoft Firmware card, which contains the same ROM as the Apple II+, or the Language System, which contains 16K of RAM. The Language System works by loading the Applesoft BASIC interpreter into its RAM from the disk drive. *Note:* Although the Applesoft language can be loaded into RAM on the Apple II, it will not allow the user access to high-resolution graphics, and some of the programs contained in this book will not function properly.

The Apple IIe is available with 64K (65,536 characters of storage) or 128K of RAM.* This memory is used to store a BASIC program, the program variables, and the images of the text screen, the low-resolution graphics screen, and the high-resolution graphics screen. When using a disk drive, the DOS (**D**isk **O**perating **S**ystem), containing the instructions to transfer data and programs between the Apple and the drive, is loaded into RAM.

Eight slots are provided inside the Apple IIe, one toward the left front and the other seven toward the back. The latter are numbered 1 through 7 and are used to connect the Apple with peripheral devices. The slot toward the front, however, is the exception. It is used only for the 80-column card or the extended 80-column card that contains an additional 64K of RAM. Slots 1 through 7 are used for communicating with external devices such as printers (usually slot 1), other computers (slot 2), and disk drives (slot 6). Other, less common peripherals include graphics tablet, clock, voice synthesis, voice recognition, plotter, and music synthesis.

The remaining integrated circuits in the Apple's core are used to generate the screen display, decode the keyboard input, and create sounds on the Apple's speaker. As with all electronic appliances, severe damage or shock can result from liquids being spilled inside the Apple. Care should be exercised.

---

*In early 1986 Apple introduced an expansion card allowing up to 1,000,000 characters of storage.

A.1.2   The Monitor (or Television)

The Apple II will output to any monochrome or color monitor. (Of course, color graphics cannot be displayed in color on a monochrome monitor.) Alternately, either a black-and-white or a color television can be used. A monitor will generally produce a sharper picture than a television; however, it is slightly more expensive. If a television is used, it is connected to the Apple with a Radio Frequency (RF) Modulator that converts the Apple's video signal to a television signal. The modulator is connected from inside the Apple to the television antenna leads. If a monitor is used, it is connected directly to the video output plug at the right rear corner of the Apple.

A.1.3   The Disk Drive

The floppy disk drive is the "file cabinet" system of the Apple. It is capable of storing 143,360 characters of information (programs and/or data) per diskette and can retrieve a single piece of information in 5/100,000 of a second. The disk drive is connected to the Apple through an interface called a *disk controller,* which is plugged into slot 6 of the Apple. Two drives can be connected to one controller, in which case they are usually labeled drive 1 and drive 2. This book utilizes only drive 1.

A.1.4   The Dot Matrix Printer

A variety of printers can be connected to the Apple through an interface plugged into slot 1. The most common and least expensive printer uses a pattern of dots to print the characters on the paper; hence the name *dot matrix printer.* The cost of a printer ranges from approximately $400 to several thousand dollars, but the printer is essential to the process of developing instructional computing materials.

A.2 HOW TO USE THE APPLE WITH THIS BOOK

A companion to this book is a diskette containing all of the sample programs described in the various chapters. This diskette will work on an Apple II+ with a minimum of 48K, an Apple IIe, or an Apple IIc system. At least one disk drive is required. A 48K Apple II system can be used if either an Applesoft Firmware or a Language System card is installed.

    It is recommended that the reader use this diskette in conjunction with the text in order to study the programs. It is further recommended that a second diskette be used to store the programs you develop from the "Posers and Problems." The following sections will explain how to boot up the Apple, initialize your own diskette, care for diskettes, and use a printer, and what to do if you get into trouble.

A.2.1   Booting Up

Using the diskette labeled "An Apple for the Teacher: Fundamentals of Instructional Computing," boot up the system as follows:

1. Open the door on the disk drive.

2. Slip the diskette into the slot in the front of the drive with the diskette label facing upward. The edge of the diskette with the oval cutout should be toward the back of the drive.

3. Push the diskette gently into the drive until it is entirely inside it. Do not force or bend the diskette. Close the disk drive door.

4. Turn on the monitor.

5. Turn on the Apple by pushing upward on the switch located at the back of the computer on your left. The red light on the disk drive will go on and the drive will make clicking sounds.

6. After a few seconds, the title of this book should appear on the screen (see Figure A.2). In a few more seconds, a menu of programs stored on the diskette will appear (Figure A.3).

7. Select a program from the menu, type in its name, and press the RETURN key. The program then may be either LOADed or RUN at your option by pressing 1 or 2 followed by pressing the RETURN key.

```
              AN APPLE FOR THE TEACHER
                  SECOND EDITION


                  BY GEORGE CULP
                  AND HERB NICKLES




            BROOKS/COLE PUBLISHING COMPANY
                MONTEREY, CALIFORNIA

          COPYRIGHT 1986 BY WADSWORTH, INC.
```

Figure A.2

```
        * * M E N U   O F   P R O G R A M S * *

      EXAMPLE PROGRAMS FROM THE TEXT:

      1     5     8     12    16    20
      2     5A    9     13    17    21
      3     6     10    14    18    22
      4     7     11    15    19

      ANSWERS TO "POSERS AND PROBLEMS":

      A354          A458          A731

      DEMONSTRATION PROGRAMS FROM THE TEXT:

      BIBLREAD      GRADEBOOK      MUSIC DEMO
      BIBLWRITE     KEYWORDS DEMO NEW SEMESTER
      FILEREAD      MENU           RAF CREATION
      FILEWRITE     MINANSWER      RAF USE

      PLEASE ENTER THE NAME OF THE PROGRAM
      YOU WISH TO ACCESS => ?1
```

[Clear screen]

```
          DO YOU WISH TO:

            1. LOAD PROGRAM 1
            2. RUN PROGRAM 1
            3. EXIT TO BASIC

          YOUR CHOICE IS (1-3) => ?1
```

[Clear screen]

```
          LOADING PROGRAM 1
```

Figure A.3

The process of powering up the Apple is called *booting DOS* by experienced Apple users. What takes place is that the DOS (**D**isk **O**perating **S**ystem) is loaded from the diskette into RAM memory and a predetermined program is executed.

To execute another program on the diskette, type RUN followed by the name of the program and press the RETURN key. To see a list of the program's statements, type LIST and press the RETURN key. For example:

RUN PROGRAM 1 (Don't forget the RETURN key.)

will load PROGRAM 1 from the diskette into the computer's memory and execute it; and

LIST (Press RETURN.)

will list all the statements of PROGRAM 1.

A.2.2 Initializing a Blank Diskette

You will want to store the programs you write on a diskette. Although you can store your programs on the diskette that comes with this book, it is best to use another diskette so that you don't accidentally delete a sample program.
   Obtain a new, blank diskette and follow this procedure:

1. After booting the sample program diskette, insert your blank diskette into the disk drive.

2. Type NEW and press the RETURN key.

3. Type 10 HOME and press the RETURN key.

4. Type INIT HELLO and press the RETURN key. The red light on the disk drive will glow and the drive will whir for about 2 minutes.

5. When the "]" character appears, remove the diskette and label the outside of the diskette with a pressure-sensitive label. Use a felt pen so that you won't damage the diskette.

   It is very important that you have a blank diskette in the drive when you follow the foregoing procedure; otherwise, you will destroy any programs on the diskette. This procedure *formats* the diskette so that it can be used with the Apple. The DOS is copied from memory onto the diskette along with whatever program is stored in memory. The diskette can subsequently be used to power up (boot) the system.

A.2.3 Care and Treatment of Diskettes

The programs you store on diskette are valuable. You have an investment in them—either time or money or both. Eliminate troubles by following these simple precautions:

1. Handle a diskette by the jacket (plastic cover) *only*. Do not allow *anything* to touch the exposed area of the diskette.

2. Never subject a diskette to a magnetic field; it may erase the diskette. Setting your diskette on top of a monitor or printer could cause problems.

3. Keep diskettes flat. Do not fold, bend, or crimp in a three-ring binder.

4. Insert diskettes carefully into the disk drive. Don't use unnecessary force.

5. Store diskettes in their envelopes away from liquids, dirty or greasy surfaces, and dust. In the classroom, chalk dust can cause serious problems with diskettes.

6. Do not expose diskettes to extreme heat or cold. Car dashboards and trunks are diskette killers.

A.2.4   How to Use a Printer

Since several different printers may be used with Apple II computers, the following instructions for using a printer are generalized. Should these instructions not work, refer to your printer manual.

1. Locate the on/off switch on the printer and turn it on.

2. Check for a switch labeled *online/offline* and set for online.

3. Type PR#1 and press the RETURN key. From now on, any text that appears on the monitor screen should also appear on the paper in the printer.

4. When a "]" appears, printing may be halted by typing PR#0 and pressing the RETURN key. Locate a switch on the printer labeled *linefeed* or *formfeed*. Use this switch to eject the paper so that the printout can be removed from the printer. (*Note:* The printer may need to be offline to eject the paper.)

The foregoing instructions require that the printer interface be plugged into peripheral slot 1 inside the Apple. This is its normal location.

The default print line length is 40 characters, the same as the Apple's screen line length. Some printers can print 80 characters per line. To print 80 characters, type the following sequence of keys:

1. Type PR#1 and press RETURN.

2. Type I while holding down the CONTROL key.

3. Type 80 and press RETURN.

A.3 WHAT TO DO WHEN ALL ELSE FAILS

A.3.1 Booting DOS Manually

Because of the number of possible configurations of Apple systems, the preceding instructions may not always boot the system, or you may wish to boot the system without turning the power off and then on again. If you follow the instructions in Section A.2.1 and the disk light does not go on, you can manually boot the DOS as follows:

1. On the Apple IIe and Apple IIc, simultaneously hold down the OPEN APPLE key and the CONTROL key and press the RESET key.

2. If a "]" or ">" appears on the screen, type PR#6 and press the RETURN key.

3. If a "*" appears on the screen, type 6; then type P while holding down the CONTROL key. Finally, press RETURN.

A.3.2 Getting Back to BASIC (Applesoft)

Through a number of different ways, it is possible to get out of Applesoft BASIC (designated by a "]" prompt) and into either Integer BASIC (designated by a ">" prompt) or the Apple monitor mode (designated by a "*" prompt).
   Follow these directions to return to Applesoft:

1. If a ">" appears on the screen, type FP and press RETURN.

2. If a "*" appears on the screen, type 3D0G and press RETURN. (That's a zero after the D.)

A.3.3 Halting a Runaway

Sometimes when you RUN a program or make a LISTing of a program you may desire to stop before it finishes. To do this, type C while holding down the CONTROL key.

A.3.4 The Last Resort

If all attempts to get yourself out of the jam you're in have failed, try pressing the RESET key and following the foregoing instructions for getting back into Applesoft. Note that pressing the RESET key during a program RUN can have disastrous results. (Some systems require the CONTROL key to be held down while pressing RESET.)

The ultimate correction for problems is to turn the power off and then boot up the Apple again. This will definitely erase the program in memory, but will not affect the diskette as long as the red light on the disk drive is not lit when you turn off the power.

If you cannot get the companion diskette to this book to boot correctly, reread Section A.2 to make sure that the Apple you are using is configured correctly.

Appendix B
BASIC Language Summary

This appendix defines the most common statements and commands used by educators on the Apple computer. It is not a complete listing of all possible statements, nor does it present a detailed description of the action of each statement. The reader who requires such information is referred to the *Applesoft BASIC Programmer's Reference Manual*, available from Apple dealers.

The assumption of this appendix is the same as that of the rest of the text: The statements and commands as described are intended to be used on an Apple II, Apple II+, Apple IIe, or Apple IIc with a minimum of 48K of RAM and one or two disk drives, for which the controller card is located in slot #6. This configuration is very common for educational users. If your system is not configured in this fashion, some of the following statements and commands will function differently than documented.

In the following summary, the general format for each statement or command is followed by an example (or examples) and a description of the action initiated. The conventions and abbreviations used are as follows:

<♦♦♦>   Required element.

{♦♦♦}   Optional element.

cond   Any logical condition.

dimension(s)   The maximum dimension(s) of an array.

expr   Any numeric constant, variable, or expression.

file   Any legal filename (only the first 30 characters are used).

key   Any key on the Apple keyboard.

line number   Any legal line number from 0 to 32767.

message   Any combination of characters.

statement   Any legal Applesoft statement.

string   Any string constant, variable, or expression.

variable   Any legal variable described in Section B.4.
or var

X   Any numeric constant, variable, or expression defining an x-axis value.

Y   Any numeric constant, variable, or expression defining a y-axis value.

B.1 BASIC STATEMENTS

DATA   line number DATA <list of variables>

```
210 DATA 4.3,"A TO Z",10
```

Provides a program with data that can be stored into variables using the READ statement. In the example, 4.3 is a real number, "A TO Z" is a string, and 10 is an integer. (See READ.)

DIM   line number DIM <variable[dimension(s)]>

```
10 DIM A(23),B(3,4),C$(4),D$(12,30)
```

Defines a variable capable of storing a list (single dimension) or a table (double dimension) of a specified length. In the example, A is a numeric variable with 23 possible entries. D$ is a string variable with a maximum of 12 rows and 30 columns.

END   line number END

```
32767 END
```

Terminates the execution of a program.

FOR   line number FOR <var> = <expr> TO <expr> {STEP <expr>}

```
45 FOR I = 2 TO 10 STEP 2
```

Creates a loop that executes all of the statements between a FOR and a NEXT statement a specified number of times. In the example, this loop would be executed for the values of I from 2 to 10 by 2s (i.e., 2, 4, 6, 8, and 10). (See NEXT.)

GET   line number GET <variable>

```
70 GET X$
```

Inputs a single character from the keyboard without the character being printed on the screen. Does not require the RETURN key to be pressed. In the example, the input character is stored in the variable X$.

GOSUB   line number GOSUB <line number>

```
220 GOSUB 10000
```

Unconditionally branches program execution to a subroutine at the indicated line number. When a RETURN statement is encountered in the subroutine, execution is returned to the statement immediately following the GOSUB. The example will cause the program to branch to the subroutine beginning at line 10000. (See RETURN.)

GOTO   line number GOTO <line number>

```
670 GOTO 10
```

Causes the execution of the program to branch to the indicated line number. In the example, program execution will branch from line 670 to line 10.

IF-THEN   line number IF <cond> THEN <statement>
line number IF <cond> THEN <line number>

```
55 IF A$ = "Y" THEN PRINT "CORRECT"
75 IF X < Z THEN 300
```

Causes the program to execute the indicated statement or branch to the indicated line number if a specified condition is true. If the condition is false, the
statement or branch is not executed and the program continues with the execution of the next numbered statement following the IF-THEN. In the first
example, the word CORRECT will be printed if A$ has the string value "Y". The
second example will cause a branch to line 300 if the value stored in X is less
than the value in Z.

INPUT   line number INPUT {string;} <list of variables>

```
240 INPUT "WHAT IS YOUR NAME? ";NAME$
800 INPUT A,B,C
```

Inputs data from the keyboard to be stored into the respective variables listed.
Optionally, INPUT can print a string on the screen before waiting for input.
The RETURN key must be pressed after the user has entered data. In the first
example, the string WHAT IS YOUR NAME?   will be printed on the screen,
followed by the cursor. The string that the user enters will be stored in NAME$.
The second example will input from the keyboard three numeric values separated by commas and store them into A, B, and C, respectively.

LET   line number LET <variable> = <expr>
line number <variable> = <expr>

```
110 LET C = 100
120 P$ = "GREAT!"
130 A = 1/2 * B + H
```

Assigns the value of <expr> to <variable>. The word LET is optional. In the
examples, the value 100 is stored in the variable C, the string GREAT! is stored
in the variable P$, and the variable A will have the value of one-half the value
of B plus the value of H.

NEXT   line number NEXT <variable>

```
80 NEXT I
```

Terminates a loop begun by a FOR statement. The <variable> must be the
same used in the corresponding FOR statement. In the example, line 80 will
terminate the preceding statement: 45 FOR I = 2 TO 10 STEP 2. (See FOR.)

ON-GOSUB   line number ON <expr> GOSUB <list of line numbers>

```
30 ON X GOSUB 10000,15000
```

Branches to the subroutine at the line numbers indicated, based on the arithmetic value of an expression. In the example, the program will branch to the subroutine at line 10000 if X is 1 and to the subroutine at 15000 if X is 2. If X is less than 1 or greater than 2, the statement immediately following the ON-GOSUB will be executed.

ON-GOTO   line number ON <expr> GOTO <list of line numbers>

```
40 ON X — Y GOTO 500,600,700
```

Branches to the line numbers indicated, based on the arithmetic value of an expression. In the example, the program will branch to line 500 if X − Y has the value 1, to line 600 if X − Y has the value 2, and to line 700 if X − Y has the value 3. IF X − Y is less than 1 or greater than 3, then the statement immediately following the ON-GOTO will be executed.

PRINT   line number PRINT <list of variables>

```
890 PRINT "YOU ANSWERED " N " QUESTIONS CORRECTLY."
```

Causes the computer to advance the cursor to the next line on the screen and print the values of the specified variables or strings. If in the example N had the value 9, YOU ANSWERED 9 QUESTIONS CORRECTLY would appear on the screen. See Section B.3, "Text Formatting Statements," for more information.

READ   line number READ <list of variables>

```
465 READ X,Y,Z
```

Used in conjunction with the DATA statement to store data into variables within a program. When a READ statement is executed, the program will set the variables listed to the next successive values in the program's DATA statements. The example will take the next three values from the DATA statements and store them in X, Y, and Z, respectively. (See DATA.)

REM   line number REM <message>

```
10 REM PROGRAM BY IMA TEACHER
```

Inserts a REMark into the program. The message only appears when the program is LISTed; the computer ignores all REMarks when the program is RUN.

RESTORE   line number RESTORE

```
360 RESTORE
```

Returns the DATA list pointer to the first value of the first DATA statement, allowing for the DATA to be reread.

RETURN   line number RETURN

```
10450 RETURN
```

Terminates a subroutine and returns execution to the next numbered statement following the GOSUB that called the subroutine. (See GOSUB.)

B.2 GRAPHICS STATEMENTS

COLOR   line number COLOR = <expr>

```
340 COLOR = 7
```

Sets the color to be plotted in low-resolution graphics. The <expr> is an integer between 0 and 15 that represents the following colors:

0 black	4 dark green	8 brown	12 green
1 magenta	5 grey	9 orange	13 yellow
2 dark blue	6 medium blue	10 grey	14 aqua
3 purple	7 light blue	11 pink	15 white

GR   line number GR

```
800 GR
```

Switches the display on the screen to low-resolution graphics (40 by 40 points) with four lines of text at the bottom. Clears the graphics screen to black and sets COLOR = 0 (black).

HCOLOR   line number HCOLOR = <expr>

```
460 HCOLOR = 1
```

Sets the color to be plotted in high-resolution graphics. The <expr> is an integer between 0 and 7 that represents the following colors:

0 black	2 violet	4 black	6 blue
1 green	3 white	5 orange	7 white

HGR   line number HGR

```
390 HGR
```

Switches the display on the screen to high-resolution graphics (280 by 160 points) with four lines of text at the bottom. Clears the graphics screen to black but does not change the value of HCOLOR.

HLIN   line number HLIN <X1>,<X2> AT <Y>

```
1010 HLIN 5,25 AT 20
```

Draws a horizontal line on the low-resolution graphics screen at the y-axis position <Y> from the x-axis position <X1> to the x-axis position <X2>. The color will be that most recently set by the COLOR statement. In the example, a horizontal line will be drawn from X = 5 to X = 25 at Y = 20.

HPLOT   line number HPLOT <X>,<Y>
           line number HPLOT <X1>,<Y1> TO <X2>,<Y2>
           line number HPLOT TO <X>,<Y>

```
200 HPLOT 100,130
210 HPLOT 0,0 TO 279,159
220 HPLOT TO 150,10
```

Plots dots or lines on the high-resolution graphics screen using the color most recently set with the HCOLOR statement. The high-resolution screen uses an (X,Y) coordinate system with 0,0 in the upper left corner. In the first example, a dot will be plotted at X = 100, Y = 130. In the second example, a line will be plotted from X = 0, Y = 0 (upper left corner) to X = 279, Y = 159 (lower right corner). In the third example, a line will be plotted from the last point plotted to X = 150, Y = 10.

PLOT   line number PLOT <X>,<Y>

```
275 PLOT 20,30
```

Plots rectangular blocks on the low-resolution graphics screen using the color most recently set by the COLOR statement. The low-resolution screen uses an (X,Y) coordinate system with 0,0 in the upper left corner and 39,39 in the lower right corner. The example will plot a block at X = 20, Y = 30.

SCRN   line number <var> = SCRN (<X>,<Y>)

```
620 Z = SCRN(27,5)
```

SCRN is a low-resolution graphics screen function that returns the color value of the graphic coordinates specified. In the example, Z will be set to the value of the color at X = 27, Y = 5.

TEXT   line number TEXT

      990 TEXT

Sets the screen to the text mode of 24 lines of text with 40 characters per line. TEXT does not clear the screen or HOME the cursor.

VLIN   line number VLIN <Y1>,<Y2> at <X>

      730 VLIN 0,39 AT 20

Draws a vertical line on the low-resolution graphics screen at the x-axis position <X> from the y-axis position <Y1> to the y-axis position <Y2>. The color will be that most recently set by the COLOR statement. In the example, a vertical line will be drawn from Y = 0 to Y = 39 at X = 20.

B.3 TEXT FORMATTING STATEMENTS

COMMA (,)   line number PRINT <var>,<var>

      370 PRINT QUANTITY,PRICE,TOTAL

Used in a PRINT statement to space data into 16-column fields. In the example, the value of the variable QUANTITY will be printed in column 1, the value of the variable PRICE will be printed in column 17, and the value of the variable TOTAL will be printed in column 33.

FLASH   line number FLASH

      1500 FLASH

Sets the text printing mode to flashing characters. All text printed after this statement is executed will flash. NORMAL reverses this action.

HOME   line number HOME

      10 HOME

Clears the text screen and returns the cursor to the home position in the upper left corner.

HTAB   line number HTAB <expr>

      550 HTAB 27

Moves the cursor to the specified column number (1 to 40). The HTAB statement is usually followed by a PRINT statement. In the example, the cursor will be moved to column 27.

INVERSE   line number INVERSE

```
345 INVERSE
```

Sets the text printing mode to black-on-white instead of white-on-black characters. All text printed after this statement will be printed in inverse. NORMAL reverses this action.

NORMAL   line number NORMAL

```
610 NORMAL
```

Sets the text printing mode to normal white-on-black characters. Reverses the action of the FLASH and INVERSE statements.

POS   line number <var> = POS(<expr>)

```
730 X = POS(0)
```

POS is a text function that returns the current horizontal cursor position (0 to 39). Although <expr> is required, the expression has no effect on the results. In the example, X will be set to the current horizontal cursor position.

SEMICOLON (;)   line number PRINT <string>;<var>

```
840 PRINT "YOU ANSWERED ";N;" CORRECTLY."
```

Used in a PRINT statement to position the cursor immediately after the string or variable preceding the semicolon. If N = 10 in the example, the printed line would read:

```
                    YOU ANSWERED 10 CORRECTLY.
```

SPC   line number PRINT <var>;SPC(<expr>);<var>

```
480 PRINT A;SPC(10);B
```

Used in a PRINT statement to insert a specified number of spaces between two variables when preceded and followed by semicolons. In the example, the value of A will be printed, followed by 10 spaces and then the value of B.

SPEED   line number SPEED = <expr>

```
160 SPEED = 200
```

Sets the speed at which characters are printed on the screen. The default speed, 255, is the fastest system speed. Zero is the slowest speed.

TAB   line number PRINT TAB(<expr>);<var>

```
80 PRINT TAB(25);R
```

Used in a PRINT statement to move the cursor to the specified column, where 1 is the left margin and 40 is the right margin. TAB can only move the cursor to the right. Use HTAB to move the cursor to the left. In the example, the value of R will be printed starting in column 25.

VTAB   line number VTAB <expr>

```
120 VTAB 18
```

Moves the cursor to the specified line number. The top of the screen is line 1; the bottom is line 24. The VTAB statement is usually followed by a PRINT statement. In the example, the cursor will be moved to line 18.

B.4 SUMMARY OF VARIABLE TYPES

INTEGER   Variable name: Single letter (optionally followed by a single letter or digit) followed by the "%" character.

Range: -32767 to $+32767$

Examples: I%, B2%, GH%

REAL   Variable name: Single letter (optionally followed by a single letter or digit).

Range: $-9.99999999 \, E + 37$ to $+9.99999999 \, E + 37$

Examples: S, R5, DE

STRING   Variable name: Single letter (optionally followed by a single letter or digit) followed by the "$" character.

Range: 0 to 255 characters

Examples: F$, K9$, XY$

Note that variable names may be longer than two characters, but only the first two characters are significant. Consequently, APPLE and APPLIANCE are the same real variable, AP.

B.5 SUMMARY OF OPERATORS

ARITHMETIC +   addition
/   division
^   exponentiation (raise to a power)
*   multiplication
—   subtraction or negation

LOGICAL   AND logical product
NOT logical negation
OR   logical sum

RELATIONAL   =   equals
>   greater than
>= greater than or equal to
<   less than
<= less than or equal to
<> not equal to

STRING   +   concatenation

B.6 MATHEMATICAL FUNCTIONS

ABS   line number <var> = ABS(<expr>)

```
100 X = ABS(-6.75)
```

Returns the absolute value of <expr>. In the example, X = 6.75.

ATN   line number <var> = ATN(<expr>)

```
100 X = ATN(1)
```

Returns the arctangent of <expr> in radians. In the example, X = .785398163.

COS   line number <var> = COS(<expr>)

```
100 X = COS(1)
```

Returns the cosine of <expr>. The <expr> must be in radians. In the example, X = .540302306.

EXP   line number <var> = EXP(<expr>)

```
100 X = EXP(1)
```

Returns the value e^<expr> where e = 2.718289. In the example, X = 2.71828183.

INT   line number <var> = INT(<expr>)

```
100 X = INT(4.53)
```

Returns the greatest integer in <expr> that is less than or equal to <expr>. In the example, X = 4.

LOG   line number <var> = LOG(<expr>)

```
100 X = LOG(2)
```

Returns the natural logarithm of <expr>. In the example, X = .693147181.

RND   line number <var> = RND(<expr>)

```
100 X = RND(1)
```

Returns a random number greater than or equal to 0 and less than 1. If <expr> is positive, a unique set of random numbers is generated. If <expr> is 0, then the last random number generated is returned. If <expr> is negative, the same set of random numbers will be generated every time the program is run.

SGN   line number <var> = SGN(<expr>)

```
100 X = SGN(-217.456)
```

Returns the sign of <expr>: +1 if positive, 0 if zero, and −1 if negative. In the example, X = −1.

SIN   line number <var> = SIN(<expr>)

```
100 X = SIN(1)
```

Returns the sine of <expr>. The <expr> must be in radians. In the example, X = .841470985.

SQR   line number <var> = SQR(<expr>)

```
100 X = SQR(16)
```

Returns the square root of <expr>. In the example, X = 4.

TAN   line number <var> = TAN(<expr>)

```
100 X = TAN(1)
```

Returns the tangent of <expr>. The <expr> must be in radians. In the example, X = 1.55740772.

B.7 STRING FUNCTIONS

ASC   line number <var> = ASC(<string>)

```
100 X = ASC("APPLE")
```

Returns the ASCII code for the first character in the string specified. In the example, X = 65.

**CHR$**   line number <string> = CHR$(<expr>)

```
100 X$ = CHR$(65)
```

Returns the ASCII character specified by the numeric value of <expr>. In the example, X$ = "A".

**LEFT$**   line number <string> = LEFT$(<string>,<expr>)

```
100 X$ = LEFT$("APPLE",3)
```

Returns a substring of the <string> from the first character to the <expr>th character. In the example, X$ = "APP".

LEN   line number <var> = LEN(<string>)

```
100 X = LEN("APPLE")
```

Returns the number of characters contained in <string>. In the example, X = 5.

**MID$**   line number <string> = MID$(<string>,<expr1>,<expr2>)

```
100 X$ = MID$("NOW IS THE TIME",5,6)
```

Returns a substring of <string> that begins with the character specified by <expr1> and has a length of <expr2> characters. In the example, X$ = "IS THE".

**RIGHT$**   line number <string> = RIGHT$(<string>,<expr>)

```
100 X$ = RIGHT$("APPLE",2)
```

Returns a substring of <string> consisting of the rightmost characters specified by <expr>. In the example, X$ = "LE".

**STR$**   line number <string> = STR$(<expr>)

```
100 X$ = STR$(24.07)
```

Converts the <expr> to a string. In the example, X$ = "24.07".

VAL   line number <var> = VAL(<string>)

```
100 X = VAL("365 days")
```

Converts the <string> to a real or integer variable. The conversion will terminate when a nonnumeric character is encountered. In the example, X = 365.

B.8 BASIC AND DISK COMMANDS

CATALOG CATALOG {,D<expr>}

```
CATALOG,D2.
```

Prints a list of all the files on a diskette. Optionally, the disk drive number, D<expr>, may be specified. In the example, a catalog of the diskette in drive 2 will be listed on the screen.

DEL   DEL <line number>,<line number>

```
DEL 350,400
```

Deletes line numbers from the program in memory, starting with the first line number specified and ending with the second line number specified. In the example, line 350, line 400, and all of the lines with numbers between 350 and 400 will be deleted.

DELETE   DELETE <file> {,D<expr>} {,V<expr>}

```
DELETE BUTTERFLIES
```

Erases a file from a diskette. Optionally, the drive number or volume number can be specified. In the example, the file BUTTERFLIES will be erased from the diskette in the drive last used.

INIT   INIT <file> {,D<expr>} {,V<expr>}

```
INIT HELLO, V25
```

Initializes a blank diskette so that it can be used. The current program in memory will be saved as the <file> specified, and that program will be run when the diskette is booted. Optionally, the drive number or volume number may be specified. In the example, the diskette in the drive most recently used will be initialized as volume 25 with the program in memory stored as HELLO.

LIST   LIST {<line number>} {,<line number>}

```
LIST
LIST 300
LIST 1000,2000
```

Lists lines of the program in memory on the screen. Optionally, a line number or range of line numbers may be specified. In the first example, the entire program will be listed. In the second example, only line 300 will be listed. In the third example, lines 1000 to 2000, inclusive, will be listed.

LOAD   LOAD <file> {,D<expr>} {,V<expr>}

```
LOAD SNOW WHITE
```

Loads the specified file from a diskette into memory. The current program in memory will be erased. Optionally, the drive number or volume number may be specified. In the example, the program SNOW WHITE will be loaded into memory from the disk most recently used.

LOCK   LOCK <file> {,D<expr>} {,V<expr>}

```
LOCK MATH DRILL
```

Protects a file from being replaced or deleted accidentally. The UNLOCK command will reverse the action. Optionally, the drive number or volume number may be specified. In the example, the file MATH DRILL will be LOCKed on the diskette in the drive most recently used.

NEW   NEW

Erases the program and variables currently in memory. Used to clear memory before writing a new program.

PR   PR#<expr>

```
PR#6
PR#1
PR#0
```

Transfers output to the specified peripheral slot number. In the examples, PR#6 boots disk drive 1; PR#1 transfers all subsequent output to a printer, assuming that the printer interface is in slot 1; PR#0 returns output to the screen.

RENAME   RENAME <file1>,<file2> {,D<expr>} {,V<expr>}

```
RENAME PROGRAM 1,MUSCLES
```

Changes the name of <file1> to <file2> on a diskette. Optionally, the drive number or volume number may be specified. In the example, PROGRAM 1 will be renamed MUSCLES on the diskette in the drive most recently used.

RUN   RUN {<file>} {,D<expr>} {,V<expr>}

```
RUN SPELL
```

Executes the program in memory if no file is specified. If a file is specified, memory is cleared, the file is loaded from a diskette, and the program is executed. Optionally, the drive number or volume number may be specified. In the example, the program SPELL will be loaded from the most recently used disk drive and executed.

SAVE   SAVE <file> {,D<expr>} {,V<expr>}

```
SAVE PICKLES
```

Saves the program currently in memory on diskette as the file specified. Optionally, the drive number or volume number may be specified. If the file specified already exists on the diskette, it will be replaced by the program in memory unless it was LOCKed. In the example, the program in memory will be saved with the name PICKLES on the diskette in the drive most recently used.

UNLOCK   UNLOCK <file> {,D<expr>} {,V<expr>}

```
UNLOCK MATH DRILL
```

Removes the accidental replace or delete lock on the file specified. Optionally, the drive number or volume number may be specified. In the example, the file MATH DRILL will be unlocked on the diskette in the drive most recently used.

B.9 SPECIAL KEYS

APPLE KEYS   OPEN APPLE
CLOSED APPLE

The APPLE keys are commonly used by application programs to signal special functions. They are actually substitutes for the game paddle buttons and are commonly used in arcade-game programs. (The APPLE keys are found only on the Apple IIe and Apple IIc.)

ARROW KEYS   LEFT ARROW ($\leftarrow$)
RIGHT ARROW ($\rightarrow$)
UP ARROW ($\uparrow$)
DOWN ARROW ($\downarrow$)

The four keys on the keyboard marked with a left arrow, a right arrow, an up arrow, and a down arrow are used to edit programs. The LEFT ARROW is used to delete characters previously typed in the current line. The RIGHT ARROW will reenter a character on the screen as though you were typing it. The UP ARROW will move up a line on the screen and the DOWN ARROW will move down a line on the screen. The ESC key must be pressed before and after using either the UP ARROW or the DOWN ARROW keys. (The UP ARROW and DOWN ARROW keys are found only on the Apple IIe and Apple IIc.)

CAPS LOCK   CAPS LOCK

The CAPS LOCK key locks the keyboard so that only uppercase letters will be printed on the screen. When the CAPS LOCK key is pressed a second time, the keyboard will be unlocked and both uppercase and lowercase letters may be typed. (The CAPS LOCK key is found only on the Apple IIe and Apple IIc.)

CONTROL (CTRL)   CONTROL <key>

CONTROL C
CONTROL G
CONTROL X

The CONTROL key is used in conjunction with other keys to specify a variety of actions. To execute a CONTROL sequence, hold the CONTROL key down and then press the other key. In the examples, CONTROL C will break the execution of a program and print the line number at which execution terminated, CONTROL G will sound a bell on the Apple speaker, and CONTROL X will delete the line currently being typed.

DELETE   DELETE

The delete key is commonly used in word processing programs to DELETE the screen character to the left of the cursor. The DELETE key has no function in Applesoft BASIC. (The DELETE key is found only on the Apple IIe and Apple IIc.)

ESCAPE (ESC)   ESCAPE

The ESCAPE key is most commonly used to edit programs. When the ESCAPE key is typed, the movable-cursor mode is entered. The arrow keys are used to move the cursor up, left, right, and down. Once the cursor is positioned, pressing the ESCAPE key will return to normal mode. The LEFT and RIGHT ARROW keys may then be used to edit.

REPEAT (REPT)   REPEAT <key>

When the REPEAT key is held down in conjunction with another key, the other key will be repeatedly typed (only on the Apple II and Apple II +).

RESET   RESET
CONTROL RESET

The RESET key immediately halts the execution of a program and sets the screen to TEXT mode. If RESET is typed while a program is being saved on a diskette, the file may be damaged. Some Apples require the CONTROL key to be held down while pressing RESET.

TAB   TAB

The TAB key is commonly used in word-processing programs to move the cursor to a specified column on the screen. It has no function in Applesoft BASIC. (Found only on the Apple IIe and Apple IIc.)

B.10 ASCII CHARACTER CODES

The following codes are used in the CHR$ and ASC functions. Codes 97 through 127 and some punctuation characters are available only on the Apple IIe and Apple IIc.

CODE	CHARACTER	CODE	CHARACTER
0	CTRL @	40	(
1	CTRL A	41	)
2	CTRL B	42	*
3	CTRL C	43	+
4	CTRL D	44	,
5	CTRL E	45	−
6	CTRL F	46	.
7	CTRL G (bell)	47	/
8	CTRL H (left arrow)	48	0
9	CTRL I	49	1
10	CTRL J (down arrow)	50	2
11	CTRL K (up arrow)	51	3
12	CTRL L (form feed)	52	4
13	CTRL M (return)	53	5
14	CTRL N	54	6
15	CTRL O	55	7
16	CTRL P	56	8
17	CTRL Q	57	9
18	CTRL R	58	:
19	CTRL S	59	;
20	CTRL T	60	<
21	CTRL U (right arrow)	61	=
22	CTRL V	62	>
23	CTRL W	63	?
24	CTRL X	64	@
25	CTRL Y	65	A
26	CTRL Z	66	B
27	CTRL [(escape)	67	C
28	CTRL \	68	D
29	CTRL]	69	E
30	CTRL ^	70	F
31	CTRL _	71	G
32	SPACE	72	H
33	!	73	I
34	"	74	J
35	#	75	K
36	$	76	L
37	%	77	M
38	&	78	N
39	'	79	O

CODE	CHARACTER	CODE	CHARACTER
80	P	104	h
81	Q	105	i
82	R	106	j
83	S	107	k
84	T	108	l
85	U	109	m
86	V	110	n
87	W	111	o
88	X	112	p
89	Y	113	q
90	Z	114	r
91	[	115	s
92	\	116	t
93	]	117	u
94	^	118	v
95	_	119	w
96	`	120	x
97	a	121	y
98	b	122	z
99	c	123	{
100	d	124	|
101	e	125	}
102	f	126	~
103	g	127	DELETE

Chapter 1

Think About This (for Fun)

One Word

Text Questions

Section 1.5.3. The output would be "close-packed" (printed with no separating spaces).

Section 1.5.5. The blank space is needed to separate the comma from the name (value of N$). Otherwise, the comma and name would be close-packed, as in HOWDY,SAMMY.

Posers and Problems

1. ```
   10 PRINT "Hello"
   20 PRINT "What's your height in
      inches";
   ```

```
30 INPUT H
40 M = 2.54 * H
50 PRINT "You are " M
   " centimeters tall!"
60 END
```

2. 25, 4, 6, .66666667, 3

3. So that the text and variable values will not be close-packed.

   The variable names are *not* enclosed in quotation marks; the text of the PRINT statement is.

4. The semicolon close-packed the "?" printed by execution of the INPUT statement (60).

5. See Section 2.4 of Chapter 2.

6. NAME   SCORE   AVERAGE
   ←15 spaces→←15 spaces→

7. Enter and RUN the program.

*8. ```
   10 PRINT "DEGREES CELSIUS";
   20 INPUT C
   ```

```
30 F = (C * 9/5) + 32
40 PRINT C " DEGREES C = " F
   " DEGREES F."
50 END
```

```
*9.  10 PRINT "HOW MANY CUPS";
     20 INPUT C
     30 PRINT "HOW MANY OUNCES";
     40 INPUT Z
     50 T = (8 * C) + Z
     60 PRINT C " CUPS " Z " OUNCES
        = " T " TOTAL OUNCES."
     70 END
```

```
*10.  10 PRINT "FIRST NAME";
      20 INPUT F$
      30 PRINT "LAST NAME";
      40 INPUT L$
      50 PRINT "HELLO, " F$ " " L$
         "!"
      60 END
```

Chapter 2

Think About This (for Fun)

A chair, a bed, and a toothbrush.

Text Questions

Section 2.3.
```
INT(10 * .999999999 + 1) = 10
INT(10 * .01 + 1) = 1
Range of INT((100 * RND(0) + 1) *
    10)/10 = 100.0 to 1.0
Range of INT(9901 * RND(0) + 100)/
    100 = 100.00 to 1.00
Range of INT(91 * RND(0) + 5) = 95
    to 5
```

Posers and Problems

1. REPLY is for *numeric input* (years);
   REPLY$ is for *string input* (state name).

3. Change PRINT statements 200 and 210 to ask for
   your age; change the "39" in statements 270,
   310, and 350 to your age.

4.
```
360 RANUM = INT(5 * RND(1) +
    1)
392 IF RANUM = 4 THEN FEEDBK$
    = "YOU OL' MEANY!"
394 IF RANUM = 5 THEN FEEDBK$
    = "BOO TO YOU!"
```

5.
```
120 PRINT "What state is the
    third"
130 PRINT "largest by land
    area";
150 IF REPLY$ = "CALIFORNIA"
    THEN PRINT "Orange you
    smart!"
160 IF REPLY$ <> "CALIFORNIA"
    THEN PRINT "IT'S
    CALIFORNIA!"
```

6.
```
  5 INPUT "What's your first
    name";F$
450 PRINT,"Bye-bye, " F$ "!"
```

7. $X = INT(151 * RND(0) + 50)$

8. 29 to 5, inclusive

```
*9.  10 PRINT "WHAT'S YOUR HEIGHT IN
        INCHES";
     20 INPUT H
     30 IF H > 72 THEN PRINT "TALL"
     40 IF H < 60 THEN PRINT "SHORT"
     50 IF H > 50 AND H < 73 THEN
        PRINT "AVERAGE"
     60 END
```

```
*10.  10 INPUT "ENTER ANY NUMBER, 1-
         10, INCLUSIVE";N
      20 A$ = "WAS ENTERED."
      30 IF N = 3 THEN PRINT "THREE "
         A$
      40 IF N = 6 THEN PRINT "SIX "
         A$
      50 IF N = 9 THEN PRINT "NINE "
         A$
      60 IF N <> 3 AND N <> 6 AND N
         <> 9 THEN PRINT "NEITHER 3,
         6, NOR 9 "A$
      70 END
```

Chapter 3

Think About This (for Fun)

In

Text Questions

Section 3.2.3. The semicolons in statement 60 close-pack the display.

Each READ assigned a new value to variable N. The value of variable C is increased by the value of N each time statement 30 or 70 is executed.

Section 3.2.4. After statement 20 is executed, the data pointer is "past" the last data element.

The error was caused by no DATA present to be READ (the data pointer is "past" the last element).

Statement 30 increases C by 1 each time it is executed. If C is not equal to 2, transfer is to statement 20. When C is equal to 2 (statement 60), statements 70 and 80 are executed.

The program would endlessly READ, PRINT, and RESTORE.

Section 3.3.2. Enter the same score for *both* the maximum *and* minimum scores.

Posers and Problems

1.  ```
    10 FOR Y = 1 TO 10
    20 READ Q$,A,C$
    30 PRINT Q$;C$;
    50 IF A = R THEN 70
    ```

    DELETE 60-70

    or

    ```
    55 RESTORE
    ```

    or

    ```
    10 DATA 4,5,6,7
    ```

2.  ```
    40 PRINT S$,S
    50 NEXT I
    60 END
    ```

3.  ```
    5 T  = 0
    42 T = T + S
    44 N = N + 1
    ```

55 ```
PRINT "THE AVERAGE SCORE IS
   " T/N "!"
```

4. LOAD, RUN, and LIST program A354 from the text diskette. (See Appendix E for listing.)

5. FOR R = 10 TO 1 STEP −1 starts at 10 and "counts" the loop to 1 in increments of −1.

    The comma in statement 40 tabs fifteen spaces before printing.

    The ";" in statement 60 close-packs the "tails" (*).

    The 80 PRINT statement "cancels" the close-packing effect of the semicolon in statement 60.

6.  ```
    10 PRINT "CELSIUS","FAHRENHEIT"
    20 PRINT "-------","----------"
    30 FOR C = 0 TO 100 STEP 5
    40    F = 32 + (C * 9/5)
    50    PRINT C,F
    60 NEXT C
    70 END
    ```

7.  ```
    10 FOR I = 1 TO 10
    20    PRINT I " CUBED IS " I ^ 3
    30 NEXT I
    40 END
    ```

8. The *minimum* changes would be:
    ```
    LOAD PROGRAM 5A
    70 PRINT "MULTIPLICATION DRILL"
    420 ANSWER = N1 * N2
    430 PRINT N1 " × " N2 " = ";
    SAVE PROGRAM 5M
    ```

9. The *minimum* changes would be:
    ```
    LOAD PROGRAM 5A
    70 PRINT "DIVISION DRILL"
    410 IF N1/N2 <> INT(N1/N2)
           THEN 360
    420 ANSWER = N1 / N2
    430 PRINT N1 " / " N2 " = ";
    SAVE PROGRAM 5D
    ```

Chapter 4

Think About This (for Fun)

A 50-cent piece and a nickel (one of the coins is not a nickel—but the other one is!)

Text Questions

Section 4.2.1. N$(3) = Phil; S(4) = 35.
The lists would be printed, but in reverse order (4 to 1).

Section 4.2.2. S(1,1) = 95; S(3,2) = 93.

Posers and Problems

1.
```
10 REM N$()=NAME;S()=SEM.
   AVE.;F()=FINAL EXAM
20 DIM N$(20),S(20),F(20)
30 FOR I = 1 TO 20
40    READ N$(I),S(I),F(I)
50    PRINT N$(I),S(I),F(I)
60 NEXT I
   .
   .
   .
1000 REM DATA FOR 20 STUDENTS
     AND THEIR SCORES
1010 DATA "JONES",80,82, etc.
   .
   .
   .
2000 END
```

2.
```
10 REM N$()=NAME,S( , )=STU-
   DENT SCORES
20 DIM N$(25),S(25,3)
30 FOR I = 1 TO 25
40    READ N$(I)
50       FOR J = 1 TO 3
60          READ S(I,J)
70       NEXT J
80 NEXT I
   .
   .
   .
1000 REM DATA FOR 25 STUDENTS,
     EACH WITH 3 SCORES
1010 DATA "ABLE",95,80,88, etc.
```

3. NUMB() was not DIMensioned; for example,
   `5 DIM NUMB(15)`

4. Three states would be randomly selected (with a random chance that one would be repeated).

5. Three states would be randomly selected without any state being repeated.

6. Five states would be printed without any repetition. *Then* the program would become an endless loop, trying to find the *sixth* state not yet printed (FOR K = 1 TO 6) when only five states were given.

7.
```
95   HNT$ = "STEPHEN F. --?--"
145  HNT$ = "DICK AND JANE'S
     DOG"
4995 MISS = 0
5020 IF REPLY$ <> ANS$ THEN
     5044
5044 IF MISS = 1 THEN 5050
5046 MISS = 1:PRINT "HINT: "
     HNT$ "...TRY AGAIN":GOTO
     5010
```

8. LOAD, RUN, and LIST program A458 on the text diskette. (See Appendix E for listing.)

9.
```
10 DIM FLAG(10)
20 FOR I = 1 TO 4
30    N = INT(10 * RND(1) + 1)
40    IF FLAG(N) = 1 THEN 30
50    FLAG(N) = 1
60    PRINT N
70 NEXT I
80 END
```

10. Do the following:
    a. LOAD MENU from the disk.
    b. Change the DATA statements to:
    ```
    290 DATA 4
    300 DATA "PROGRAM 5",
        "SUBTRACTION DRILL"
    310 DATA "PROGRAM 5A",
        "ADDITION DRILL"
    320 DATA "PROGRAM 5M",
        "MULTIPLICATION DRILL"
    330 DATA "PROGRAM 5D",
        "DIVISION DRILL"
    ```
    c. SAVE DRILL MENU
    d. Add PRINT CHR$(4) "RUN DRILL MENU" as the last executable statement in each of the drill programs.

    The DRILL MENU program must be SAVEd prior to RUNning, because if it successfully executes, it will LOAD and RUN another program. This erases the DRILL MENU program from memory.

Chapter 5

Think About This (for Fun)

The man opened one carton, took one package, opened it, and then dropped one cigarette overboard. This made the raft a cigarette lighter!

Posers and Problems

1. 70 IF PW$ = "<your choice>" THEN PRINT ...

4. See PROGRAM 13.

Chapter 6

Think About This (for Fun)

There are six F's (the "of's" are often overlooked).

Posers and Problems

1. LOAD PROGRAM 9
```
91 REM C() - The count for a
   given score
92 DIM C(100)
302 C(SCRE(I)) = C(SCRE(I)) +
    1
641 HOME : PRINT ,"SCORE COUNT"
    : PRINT
642 FOR I = 100 TO 0 STEP -1
644    IF C(I) = 0 THEN 648
646    PRINT "SCORE = " I,
       "COUNT = " C(I)
648 NEXT I
649 VTAB 24 : HTAB 30 : INPUT
    "RETURN =>";Z$
692 FOR I = 1 TO 100 : C(I) =
    0 : NEXT I
```
SAVE PROGRAM 9 (optional).

Chapter 7

Think About This (for Fun)

Bookkeeper

Text Questions

Section 7.3.1. LOAD, RUN, and LIST program A731 on the text diskette. (See Appendix E for listing.)

*5. For PROGRAM 19:
```
22   HOME : VTAB 12
24   INPUT "PLEASE ENTER YOUR
     NAME";STUDNT$
26   PGM$ = "PROGRAM 19"
531  D$ = CHR$(4)
532  PRINT D$ "OPEN P19 SCORES"
533  PRINT D$ "APPEND P19
     SCORES"
534  PRINT D$ "WRITE P19 SCORES"
535  PRINT STUDNT$ : PRINT PGM$
     : PRINT SCRE
536  PRINT D$ "CLOSE P19 SCORES"
```

For PROGRAM 20:
```
22   HOME : VTAB 12
24   INPUT "PLEASE ENTER YOUR
     NAME";STUDNT$
26   PGM$ = "PROGRAM 20"
9951 D$ = CHR$(4)
9952 PRINT D$ "OPEN P20 SCORES"
9953 PRINT D$ "APPEND P20
     SCORES"
9954 PRINT D$ "WRITE P20
     SCORES"
9955 PRINT STUDNT$ : PRINT PGM$
     : PRINT C
9956 PRINT D$ "CLOSE P20
     SCORES"
```

Chapter 8

Think About This (for Fun)

SLEEPLESSNESS (as in programming)

Posers and Problems

1.
```
10 HGR
20 HCOLOR = 3
30 HPLOT 10,10 TO 100,100
40 END
```

2.
   •
   •
   •

```
440 REM PLOT SQUARE
460 LET A = INT(RND(1) * 40)
470 HLIN 0,A AT 0
480 VLIN 0,A AT 39
490 HLIN A,0 AT 39
500 VLIN A,0 AT 0
510 NEXT I
520 END
DEL 530,680
```
   •
   •
   •

3. The screen will change from text to high-resolution graphics, and the entire screen will be colored violet.

4.
```
10 HOME
20 GR
30 FOR I = 0 TO 15
40 COLOR = I
50 VLIN 0,38 AT I * 2 + 5
60 VLIN 0,39 AT I * 2 + 6
70 NEXT I
80 END
```

5.
```
10 HOME
20 GR
30 COLOR = 6
40 FOR Y = 0 TO 39
50 HLIN 0,39 AT Y
60 NEXT Y
70 COLOR = 13
80 FOR Y = 0 TO 38 STEP 2
90 FOR X = 0 TO 38 STEP 2
100 PLOT X,Y
110 NEXT X
120 NEXT Y
130 FOR Y = 1 TO 39 STEP 2
140 FOR X = 1 TO 39 STEP 2
150 PLOT X,Y
160 NEXT X
170 NEXT Y
180 END
```

6.
```
10 HOME
20 HGR
30 HCOLOR = 3
40 FOR Y = 0 TO 159
50 X = SQR(Y) * 20
60 HPLOT X,Y
70 NEXT Y
80 END
```

or

```
10 HOME
20 HGR
30 HCOLOR = 3
40 HPLOT 0,0
50 FOR Y = 1 TO 159
60 X = SQR(Y) * 20
70 HPLOT TO X,Y
80 NEXT Y
90 END
```

Chapter 9

Think About This (for Fun)

$50\frac{1}{2} + 49\frac{38}{76} = 100$

Chapter 10

Think About This (for Fun)

Twenty-eight jumps (after twenty-seven jumps, the frog is 3 feet from the top of the well; one more jump of 3 feet is needed).

Appendix D
Making Music with the Apple

Applesoft BASIC does not have any built-in functions for the creation of sound effects and music as do some microcomputers. However, the Apple's internal speaker can be activated by a special machine-language program. This appendix describes the various statements and procedures necessary to enter and use this program to play music on the Apple II, Apple II+, Apple IIe, and Apple IIc. It is included as an appendix rather than a chapter section because some of the statements require a knowledge of music that not all readers may have, and the programming steps to create a score may be tedious. (In other words, if you don't have a lot of patience and you can't read music, you had better skip this appendix!)

D.1 THE MUSIC SUBROUTINE

The first step to generating music on the Apple is to enter the machine-language tone routine. This routine was developed by P. Lutas and first appeared in the January 1978 edition of the *Apple II Reference Manual*, published by Apple Computer, Inc. The authors have adapted this routine for use on all the Apple II models, regardless of the available memory.

The machine-language tone routine can easily be entered by using a BASIC subroutine that POKEs the machine-language commands into the appropriate memory locations in the computer. The BASIC routine listed here appears on the diskette accompanying this book as MUSIC SUBROUTINE.

```
10000 REM ----------------
10010 REM MUSIC SUBROUTINE
10020 REM ----------------
10030 REM
10040 P = PEEK (116) * 265 + PEEK (115) - 22
10050 HIMEM: P - 1
10060 D = P + 1:T = P + 2
10070 POKE T,173: POKE T + 1,48: POKE T + 2,192: POKE T + 3,136: POKE T
      + 4,208: POKE T + 5,5: POKE T + 6,206
10080 POKE T + 7,D - INT (D / 256) * 256: POKE T + 8, INT (D / 256)
10090 POKE T + 9,240: POKE T + 10,9: POKE T + 11,202: POKE T + 12,208:
      POKE T + 13,245: POKE T + 14,174
10100 POKE T + 15,P - INT (P / 256) * 256: POKE T + 16, INT (P / 256):
      POKE T + 17,76
10110 POKE T + 18,T - INT (T / 256) * 256: POKE T + 19, INT (T / 256):
      POKE T + 20,96
10120 RETURN
```

To use the MUSIC SUBROUTINE in a program, follow these steps:

1. Type NEW.

2. LOAD MUSIC SUBROUTINE from the diskette accompanying this book or type in the routine carefully, following the listing.

3. Enter the first statement in your program as GOSUB 10000. This will branch to the MUSIC SUBROUTINE and the machine-language routine will be POKEd into memory.

4. Enter additional statements to your program to achieve your objectives. Do not use statement numbers from 10000 to 10120, and do not use the variables P, D, or T, as these are used by the MUSIC SUBROUTINE.

The following sections describe the BASIC statements you will need to add to your program to play music.

D.2 PLAYING MUSIC

After the GOSUB to the MUSIC SUBROUTINE has been executed at the beginning of the program, music can be played at any time by specifying which notes are to be played. Each note played requires three statements to generate the tone: one to set the frequency of the note, one to set the duration of the note, and one to execute the machine-language tone routine. These three statements are repeated for each note in the song. Unfortunately, there is no way to adjust the volume on the Apple II+ or Apple IIe, due to the design of the internal speaker.

D.2.1 Note Frequencies

```
line number POKE P,32767/<expr>
```

This statement sets the frequency of the note to be played, based on the following formula:

frequency $= 110 * (2 \char`\^ (^1\!/_{12})) \char`\^$ note

where "note" is a number from 3 to 38, representing the 36 notes in the following table. The frequency is specified by <expr>. The variable P must always be used, because it specifies a memory location calculated by the MUSIC SUBROUTINE. This formula was used to calculate the note frequencies in the following table.

Octave 1		Octave 2		Octave 3	
Note	*Frequency*	*Note*	*Frequency*	*Note*	*Frequency*
C	131	C	262	C	523
C#	139	C#	277	C#	554
D	147	D	294	D	587
D#	156	D#	311	D#	622
E	165	E	330	E	659
F	175	F	349	F	698
F#	185	F#	370	F#	740
G	196	G	392	G	784
G#	208	G#	415	G#	831
A	220	A	440	A	880
A#	233	A#	466	A#	932
B	247	B	494	B	988

For example, the statement POKE P,32767/262 will set the frequency for a C note in the second octave.

D.2.2 Note Duration

```
line number POKE D,<expr>
```

This statement sets the duration for which the note will be played. The duration of the note is specified by <expr>. The variable D must always be used, because it specifies a memory location calculated by the MUSIC SUBROUTINE. Use the following table as a rule of thumb for choosing the value of <expr>.

<expr>	Length of Note
168	Whole note
84	Half note
42	Quarter note
21	Eighth note

D.2.3 Executing the Tone Routine

```
line number CALL T
```

This statement CALLs (executes) the machine language tone routine and plays the note specified by the previous two statements. The variable T must always be used, because it specifies a memory location calculated by the MUSIC SUBROUTINE.

D.3 MUSICAL EXAMPLES

The following program is a short example of the statements previously described (see if you can "name that tune" in two notes):

```
NEW
LOAD MUSIC SUBROUTINE
10 GOSUB 10000      :REM EXECUTE MUSIC SUBROUTINE
20 POKE P,32767/392 :REM SET FREQUENCY FOR NOTE 1
30 POKE D,168       :REM SET DURATION FOR NOTE 1
40 CALL T           :REM PLAY NOTE 1
50 POKE P,32767/523 :REM SET FREQUENCY FOR NOTE 2
60 POKE D,84        :REM SET DURATION FOR NOTE 2
70 CALL T           :REM PLAY NOTE 2
80 REM
90 REM CONTINUE PLAYING NOTES
RUN
```

An additional sample musical program appears on the diskette accompanying this book as RED WHITE AND BLUE. This patriotic program draws three American flags in random locations on the screen using low-resolution color graphics and plays a "rousing" tune.

```
10 REM     RED, WHITE, AND BLUE
20 REM
30 REM ------------------------------------------------------------
```

```
40 REM         STEP 1 - INITIALIZE MUSIC ROUTINE
50 REM
60 GOSUB 10000
70 REM ------------------------------------------------------------------
80 REM         STEP 2 - DRAW GRAPHICS ON SCREEN
90 REM
100 GOSUB 2000
110 REM -----------------------------------------------------------------
120 REM          STEP 3 - READ DATA AND PLAY TUNE
130 REM
140 FOR I = 1 TO 74
150 READ F,L
160 POKE P,(32767 / F)
170 POKE D,L
180 CALL T
190 NEXT I
200 END
210 DATA 392,42,392,84,349,42,330,42,330,84
220 DATA 311,42,330,42,330,252,311,42,330,42
230 DATA 330,84,311,42,330,42,392,84,330,42
240 DATA 392,42,349,168,294,126,294,42,294,84
250 DATA 277,42,294,42,294,84,277,42,294,42
260 DATA 349,252,330,42,294,42,330,42,392,84
270 DATA 392,42,440,84,440,84,294,252,392,42
280 DATA 392,84,349,42,330,42,330,84,311,42
290 DATA 330,42,330,252,311,42,330,42,330,84
300 DATA 311,42,330,42,349,42,330,42,294,42
310 DATA 247,42,294,168,262,126,262,42,262,84
320 DATA 247,42,262,42,262,84,247,42,262,42
330 DATA 392,210,262,42,294,42,330,42,392,42
340 DATA 262,42,294,42,330,42,392,42,262,42
350 DATA 294,42,330,42,294,168,262,168
2000 REM ----------------------------------------------------------------
2010 REM         GRAPHICS SUBROUTINE
2020 REM
2030 DIM R(3),S(3)
2040 FOR J = 1 TO 3
2050 H = INT ( RND (1) * 20 + 1)
2060 FOR K = 1 TO J - 1
2070 IF H < R(K) + 6 AND H > R(K) - 6 THEN 2050
2080 NEXT K
2090 R(J) = H
2100 V = INT ( RND (1) * 25 + 1)
2110 FOR K = 1 TO J - 1
2120 IF V < S(K) + 6 AND V > S(K) - 6 THEN 2100
2130 NEXT K
2140 S(J) = V
2150 NEXT J
2160 FOR I = 1 TO 3
2170 FOR J = 1 TO I - 1
```

```
2180 IF S(I) > S(J) THEN 2250
2190 K = S(J)
2200 S(J) = S(I)
2210 S(I) = K
2220 K = R(J)
2230 R(J) = R(I)
2240 R(I) = K
2250 NEXT J
2260 NEXT I
2270 GR : HOME
2280 FOR J = 1 TO 3
2290 H = R(J)
2300 V = S(J)
2310 COLOR = 2
2320 FOR I = 0 TO 12
2330 FOR I = 0 TO 6
2340 HLIN H,H + 6 AT V + I
2350 NEXT I
2360 FOR I = 0 TO 12
2370 COLOR = 15
2380 IF (I / 2) - INT (I / 2) = 0 THEN COLOR = 1
2390 IF I < 7 THEN HLIN H + 7,H + 17 AT V + I
2400 IF I > 6 THEN HLIN H,H + 17 AT V + I
2410 NEXT I
2420 COLOR = 0
2430 HLIN H - 1,H + 18 AT V - 1
2440 VLIN V,V + 12 AT H + 18
2450 HLIN H - 1,H + 18 AT V + 13
2460 VLIN V,V + 12 AT H - 1
2470 NEXT J
2480 VTAB 22
2490 PRINT TAB( 10);"RED, WHITE, AND BLUE"
2500 RETURN
10000 REM ----------------
10010 REM MUSIC SUBROUTINE
10020 REM ----------------
10030 REM
10040 P = PEEK (116) * 256 + PEEK (115) - 22
10050 HIMEM: P - 1
10060 D = P + 1:T = P + 2
10070 POKE T,173: POKE T + 1,48: POKE T + 2,192: POKE T + 3,136: POKE T
      + 4,208: POKE T + 5,5: POKE T + 6,206
10080 POKE T + 7,D - INT (D / 256) * 256: POKE T + 8, INT (D / 256)
10090 POKE T + 9,240: POKE T + 10,9: POKE T + 11,202: POKE T + 12,208:
      POKE T + 13,245: POKE T + 14,174
10100 POKE T + 15,P - INT (P / 256) * 256: POKE T + 16, INT (P / 256):
      POKE T + 17,76
10110 POKE T + 18,T - INT (T / 256) * 256: POKE T + 19, INT (T / 256):
      POKE T + 20,96
10120 RETURN
```

Appendix E
Listing
of
Poser and Problem Programs

```
] LIST


10 REM        A354 (PROGRAM 4 MODIFICATION)
20 REM
30 REM ----------------------------------------------------------------
40 HOME : HTAB 4: INVERSE : PRINT "FRAME 1 - TITLE DISPLAY WITH PAUSE":
   NORMAL
50 REM
60 VTAB 12: HTAB 8
70 PRINT "SEEK AN EYE COLOR"
80 FOR P = 1 TO 4000: NEXT P
90 REM ----------------------------------------------------------------
100 HOME : HTAB 10: INVERSE : PRINT "FRAME 2 - INTRODUCTION": NORMAL
110 REM
120 VTAB 4
130 PRINT "THIS PROGRAM WILL SEARCH A DATA LIST": PRINT
140 PRINT "CONSISTING OF NAMES, EYE COLOR AND": PRINT
150 PRINT "HAIR COLOR FOR A MATCH WITH AN": PRINT
160 PRINT "EYE COLOR THAT YOU SPECIFY."
170 VTAB 20: HTAB 30: INPUT "RETURN =>";Z$
```

```
180 REM ----------------------------------------------------------------
190 HOME : HTAB 4: INVERSE : PRINT "FRAME 3 - INITIALIZE; GET VALUES":
    NORMAL
200 REM
210 VTAB 10: HTAB 6:COUNT = 0
220 INPUT "THE EYE COLOR SOUGHT IS? ";EC$
230 REM       STATEMENTS 230 AND 240 DELETED FROM PROGRAM 4
250 REM ----------------------------------------------------------------
260 HOME : HTAB 2: INVERSE : PRINT "FRAME 4, STEP 1 - DISPLAY HEADING":
    NORMAL
270 REM
290 PRINT "PEOPLE WITH THE EYE COLOR OF "EC$" ARE:": PRINT
300 PRINT "NAME","EYES","HAIR"
310 PRINT "----","----","----"
320 REM ----------------------------------------------------------------
330 HTAB 2: INVERSE : PRINT "FRAME 4, STEP 2 - DO THE LOOP SEARCH": NORMAL
340 REM
350 FOR I = 1 TO 50
360 READ NAME$,EYE$,HAIR$
370 IF NAME$ = "END OF NAMES" THEN 400
380 IF EC$ = EYE$ THEN PRINT NAME$,EYE$,HAIR$:COUNT = COUNT + 1
390 NEXT I
400 PRINT : PRINT "THIS SEARCH FOUND "COUNT" MATCH(ES).": PRINT
410 REM ----------------------------------------------------------------
420 HTAB 2: INVERSE : PRINT "FRAME 4, STEP 3 - ANOTHER SEARCH OPTION":
    NORMAL
430 REM
440 INPUT "DO YOU WISH ANOTHER SEARCH (Y OR N)? ";Z$
450 IF Z$ = "Y" THEN RESTORE : GOTO 190
460 REM ----------------------------------------------------------------
470 HOME : HTAB 4: INVERSE : PRINT "FRAME 5 - PROGRAM CONCLUSION": NORMAL
480 REM
490 VTAB 12: HTAB 8
500 PRINT "* SEARCH COMPLETED *"
510 END
520 REM ----------------------------------------------------------------
530 REM       DATA LIST - HYPOTHETICAL NAMES, EYE AND HAIR COLORS
540 REM
550 DATA "HERB","BLUE","BROWN","BUCK","BLUE","BLOND"
560 DATA "KAY","GREEN","BROWN","KARYN","BLUE","BLACK"
570 DATA "TRACY","GREEN","BLOND","MICHAEL","BROWN","BROWN"
580 DATA "PJ","BROWN","BLOND","GEORGE","RED","BALD"
590 REM ----------------------------------------------------------------
600 REM       SPACE FOR ADDITIONAL DATA SETS TO BE INSERTED
970 REM ----------------------------------------------------------------
980 REM       THE FINAL DATA SET TO IDENTIFY THE END OF THE DATA LIST
990 REM
1000 DATA "END OF NAMES","X","X"
```

```
] LIST


10 REM        A458
20 REM
30 REM  ------------------------------------------------------------------
40 REM        FRAME 1, STEP 1 - TITLE AND ASSIGNMENTS
50 REM
60 HOME : VTAB 8
70 PRINT "FIVE RANDOM SENTENCES SELECTED FROM": PRINT
80 PRINT "3 LISTS OF 7 SUBJECTS, VERBS, AND": PRINT
90 HTAB 10: PRINT "DIRECT OBJECTS"
100 VTAB 23: HTAB 30: INPUT "RETURN =>";Z$
110 DIM SUBJ$(7),VRB$(7),DOBJ$(7)
120 REM  -----------------------------------------------------------------
130 REM        FRAME 1, STEP 2 - ASSIGN SUBJECTS
140 REM
150 FOR I = 1 TO 7: READ SUBJ$(I): NEXT I
160 REM  -----------------------------------------------------------------
170 REM        FRAME 1, STEP 3 - ASSIGN VERBS
180 REM
190 FOR I = 1 TO 7: READ VRB$(I): NEXT I
200 REM  -----------------------------------------------------------------
210 REM        FRAME 1, STEP 4 - ASSIGN DIRECT OBJECTS
220 REM
230 FOR I = 1 TO 7: READ DOBJ$(I): NEXT I
240 REM  -----------------------------------------------------------------
250 REM        LOOP FRAMES, STEP 1 - GET 3 RANDOM VALUES, 1-7
260 REM
270 FOR I = 1 TO 5
280 S = INT (7 * RND (1) + 1)
290 V = INT (7 * RND (1) + 1)
300 D = INT (7 * RND (1) + 1)
310 REM  -----------------------------------------------------------------
320 REM        LOOP FRAMES, STEP 2 - POSITION AND DISPLAY SENTENCE
330 REM
340 HOME : VTAB 12
350 PRINT SUBJ$(S)" "VRB$(V)" "DOBJ$(D)"!"
360 VTAB 22: HTAB 36: INPUT "=>";Z$
370 NEXT I
380 REM  -----------------------------------------------------------------
390 REM        FRAME 3 - OPTION FOR MORE
400 REM
410 HOME : VTAB 12
420 INPUT "WANT TO DO IT AGAIN (Y/N)? ";Z$
430 IF Z$ = "Y" THEN 270
440 END
450 REM  -----------------------------------------------------------------
460 REM        DATA FOR THE SUBJECTS
```

```
470 REM
480 DATA "JIM","THE DOG","THE CAT"
490 DATA "SUE","THE GOLD FISH","BILL"
500 DATA "JACK AND JILL"
510 REM -------------------------------------------------------------------
520 REM        DATA FOR THE VERBS
530 REM
540 DATA "HATED","LOVED","WORE","KISSED"
550 DATA "TOSSED","CAUGHT","ATE"
560 REM -------------------------------------------------------------------
570 REM        DATA FOR THE DIRECT OBJECTS
580 REM
590 DATA "THE BALL","THE HILL","THE HAT"
600 DATA "THE COOKIES","THE BAT","THE CRACKER"
610 DATA "THE MICROCOMPUTER"


] LIST



10 REM        A731
20 REM
30 REM -------------------------------------------------------------------
40 REM        FRAME 1 - TITLE AND ASSIGNMENT
50 REM
60 HOME : VTAB 12: HTAB 4
70 PRINT "ALPHABETIZING A LIST OF NAMES"
80 FOR P = 1 TO 2000: NEXT P
90 DIM L$(250)
100 REM -------------------------------------------------------------------
110 REM        FRAME 2 - INTRODUCTION
120 REM
130 HOME : VTAB 4
140 PRINT "THIS PROGRAM WILL ALPHABETIZE": PRINT
150 PRINT "A LIST OF NAMES INPUT IN THE": PRINT
160 PRINT "SEQUENCE: LAST NAME FIRST NAME.": PRINT
170 PRINT "YOU MUST ENTER THE WORD 'STOP' TO": PRINT
180 PRINT "GET THE ALPHABETIZED LIST."
190 VTAB 23: HTAB 30: INPUT "RETURN =>";Z$
200 REM -------------------------------------------------------------------
210 REM        FRAME 3 - INPUT NAMES TO L$() ARRAY
220 REM
230 FOR I = 1 TO 250
240 HOME : VTAB 12
250 INPUT "LAST NAME FIRST NAME ";L$(I)
260 IF L$(I) = "STOP" THEN 280
270 NEXT I
280 NAMES = I - 1
290 REM -------------------------------------------------------------------
300 REM        FRAME 4 - SORT THE NAMES ALPHABETICALLY
310 REM
```

```
320 HOME : VTAB 12: HTAB 10: PRINT "SORTING NAME"
330 FOR J = 1 TO NAMES: VTAB 12: HTAB 23: PRINT J
340 TEMP$ = L$(J)
350 FOR K = J - 1 TO 1 STEP - 1
360 IF L$(K) < = TEMP$ THEN 400
370 L$(K + 1) = L$(K)
380 NEXT K
390 K = 0
400 L$(K + 1) = TEMP$
410 NEXT J
420 REM -----------------------------------------------------------------
430 REM        FRAME 5, STEP 1 - OPTION FOR A PRINTER COPY
440 REM
450 HOME : VTAB 12
460 INPUT "DO YOU WANT A PRINTER COPY (Y/N)? ";P$
470 IF P$ = "Y" THEN PRINT CHR$ (4)"PR#1"
480 REM -----------------------------------------------------------------
490 REM        FRAME 5, STEP 2 - OUTPUT OF ALPHABETIZED LIST
500 REM
510 PRINT : PRINT "ALPHABETIZED LIST:": PRINT
520 FOR I = 1 TO NAMES
530 PRINT I TAB( 5)"- "L$(I)
540 NEXT I
550 IF P$ = "Y" THEN PRINT CHR$ (12): PRINT CHR$ (4)"PR#0"
560 VTAB 24: HTAB 36: INPUT "=>";Z$
570 REM -----------------------------------------------------------------
580 REM        FRAME 6 - OPTION FOR ANOTHER LIST OF SAME NAMES
590 REM
600 HOME : VTAB 10
610 PRINT "DO YOU WANT ANOTHER LIST": PRINT
620 INPUT "OF THESE NAMES (Y/N)? ";Z$: IF Z$ = "Y" THEN 450
630 END
```

INDEX